Happiness in Action

Happiness
in Action

A Philosopher's Guide to the Good Life

Adam Adatto Sandel

Harvard University Press

CAMBRIDGE, MASSACHUSETTS LONDON, ENGLAND 2022

First printing

Library of Congress Cataloging-in-Publication Data

Names: Sandel, Adam Adatto, author.
Title: Happiness in action : a philosopher's guide to the good life /
    Adam Adatto Sandel.
Description: Cambridge, Massachusetts : Harvard University Press,
    2022. | Includes bibliographical references and index.
Identifiers: LCCN 2022003930 | ISBN 9780674268647 (cloth)
Subjects: LCSH: Well-being—Philosophy. | Self-realization—
    Philosophy. | Self-actualization (Psychology)
Classification: LCC HN25 .S344 2022 | DDC 301—dc23/eng/20220325
LC record available at https://lccn.loc.gov/2022003930

For Helena, with love

Contents

Happiness in Action

Introduction

We've all been there before—the morning after landing a new job, earning a promotion, winning a race, passing a test, getting a candidate elected, or achieving some change in the world for which we fought long and hard. We wake up in the afterglow of last night's celebration relieved that today, at least, there is no interview to practice, mock exam to take, speech to refine, or result to await. Finally we have a break, and the world is wide open for whatever we want to do, at least now, at least for a moment. So we kick up our heels, take a vacation (if time and resources permit), or perhaps just indulge for a little while in the Netflix shows we've been meaning to catch up on. Intermittently we reflect on the accomplishment of yesterday and look back on it with pride. But all the while we are unable to entirely suppress the nagging sense that our newfound happiness is slipping away almost as fast as it came. Sooner or later, we find ourselves asking, "What now?"

We realize that the milestone that was supposed to make us happy and that was supposed to justify the arduous process of self-sacrifice leaves us empty. We learn once more, but almost as if for the first time, that, after all, we are the same person, now with one more accomplishment in the hopper of achievements, but no closer to the good life and already looking for the next hill to climb. Soon our celebratory break comes to a close and we plunge back into striving for a new goal, with all the anxieties that accompanied the first.

Deep down we sense that there must be more to life than the cycle of striving, achievement, and emptiness. But how to articulate that "something more" is not easy. Being goal-oriented is a good thing, right? Isn't that what makes us responsible, dedicated people rather than couch potatoes or those who get pulled this way and that by the myriad distractions that contemporary life throws our way? It seems that everywhere we turn, from the latest self-help literature on how to be more productive to the advertising slogan for Fitbit's fitness tracker app—"crush your goals!"—we are encouraged to be more goal-oriented. We might think, "Maybe it's a new *kind* of goal that I need—something of greater meaning or social significance to replace or to complement what I've been after." But we soon discover that whether we have one goal or two, a personal goal or a public one, the same problem arises. Orienting our lives to achievement somehow leaves us perpetually unsatisfied. What are we missing?

We sense it in the feeling of becoming one-dimensional, as if the whole of our person were getting contorted and stuffed into a tiny box, or perhaps chopped up and dispersed into multiple buckets, depending on how many goals we're juggling at once. We feel everywhere and nowhere at the same time. The manifestations of this condition are many: spending hours in the office in front of a screen while losing touch with the outdoors; beating ourselves up over how close we are to finishing the project and losing the intrinsic joy that attracted us to the activity in the first place; losing our sense of self by constantly focusing on helping our children achieve their goals; feeling too busy to spend time with friends; sacrificing our dignity for the sake of making the right impression and getting ahead. "It's for a good cause," we tell ourselves, as we try to suppress the shame of making a false compliment or of catering to someone who belittles us.

As we reflect on our predicament, we begin to catch sight of certain qualities of character, or ways of being, that we would like to make good on but that we sacrifice in our narrow focus on getting stuff done. The aim of my book is to identify and articulate these ways of being and thus to offer a conception of the good life beyond goal-oriented striving.

Activity for the Sake of Itself: Three Virtues

At the root of our unhappiness, I suggest, is a falling away from three virtues that tend to get displaced and distorted by our goal-oriented striving: self-possession, friendship, and engagement with nature. Disparate though these virtues may seem, they are all ways of conceiving what we might call "activity for the sake of itself"—activity that is intrinsically meaningful and that does not await some future accomplishment or acquisition for its justification. Such activity, I suggest, is the key to a happiness that lasts. Unlike goal-oriented striving, which always terminates with the accomplishment and must restart itself in search of some new achievement, the commitment to being one's self, to being a friend, and to engaging with nature comes with its own inspiring challenge and reward at every moment.

Another way to understand these virtues is as channels through which we can realize the ideal of living in the moment and being fully present in what we do. We know that such an embrace of the here and now is precisely what is missing from a goal-oriented life that is anxiously looking ahead to the next potential victory or dejectedly looking back on what we perceive as a past failure. But the ways we go about realizing "presence" tend to occur in momentary respites only. We attend a yoga class, practice meditation, attempt to block out the noise of the workday by focusing on the bare sounds of the world around us, and then jump right back into the same goal-oriented, pressure-packed way of life. Our "living in the moment" turns out to be just as fleeting as our achievements.

What we need is a kind of living in the moment that is more than momentary, a presence that pervades the whole of what we do and that is not merely an escape from the rest of the day. But this requires a transformation in the whole of the way we live, a revised conception of what it means to be active. What we need is renewed attention to those ways of being and exercises of virtue that aim at nothing beyond themselves.

The perspective I suggest does not require or recommend giving up on our goals. A life without goals would be hard to imagine and perhaps impossible to live. We need to acquire things, complete projects, and attain certain positions and states of the world if only to put food on the table and a roof over our heads. And the pursuit of goals that go beyond the bare necessities of life can be inspiring and thrilling. The problem arises when we begin to regard our goals as the primary source of meaning in our lives, or when we convert activities that are valuable for their own sake into tasks at which we might succeed or fail.

Consider how a passion for artistic creation that finds expression with each stroke of the brush can devolve into the pressure of producing something that will be accepted by the artistic community and finished on time for display in an upcoming exhibition. Or consider how a weekend hike, which promises the learning experience of negotiating with the terrain at every turn and the opportunity for unexpected encounters and vistas, can turn into a harried march to the summit—to log a good time, to behold the view advertised in the guidebooks, or to add a photo to one's Instagram story. Consider the familiar worries that if one doesn't get married or land the right job or have kids or buy the house, one's life will be, in some respect, a failure. We are well schooled in confronting such concerns with a critique of conventional goals and notions of success. True though such critiques may be, the deeper problem lies in defining a meaningful life in terms of goals in the first place.

I propose that we reinterpret the very meaning of a goal in light of self-possession, friendship, and engagement with nature. The point of a goal—whether great or small, personal or social—lies not in the goal itself but in the path that one walks in its pursuit. The path is to be understood not merely as a way to a destination but as an opportunity to cultivate and bring to expression virtues that are ends in themselves.

Life as an Open-Ended Journey

We often remind ourselves that life is "not about the end but the way." We tell ourselves to "embrace the journey of life" instead of being fixated on the endpoint we seek. Every now and then a graduation speaker will quote the early twentieth-century poet C. P. Cavafy from his famous "Ithaca." The poem recalls the fabled homecoming journey of Odysseus, who, after his stunning public achievement of defeating Troy, finds himself amid even greater challenges at sea. Cavafy writes: ". . . do not rush the voyage in the least. / Better it last for many years . . . / Ithaca gave you the wondrous voyage. / Without her you'd never have set out. / But she has nothing to give you any more. / If then you find her poor, Ithaca has not deceived you. / As wise as you've become, with such experience, by now / you will have come to know what Ithacas really means."[1] The lesson that Cavafy finds in Homer and that resonates as worthy of marking a rite of passage is that what matters most in life is not what you achieve (even a great public goal) or what you seek to reach (even a beloved home) but what you discover about yourself and about the world on the way. In a reversal of our typical conception of the relation of the means to the end, Cavafy suggests that the destination is for the sake of the journey, not the other way around. Or we might say, the very meaning of the destination, of home, is determined by the path to reach it. Life is ultimately a boundless opportunity for character formation and self-discovery in which each goal, each endpoint, is but an episode in the ongoing quest for self-knowledge.

But rarely do we take such sentiments thoroughly to heart, or grasp their implications. In the same breath with which the

graduation speaker quotes Cavafy and lauds the ideal of a journey
that never ends, they impress upon the audience that the real point
of one's education is to be equipped to solve society's greatest problems or to go out into the world and make it a better place. Thus
the goal-oriented perspective reappears, this time decked out in altruistic and socially minded regalia, but goal-oriented nonetheless.

Even our most earnest invocations to embrace the process often
come with a postscript: "Before you know it, you'll reach your goal."
And more often than not, our exhortations to appreciate some aspect
of the journey of life come as a form of consolation for those who
have fallen short. "It's not whether you win or lose but how you play
the game." That's for losers, we assume, not for winners.

The predominance of the goal-oriented outlook is strikingly revealed in the ubiquitous advertising slogans for cutting-edge self-
monitoring devices such as Apple Watches and Fitbits, which track,
quantify, and record just about every daily activity imaginable, while
promising to "virtually take you to places you might not visit otherwise—like three breathtaking routes in California's Yosemite National Park." The subtle tension between the longing for unexpected
discovery and the security of a sure course is captured in the mar-
keting for the Fitbit adventures app: "With each step, you advance
on a pre-set route and discover landmarks and treasures along the
way. The goal is simply to finish." Of course, a genuine adventure
is entirely at odds with a preset route, especially a virtual one that
guarantees we won't get lost. We thus remain trapped in a goal-
oriented framework, even while, at times, invoking the idea of life
as a journey.

The reason for our equivocation between these two ideals, goal
orientation and activity for the sake of itself, is, I believe, that we
lack a framework for understanding two seemingly paradoxical
aspects of a good life: experiencing life as a journey without a fixed
destination while, at the same time, appreciating that the *way* to
a goal can have intrinsic significance. We will begin to build such a

framework as we come to more deeply understand activity for the sake of itself in its concrete manifestations in self-possession, friendship, and engagement with nature.

I expect that these three virtues will strike the reader as in some sense familiar and as relevant to a life well lived. We all know the exhilarating feeling of standing up for ourselves against the pressures of social conformity, the sense of empowerment that comes from celebrating with friends in good times and taking comfort with them in bad, and the thrill of engaging with nature by going on a hike, diving into the ocean, or simply contemplating a beautiful sunset. We are reminded by self-help books to spend time with the people who care about us and to appreciate the small things in life. But there is far more to these virtues than we realize.

First, they are difficult to live up to consistently in the face of pressures to accomplish and achieve. Second, and more fundamentally, their very meaning gets distorted in subtle ways by precisely the goal-oriented disposition from which they are meant to liberate us. For example, we readily equate self-possession with the spirit of "leaning in"—a kind of self-assertiveness in the workplace aimed at having an impact and climbing the corporate ladder. We lose sight of the ways in which we might stand up for ourselves and hold our own that have nothing to do with attainment or esteem and that may even involve risking our careers or cherished goals for the sake of our dignity.

Similarly, we easily mistake for friendship various forms of alliance in service of shared aims, or pleasurable associations in which we indulge while on a break from work. We overlook the kind of friendship that consists in a shared history and involves rising to new wisdom and self-understanding in each other's company. The ease with which we apply the term "friend" to those who follow us on social media and count and display how many friends we have speaks to a hollowing out of what genuine friendship entails. Of course we know that most of our social media friends are not real friends. But the fact that we have become acclimated to using "friend" in this way speaks to our unwitting slide in the direction of instrumental and goal-oriented relationships.

When it comes to engaging with nature, we face the immense difficulty of squaring our momentary appreciation of natural wonders and the great outdoors with all the ways in which we try to shield ourselves from nature and to exploit the earth and sky for our purposes. Our stance toward nature, on examination, turns out to be equivocal: We take pleasure in certain aspects of nature that fit easily with our daily routine, or that strike us as exotic novelties, and then turn our backs on the landscapes, forests, lakes, and oceans that we exploit for industry.

Even the care we take for nature is motivated by a certain goal-oriented striving under the heading of "conservation." We treat nature as a scarce resource to be preserved for the health of the planet and the security of future generations. But rarely do we attempt to appreciate and protect nature for its own sake, as a source of wonder and awe in the face of which we stand to gain new perspectives on ourselves and the goals we pursue. When pressed to articulate why biodiversity matters, for example, we turn almost automatically to some account of how, when one species goes extinct, others will suffer, including, in the end, ourselves. We lack the vocabulary in which to understand the diversity of nature as intrinsically meaningful and as worthy of our engagement.

In the case of more formidable aspects of nature—hurricanes, earthquakes, floods, and illnesses—we tend to drop our appreciative stance and treat them as threats to be eradicated from our lives. We take up arms against nature in our myriad efforts to predict and control it, as if someday at least we might get the better of nature entirely and ward off even death. Seldom do we pause to consider that nature, in even its most frustrating and seemingly hostile forms, might have something to teach us of the meaning of existence and of our own humanity.

Philosophy as a Guide to the Good Life

To develop an account of the good life in terms of activity for the sake of itself, and to explore it concretely in terms of self-possession, friendship, and engagement with nature, I go back to a source that may, at first glance, seem inaccessible but that I have come to see as indispensable for thinking through the meaning of life today: the tradition of philosophy, ancient and modern.

For many, philosophy may evoke the image of an academic discipline that perhaps offers some interesting abstract reflections on the world but is of little direct relevance for everyday life. But philosophy as it was originally conceived in ancient Greece was not mainly an academic subject. Philosophy was about how to live. The connection of philosophy to everyday life is no clearer than in the person of Socrates, who never taught in a formal setting and never even wrote books. His teaching comes down to us primarily through the dialogues of his devoted student, Plato, in which Socrates figures as the main character. We learn from Plato that Socrates pursued philosophy in a very practical sense, spending his days mixing and mingling with people on the streets and in their homes, conversing on the meaning of happiness and the good life. He did so not out of idle curiosity, or merely for the sake of argument, but with the firm belief that through sustained dialogue and reflection, he could reach greater clarity on how to live his own life.

The motto by which Socrates lived was the two-word command of the Delphic Oracle, the messenger of the god Apollo: "Know thyself." Socrates took it thoroughly to heart. When he was once asked whether, as a matter of fact, he believed in the events of the religious tradition and in ferocious mythical monsters such as centaurs, Chimeras, and the like, Socrates was said to have replied that he didn't know and had no time to consider it. His focus was on the development of virtues in his own soul. Instead of asking whether the events really happened or whether the creatures really existed, he would interpret the mythical tradition with respect to his own action, asking himself whether he might harbor monstrous tendencies in his own person or whether he was of a gentler nature. His abiding focus was on how best to live his life.[2]

Central to the question of how to live, for Socrates, was the relationship between happiness and accomplishment. He lived at a time when the greatest aspiration of ambitious citizens was to make a mark in public life and to be remembered in the fashion of Achilles, the mythic hero of the Trojan War. But Socrates called into question the preoccupation with fame, fortune, and worldly success. He did so not from the perspective of inward reflection or abstract contemplation but from the standpoint of a certain notion of rigorous activity. In contrast to the assertions of famous orators and luminaries of his day, who sought victory in the law courts and acclaim in the public assembly, Socrates suggested that true happiness consists in the passionate pursuit of self-knowledge for the sake of itself. In the teaching of Socrates, we thus find a searching examination of the very tension we face today between goal-oriented striving and the embrace of life as a boundless journey.

We also find profound and counterintuitive suggestions of how we might conceive of self-possession, friendship, and engagement with nature. As we will see, Socrates helps us distinguish genuine self-possession from the kind of self-assertive individualism that may first come to mind when we think of the virtue. Socrates's remarkable ability to withstand social pressures and to remain grounded in situations that threatened his integrity, and even his life, had to do with his devotion to philosophy, which he conceived as a shared quest for wisdom among those equally committed to self-knowledge. Socrates's self-possession was thus, at the same time, a certain form of friendship. It found expression in a common venture through dialogue, a form of community grounded in a shared concern for the subject matter of the discussion. Socrates often describes philosophy as a mode of "friendly" dialogue, in which each participant attempts to strengthen the view of the other by clarifying and developing it, in contrast to the oppositional discourse of argument and refutation that prevailed in the Athenian law courts. Socrates thus underscores a deep connection of self-possession and friendship that we often overlook. This connection, as we will see, comes to further expression in Aristotle, the philosophical successor to Socrates and Plato, who develops a conception of the self, or, in his terms, the soul, as a locus of shared activity that comes into its own in friendship.

Running through Plato's and Aristotle's accounts of the soul and of virtue is also an understanding of nature from which we can learn. Though Aristotle's conception of physics, according to which things move in search of their proper place, is often dismissed today as naïve and unscientific, it offers, I suggest, an illuminating contrast to the mechanistic accounts of nature that we often take for granted. By reexamining Aristotle's understanding of motion from the perspective of the soul, and by considering Socrates's interpretation of nature in the context of understanding the good life, we find a way of engaging with nature as a kind of friend rather than as an opponent. In contrast to our contemporary oppositional stance toward nature according to which human values lie on one side and the forces of nature on the other, we will explore what could be called a Socratic stance, by which we learn from nature as a partner in dialogue as we strive for self-knowledge.

The Problem with Progress

There is another reason for turning to philosophy, and especially to ancient philosophy, that goes beyond the profundity of reflection on the good life that we find in Plato and Aristotle. The difficulty we face in attempting to articulate a conception of the good life beyond goal-oriented striving, and the reason that, when pressed to articulate a source of meaning beyond our career and personal aspirations, we tend to cite higher and more meaningful goals (and thus never really break out of the goal-oriented framework), is that we remain beholden to implicit philosophies that came to prominence in early modern times and that pervade our ways of thinking and being today. Chief among them is a conception of human agency that came to define the Enlightenment: the idea that we rise to our highest calling as agents of *progress.*

What it means to live a good life, according to this view, is to participate in bringing about a world that is freer, more peaceful, more just, more productive, more prosperous, or more advanced in some sense or other. Though the standard varies by different accounts, conceiving agency in terms of progress assumes that it consists in striving for an ideal already in sight but not yet actualized. Due to the contingencies of human affairs and the stubborn resistance of nature, the ideal may not come to fruition for a long time. Thus it is perfectly consistent to question the feasibility of progress on any given timetable, and even to accommodate periods of regression, while holding onto the faith in progress itself. According to that faith, the basic motivating force of human action lies outside the here and now in practice but is already here in theory (or in our thought). We know the direction in which life is headed and need only take the path. The path, or the way, becomes the means; the ideal becomes the end. The zeal to reach the end as fast as possible easily leads to the search for any means that will expedite the process, even if those means require sacrificing one's own dignity or the dignity of others. From this perspective, being oneself in the genuine and highest sense means being an agent in service of a goal. Friendship gives way to alliance for the efficient realization of the goal. And engagement with nature becomes the project of bending nature to our design.

The extent to which this progressivist way of thinking animates contemporary life cannot be underestimated. It is at work, quite obviously, in those who explicitly champion versions of progress, such as one popular author and scholar who proposes that, despite appearances, violence is on the decline, thanks to the continuous development of reason and science, and who tellingly defines reason itself as "the use of knowledge to attain a goal."[3] More subtly, the framework is at work in our everyday social and political discourse, such as the imperative to be "on the right side of history" or the reassurance that the "arc of the universe bends toward justice."

Perhaps most pervasively, it is at work even as we disavow grand narratives of progress or historical change yet define the meaning of our individual lives in terms of making the world a better place, however we might conceive of that, or simply executing a life plan consisting of certain personal milestones. The language of making, planning, and bringing to fruition is all of a piece. What gets lost in such a goal-oriented perspective is an appreciation for life in its unfolding. Rather than thinking of one's life as a plan to be executed, we should conceive a good life as coming to clarity and articulation through encounters with the unbidden.

One could also state the shortcoming of the progressivist ideal in the reverse: A life that stakes its meaning on the attainment of a goal, whether the technological conquest of nature, the eradication of injustice from the world, or whatever the goal may be, will always run up against an insurmountable limit in the form of unforeseeable upheaval, undeserved suffering, and unfathomable turns of fate. And when it does, one is liable to cope with such resistance in self-destructive ways: construing suffering as a punishment for sin or as a necessary evil for the greater health of the universe or simply as a persistent and inexplicable cloud that hangs over every auspicious beginning and that sullies every accomplishment.

What we need is a framework that enables us to understand suffering as integral to life and not its mere negation. And here philosophy can be an indispensable guide. Philosophy can help us find our way to an account of those virtues that involve the redemption of suffering and that offer the path to a life worth living at every moment.

Taking seriously premodern ways of thinking can help us reconsider the notion of progress that has taken hold of our daily lives. In contrast to our progressivist ways of thinking, we might consider the surprising equanimity and matter-of-factness with which Plato and Aristotle write of the transition from one political regime to another—from democracy to tyranny, from tyranny to oligarchy, and then back again, as if the instability of political reform and all human achievement was no great shock or testament against life but rather a spur to keep in check our utopian aspirations and to reorient our lives to virtue, character, and interpretive capacity.

Philosophy and Everyday Life

In the spirit of Socrates's suggestion that philosophy is helpful, even indispensable, for making sense of everyday life, and to show how one might draw upon philosophy in the struggle to put goal-oriented striving in its place, I weave throughout the book aspects of my own life that philosophy has helped me come to understand with greater clarity. I also draw upon characters and episodes from literature, film, and popular television series, showing how philosophy can help us find new depth in the things we appreciate as entertainment and how these things, for their part, can give concrete expression to broader philosophical perspectives on how to live.

The focal point of my personal anecdotes is a passion that seems to have nothing to do with philosophy and that is, in one sense, about as narrow a goal-oriented pursuit as one can imagine: training to excel at a single exercise that flies under the radar of mainstream sporting activities but that is a staple of workout routines and military tests worldwide—the pull-up. At the time of writing this book, I am training to reclaim the Guinness World Record for Most Pull-Ups in One Minute, which I held from 2018 to 2020 until it was recently broken. But the record has been the source of an ongoing personal challenge for years, as I've set it and been surpassed three times since 2014.

My path to this unique exercise could be traced to a series of chance encounters, but it grows out of a lifelong love of sports—first baseball and tennis, which I played from age eight through college, and then weightlifting, which I first took up to get stronger for baseball and then pursued for its own sake with the Oxford University Powerlifting Club while studying for my doctorate in philosophy. But what has sustained me in the niche activity of the pull-up, believe it or not, is something philosophical. Strange though it may seem, what appears, from a certain perspective, to be the absurd task of hanging from a bar and then raising oneself until one's chin is over the bar, again and again, is one of the ways in which I've come to understand the meaning of activity for the sake of itself.

Throughout the months of training leading up to a record attempt, I learn to deal with injury and to accept failure as integral to the joy of struggle and overcoming. As I summon the energy in the midst of a tough workout to shout encouragement to training partners, and as I draw strength from their support when I'm ready to give up on a hard set, or find myself sprawled out on the gym floor after an all-out effort that comes up short, I develop friendships and acquire a voice of free and honest self-expression that I struggle to find in other settings. I cross paths with people I might not otherwise meet, discover unlikely mentors, and come to understand life through new and illuminating perspectives. As I descend from the top of the pull-up and rebound for the next rep, I learn to engage with the force of gravity not as a barrier to my striving or some external feature of the world, but as a partner in a shared activity. In these ways and more, the act of doing pull-ups is more than a means to an end. It's an ongoing journey of character formation and self-discovery.

A glaring reason that such a pursuit would seem an unlikely source of activity for the sake of itself is that much of it is still oriented to setting a record—which would appear, at first glance, to be what justifies the long hours of daily training that few would otherwise embrace. But it is precisely the tension between the goal-oriented aspect of the activity and the intrinsic significance of it, which is far from easy to recognize at first, that makes the activity fertile ground for philosophy.

In fact, it was in the context of struggling with the pressure of competition, the fear of failure, and the fleeting nature of success, and of searching for a broader perspective in which to understand the point of what I was doing, that I began to formulate the contrast between activity for the sake of a goal and activity for the sake of itself. Of course, the philosophy I have studied has deeply influenced this way of seeing things. But it was during training—first as a graduate student competing in powerlifting, later as a philosophy teacher in the crazy pursuit of a pull-up record—that I came to a deeper understanding of the very philosophy I was reading, presenting, and interpreting. My hope is that by drawing on my own experiences and how I have come to appreciate the significance of philosophy for the pursuit of happiness, I can make philosophy accessible for readers who, in their own infinitely various ways, struggle with the same fundamental tension of goal-oriented striving and activity for the sake of itself.

Where Stoicism Goes Wrong

As a further word of introduction to our exploration of the good life beyond goal-oriented striving, I should mention, by way of contrast to the approach I propose, another effort to bring ancient philosophy to bear on contemporary living that has become quite popular and that will serve as a counterpoint throughout the book to the conception of activity for the sake of itself: the revival of Stoic philosophy.

The appeal of the Stoics has undoubtedly to do with their encouragement of equanimity in the face of life's challenges and their provision of a framework for recovering self-command amid the pressures of work, family life, and unexpected travails. On the surface, at least, the contemporary Stoic revival seems to offer a refreshing alternative to goal-oriented striving: What really matters, according to the Stoics, is not achievement but virtue. To live a good life is to withstand setbacks and misfortune with composure and self-command, to remain virtuous in a world where the just often suffer and the unjust prevail. Stoicism teaches that virtue is an end in itself, a source of satisfaction that accomplishment and acclaim can never provide.

But the Stoic interpretation of virtue, I suggest, is too passive and self-effacing to promote true happiness. As we will see, the source of Stoic self-command turns out to be the supposedly enlightened realization that our words, deeds, and affairs are cosmically insignificant gestures playing themselves out within a minuscule interval of time in a tiny corner of the universe. "Look at how soon we're all forgotten . . . the abyss of endless time that swallows it all," writes Stoic and Roman emperor Marcus Aurelius, as he counsels against an obsession with reputation.[4] Even our closest relationships, according to Stoicism, mean little in the larger scheme of things. As the father kisses his son at night, teaches the ancient Stoic philosopher Epictetus, he should remember that his son is but a mortal and can be taken from the world at any moment. The lesson is to take joy in the company of loved ones without becoming too attached. According to one contemporary Stoic author, we should learn to regard friendship as a "preferred indifferent," something we would rather have than not but that is inessential to a life well lived.[5]

Though Stoic virtue may outwardly appear to encourage activity, in the form of earnest work and political leadership, for example, the source of its worldly engagement is the passive acceptance of "the way things are." On the basis of this ultimate acceptance, the Stoic is able to forge ahead with their responsibilities on earth, unperturbed by the fear of defeat. The motive for forging ahead, however, or for committing oneself tenaciously to anything at all, remains, for the Stoic, unclear.

The Stoic demotion of human agency ultimately bespeaks a failure to overcome the goal-oriented perspective. For all its critique of worldly success, Stoicism fails to imagine an alternative conception of human affairs beyond the cycle of success and defeat. It is a philosophy demoralized by the fragility of achievement that misinterprets and underestimates self-possession, friendship, and engagement with nature, and that fails to recognize the enduring character of activity for the sake of itself.

In preaching the impermanence of human things, Stoicism overlooks the sense in which the lives of people and cultures of old were not just aimed at erecting buildings, founding empires, and reaching milestones but in bringing to expression understandings of virtue and the good that can, in principle, be taken up at all times. Though ancient Athens, conceived as a small-scale democracy in rivalry with Sparta, was but a brief moment in world history, its majestic Parthenon now reduced to a tourist attraction, the notions of virtue and heroism that arose from the great thinkers of Athens—such as Socrates, Plato, and Aristotle—continue to be available as possibilities for us today. These thinkers, long relegated to scholarly debate and interpretation, remain alive for anyone engaged in the quest for self-knowledge. We can turn to them for advice. We can attempt to carry on the moral and spiritual projects they set forth.

In its contemporary self-help incarnation, Stoicism plays up the distinction between what we can and can't control. What we can control, at least to a significant degree, are our own thoughts and emotions. What we can't control is the external world—in forms such as disease, natural disasters, and the reactions of other people. Though such a distinction may help counteract the arrogant delusions of mastery that constantly frustrate and distract us, it also leads us away from the interpretive engagement with things by which we rise to self-possession and participate in constituting a world in which we might find ourselves at home.

Stoicism's ultimate flaw is its failure to think its way beyond the dualisms of inner and outer, subject and object, self and world. Instead of empowering us to encounter new and alien circumstances and to make them our own, Stoicism indulges our tendency to solipsistic escapism. The contemporary appeal of Stoicism, I think, is that it is just critical and familiar enough to satisfy our search for meaning without challenging us too much. We need to go further. We need to reconceive the very meanings of self and world and envision a life in which what appears to be external or alien can be embraced as an occasion for interpretation and creative redemption.

Reconceiving the Meanings of Self and World

As we will see throughout our investigation of self-possession, friendship, and engagement with nature, we find the meaning of life when we are immersed in activity for its own sake, when we aren't turned inward, scrutinizing our thoughts and emotions, or turned outward, toward the finish line of some project. To be so immersed is to overcome the distinction between "in my mind" and "out there." For what I face, so to speak, in the midst of activity, is nothing but my very self—a self that is, at the same time, a world.

Though difficult to maintain consistently, such a unity of self and world is hardly a remote ideal. One need only consider an instance of committed engagement with things in which self-conscious scrutiny gives way to a sort of being-in-the-flow of an activity. When I am absorbed in a pull-up training set, for example, the "I" who might succeed or fail in the competition two months from now vanishes into a rhythmic struggle with gravity and the journey of training to which the movement attests. Even the pull-up bar, an apparently external object, foreboding in its stark physical presence as I step into the gym and look up at it before warming up, withdraws from my perceptual awareness as I engage with it in a maximum-effort set. In such moments of absorption, which span the range of human activity from sports, to musical performance, to craftsmanship, to engrossed conversation, one finds one's self at home in what, at times, appears to be an external world.

In the engagement in activity for the sake of itself, one comes to understand that self and world are not two separate entities—as if the self were a private sphere of consciousness confronted by a world that exists outside. The things that one can see and touch and that one may be inclined to ascribe to the external world are not, first and foremost, meaningless arrangements of matter that may eventually come to be invested with various subjective values. They are rather extensions of the self from the start—defined in their very being by meanings already constituted by some enacted story. Strange though this suggestion might sound, it will become clearer, I hope, in our consideration of engagement with nature and contending with time. I aim to show that true self-possession involves the recognition that one's own life in its specific intensity and commitment participates in constituting the world—that there *is no world* external to our consciousness, and no consciousness that does not find itself already at work in the world.

Another way of expressing this idea is that the self is not an individual sphere of consciousness that, from time to time, becomes absorbed in the flow of activity and thus "at one" with the world momentarily. As soon as one is self-aware, and can say "I" in contrast to "this" or in contrast to "you," one is already thinking of the self in terms of a relation to something, or to someone, who is part of a shared activity. "I am so fed up with this damn pull-up bar that keeps slipping from my grip" does not refer to a subject, "I," in contrast to an object, the bar. We are inclined to think in this way only because we are biased by a long tradition of modern thought that defines the person as a mind separate from the world and assumes that there would be some sort of world—matter, stuff, things "out there"—apart from human existence. But the expression of frustration with the pull-up bar in which I seem to distinguish subject from object can readily be given a different interpretation: The distinction between myself and the pull-up bar is really a modification of an engaged relation in which the two of us are inseparable. The "I" to which I refer is an active self, oriented to the resumption of the training session. The bar is a necessary partner in that activity; it has simply become a resistant partner rather than a cooperative one.

On the basis of the bar's continuing resistance, I can further distance myself from it by examining it with respect to its material composition, comparing it to other bars that might be better made. But this sort of scrutiny, which we may be inclined to view as penetrating into the inner matter of the thing, is a kind of *distancing* within a framework opened up by an active, engaged partnership. When I indulge in this apparently detached reflection, I by no means break all ties with the bar and at last become acquainted with its objective features. I continue to engage with it, though now in a mode of frustration and problem-solving rather than thoroughly absorbed partnership.

It is the absorbed partnership, however, that is the basis of the self-conscious problem-solving, not the other way around. Whereas we typically regard absorption as the exception and self-conscious reflection as the rule, we should consider that matters stand in reverse: We are primarily active beings, absorbed in what we do, the things we use, and the people with whom we move in concert. Only derivatively are we self-conscious planners and calculators who stand back from what we do and look upon the world at some distance. What we take to be the ego, or subjective consciousness, that so often intrudes in daily life, drawing comparisons to others, separating itself from what it does and what it uses, worrying that things might fall apart, turns out to be a derivative reality subordinate to the enacted story expressed in the flow of activity.

As Aristotle puts it, we are most ourselves not when we are at rest, passively enjoying a pleasurable state, or reflecting on some achievement, but when we are *en energeia,* "in action." To be in action is to exercise the capacity to deliberate and judge competing possibilities in the various situations that life throws one's way. The point of judgment, suggests Aristotle, is not simply to make the "right" decision, in the sense of accomplishing a goal or maximizing utility, but to take a stand on *who* one is, to declare, as it were, that "all things considered, I stand by this decision; I will continue to live with it and learn from it."

From this perspective, contemporary efforts of social policy to "nudge" us into "better" judgments by surveying and analyzing certain psychological tendencies, or to replace human judgment altogether with algorithmic decision-making, misses the very point of judgment, conceiving it as a means to an end rather than as an expression of self-possession. While technology backed by rational choice theory promises to satisfy our current preferences better than we could ourselves, it deprives us of the agency through which we develop character, learn skills, and form our goals in the first place.

Self-Possession

In Chapters 1 and 2, we will explore self-possession as a virtue both widely recognized and superficially understood. The virtue calls up the image of a person who is difficult to sway and who responds to opposition with poise. But it goes far deeper than the outward manifestation of being unflappable. For as we know from those who might first come to mind when we think of self-possession, looks can be deceiving. Consider the dapper ad exec making a smooth, high-stakes pitch to a room full of clients, as Don Draper does in the hit television series *Mad Men*. When Draper leaves the bright lights of his Madison Avenue office, his life spirals into a dissolute freefall of affairs, alcohol, and failed attempts at personal renewal.

The crisp white shirt that he buttons up every morning, often after a night of debauchery, masks the disarray of his inner life.

With the help of ancient philosophy, we will see that self-possession rightly understood is not confidence in this or that task or domain. It involves being at one with one's self in the full range of one's commitments, coming to understand the different aspects and moments of one's life as belonging to each other and constituting a "whole" that is always in the works and that gives one the direction and courage to confront the unbidden.

To understand this notion of self-possession concretely in its many aspects, we will consider two main philosophical perspectives: Aristotle's account of virtue, in particular, what he calls "greatness of soul," which is the focus of Chapter 1, and Plato's portrayal of the life and death of Socrates, the focus of Chapter 2. Though scholars often contrast Aristotle's account of virtue with Plato's, I suggest that we understand them as mutually reinforcing. What we find in Aristotle's description of greatness of soul, I propose, is a nuanced and remarkably precise account of the virtue that Socrates displays in action throughout the course of Plato's dialogues. Our study of self-possession will culminate in the trial and execution of Socrates, and a consideration of his mysterious, almost superhuman poise in the face of condemnation for allegedly "corrupting the youth of Athens" by leading them to question conventional authority. Along the way, we will consider self-possession in its many aspects, guided by ancient philosophy and a range of references from film, television, popular culture, and everyday life.

Some of the key dimensions of self-possession that we will explore include standing up for one's self yet not insisting on recognition or honor when unjustly denied it; exercising one's own judgment in the face of the many ways in which technology and so-called expert knowledge threaten to leap in and disburden us of agency; making the effort to understand those who disagree with us—not simply by explaining their views psychologically, as if we were diagnosing a condition of sickness, but by trying to find in them a partial insight with which we can relate; coming to recognize that those who surround us, even in their ignorance and hostility, are not inexplicable aberrations or threatening mysteries, but are, in some sense, like us; learning to understand our duty to others as first and foremost a duty to ourselves; coming to reconceive morality as a form of self-affirmation that has its end in itself rather than a form of self-sacrifice that longs for an extrinsic reward; avoiding forms of moralizing self-evasion whereby we classify our own weaknesses as virtues; and cultivating the capacity to gather ourselves when things fall apart and to redeem misfortune.

What Friendship Really Means

From our examination of self-possession, the topic of Chapter 3 will have already begun to emerge: friendship. Though self-possession and friendship may at first strike us as separate virtues, each a different component of the good life, we will see that they are intertwined, so much so that it is impossible, even, to conceive of one without the other. Beginning from the observation that what motivates and constitutes some of the most resonant instances of self-possession is a devotion to friends and loved ones, we will investigate friendship as a mode of self-possession, and vice versa.

Our leading theme will be friendship for the sake of itself in contrast to friendship for the sake of a goal. To get a handle on the distinction, we will consider Aristotle's famous contrast between friendship for utility and friendship for virtue. But we will also come to see that what Aristotle means by friendship for virtue can be adequately understood only in light of self-possession, or, in his terms, greatness of soul.

What constitutes genuine friendship, Aristotle proposes, is rising to self-possession in each other's company. In the opposite direction, looking at self-possession as a mode of friendship, Aristotle makes the thought-provoking suggestion that only one who is self-possessed and thus a friend to one's self is prepared to be a friend to others. By considering what it might mean to be a friend to one's self, we will gain a deeper understanding of self-possession as bearing the structure of friendship, or of a certain harmony out of difference within one's own person.

Without the connection of friendship and self-possession in view, we would be liable to mistake Aristotle's bold claim that true friendship can prevail only among the virtuous with the simplistic yet widely accepted view that he believed that only the virtuous, in the sense of the just, could be true friends. As we will see, friendship may require giving a friend special preference, or even covering up for a friend's misdeed. To explore the tension between friendship and justice, we will consider examples from literature, film, and everyday life.

Another theme of the chapter is the sense in which our tendency to neglect friendship in favor of alliance has deep philosophical roots in the Enlightenment idea of progress and in providential views of history that still very much influence us. From such a perspective, the highest human calling becomes working to bring about an ideal state of affairs, for which allies, but not friends, are needed. What was once regarded by ancient philosophy as the highest virtue— friendship for the sake of itself—gets demeaned as parochial and divisive. Friendship gets conceived as but one step away from egoism or selfishness, a kind of tribal love of one's own at odds with disinterested justice and grand visions of reform. Of note is that with very few exceptions, modern philosophers have much to say about justice, class solidarity, and other forms of alliance, but next to nothing about friendship. But the modern degradation of friendship is deeply misguided.

What the ancient philosophers and tragic poets understood, and Enlightenment thought overlooks, is that unforeseen upheaval and injustice is not simply a creature of human folly and thus amenable to social reform. It is an essential dimension of existence with which we must constantly come to grips. Without friends, we would find ourselves unable to rise to this ultimate calling. It is only in friendship that we gain the strength to redeem misfortune, rise to self-possession, and come into our humanity. The familiar idea that friendship is a rival to universal concern, which is common to philosophies ranging from the Stoics to Adam Smith, turns out to be a mistake. We cannot appreciate humanity in general except by reference to how those "far" from us might become potential friends. The imperative to seek friends rather than allies remains paramount for living a good life.

Engagement with Nature

Just as friendship and self-possession form a pair, so engagement with nature forms with them a unity, which we explore in Chapter 4. Here we will consider that a pervasive source of our dispossession and unhappiness is a kind of disengagement from nature, whereby we lose touch with the promptings and potential insights to be gleaned from the things we do not make or produce but encounter. Instead of attending to nature as a source of meaning and self-knowledge, as we might do in a moment of awe inspired by a natural wonder that summons our interpretive power to articulate the beauty and sublimity of our surroundings, we too often regard nature as a merely external context or environment to be appropriated for our goals.

This attitude finds its starkest expression in our wanton neglect of the beauty and mystery of nature as we thoughtlessly clear rainforests to make way for farmland, or turn a blind eye to landscapes, lakes, and stars as we pursue industry, erect factories, and pollute the air through which we might behold the sky. But this attitude finds equal expression in the prevailing environmentalism that treats nature as a scarce resource to be conserved, or that understands what's wrong with pollution primarily in terms of global climate change and the destructive effects it will have on human or planetary health and well-being.

More subtly still, this attitude pervades our most widely accepted ways of studying and conceiving of nature—the theories we tend to accept uncritically as unqualified advances of modern science, such as Darwinian understandings of animal behavior in terms of traits conducive to survival, or modern accounts of motion in terms of the laws of gravity. In such theories we understand only as much of things as we can turn into an object to be predicted and controlled. But such objectification, like all forms of goal-oriented striving, involves a narrowness of vision, a profound neglect, a looking *away* from things, which, when it loses consciousness of itself as such, turns into a form of ignorance that is, at the same time, a form of self-loss. In our abstract conceptions of the physical world, such as "bodies in motion," which enable us to calculate things such as the velocity necessary to project a rocket into outer space, or in our focus on the blind instinct to survive, which allows us to predict the phenotypes that might prevail among a species of living organism in years to come, we lose touch with the visible, tangible world as it first strikes us in its infinite richness, mystery, and range of possible motivation.

The world as it first appears in the course of everyday life—as a source of resistance and inspiration—can be adequately understood only in an attempt to bring nature to expression as a way of understanding ourselves. The mode of discourse proper to such an undertaking could be conceived as a certain poetic or literary language of the kind familiar to ancient accounts of nature as personified in ways that challenge us to rise to self-possession. Such an interpretive engagement with nature could also be understood along the lines of a Socratic dialogue. Of course, unlike a human partner in dialogue, the sun, the moon, and the stars do not speak back to us directly if we ask them a question (though, as Socrates points out, neither does a written text). But, like any partner, these aspects of nature can be seen to offer certain meanings and suggestions of their own, in simply being as they are, on which we may follow up through a dialogue within ourselves and with friends. The way in which Socrates invokes the image of the sun to articulate the idea of the good is one example that we will examine. And as we attempt to interpret meanings that find expression in nature, nature itself appears in new ways.

Modern ways of thinking tend to dismiss such an understanding of nature as the undisciplined human projection of meaning onto a morally indifferent universe. But as we will see, the charge of anthropocentrism itself presupposes a very questionable conception of the "anthropos," or human, in terms of a subjective consciousness that is separate from the objects it observes. Such a subject-object distinction, which places human values and aspirations on one side and nature on the other, overlooks the engaged and committed immersion in things that constitutes our basic way of being and perceiving. On close examination, the ways of observing and explaining that we are inclined to take as objective and freed of all anthropocentrism, such as our conceptions of nature in terms of "body," "mass," "quantity," and "cause," subtly attest to certain questionable self-conceptions that easily conceal themselves in the cloak of a self-evident, merely descriptive language.

To recover and elaborate the virtue of engagement with nature, we will consider it in contrast to two rival attitudes. The first we might call an oppositional stance toward nature characteristic of a technological outlook. This is the idea that the nature we confront is infinitely malleable for whatever purpose we may seek to impose on it. However resistant nature may first appear, it is ultimately ours to subjugate and repurpose for our own aims. The radical statement of the technological outlook is that there is really no such thing as nature, in the sense of an external constraint on our productive power. For what appears to be a force to which we are subject—a mere given—is really given *to us* to be subdued in proportion to the advance of our technological mastery. The life-extension movement gaining traction today is a perfect example of this type of oppositional stance toward nature. It bespeaks the faith that even death, the supposedly ultimate natural limit on our striving, can be conquered. As we will see, such a faith not only represents an unrealistic promethean aspiration; the aspiration itself depends upon the reduction of death to something that can be observed and studied, predicted and postponed. It overlooks the sense in which death has to do with the meaning of the lives we live, the radical exposure of our lives to disruption at every moment.

The second attitude that stands in contrast to an interpretive engagement with nature is, in a sense, the opposite of the technological. This is a resigned stance characteristic of certain premodern outlooks but that finds voice today in the view that nature simply "is": the idea that nature does impose certain insurmountable limits on our striving and that we must come to accept those limits as a part of life. This view is central to the contemporary revival of Stoic philosophy, which teaches equanimity in the face of what we can't control and directs our attention to the infinite power of nature according to which all things disperse and join once more in an infinite cycle.

In contrast to both the resigned and oppositional attitudes is the engagement with nature that we will explore: a Socratic understanding whereby we come to understand nature—even in its oppositional forms of disaster, injury, illness, and death—as offering lessons and insights for how we might reinterpret our lives and the very goals we pursue.

Contending with Time and What It Means to Be Free

Finally, we will explore two implications of a life oriented to self-possession, friendship, and engagement with nature: how we understand and relate to time, and how we conceive of what it means to be free.

In Chapter 5, we will consider the contrast of goal-oriented striving and activity for the sake of itself in terms of the understanding of time to which each gives rise. We will examine the way in which our familiar anxieties concerning time—that time seems to fly by too fast, that it perpetually runs out and pulls us away from what we are doing, that, ultimately, it carries us ineluctably toward old age and death—can be traced to a certain distortion of time characteristic of a life spent in constant anticipation of a goal that lies outside itself.

Our most seemingly self-evident conception of time in terms of passage and succession is the companion of goal-oriented striving in which one event must follow before or after another. It is only from within the grip of such striving that time can be said simply to pass and that such passage can become the object of measurement in terms of seconds, minutes, hours, days, and years. What appears to be "real" or "objective" time in contrast to our subjective perceptions of it thus turns out to be a symptom of our falling out of touch with activity for the sake of itself.

From the perspective of life as an ongoing journey, defined by self-possession, friendship, and engagement with nature, time never simply passes. For each moment that comes can be understood as a redemption and reintegration of what has gone by. Past and future, we will see, are not points on a timeline, one following after the other, but constitutive dimensions of every moment—the past denoting the closure and unity of the present, the future its openness and mystery. Life so understood does not play itself out in a sequence of moments stretching from birth to death. Its movement is rather to be understood in terms of the openness and closure of a single moment that can be seen to traverse "all times."

To understand time in this manner is to reconceive the very meaning of life and death. Our familiar understanding of death as the negation of life, or the point at which life comes to an end, is born of the reduction of life to the "presence" of a consciousness that comes into the world at a certain point in time, remains alongside the world for a stretch, and then, one day, is extinguished or removed. To conceive of life in this way is to place one's self within the sequence of moments that appears to constitute time from the standpoint of goal-oriented striving and to overlook the sense in which self-possession, friendship, and engagement with nature constitute ways of being that exceed the bounds of one's own consciousness and that participate in constituting any possible world to which one might arrive and from which one might depart.

Or, seen from the direction of the world, one's life, or personal identity, can never be reduced to a sphere of consciousness for the simple reason that it is inseparable from the world that solicits one's interpretive energy and that, in the exercise of which, one participates in bringing the world to expression. In constituting the world in one's own action, and, in turn, being constituted by the world on which one acts, one is constantly bringing life to a certain closure from which an open horizon can appear. Death, if it is to mean anything at all, can be nothing more or less than the unfathomable dimension of the unbidden and unknowable that encircles and pervades life, the very condition and source of our deepest commitments and the quest to know ourselves. From this perspective, the question of what may be "after death"—the fate of one's consciousness, the rewards or punishments that may be in store—loses its urgency. For the mystery and possibility of any moment that lies ahead is no deeper or more profound than that of the moment in which one is living now.

In Chapter 6, we will examine the conception of freedom to which activity for the sake itself gives rise. From our examination of self-possession, the theme of freedom will have already emerged in the capacity for judgment, independence of mind, and the creative overcoming of hardship. But such capacities, and the very notion of self-possession, are easily misunderstood in terms of a familiar but misguided conception of freedom as *choosing,* or *forging,* a life for one's self instead of being swayed by one's environment. This understanding commonly takes the form of the opposition of free will and determinism. On one end is the unbounded capacity to live by one's own choices and decisions and on the other is the constraint of external necessity in the form of natural inclination and social pressure. But such a contrast grows out of a misguided tradition of thought that understands the self as a subject placed amid a world of objects against which it must constantly try to maintain itself. Such a subject-object distinction utterly neglects the mutual constitution of self and world.

As we will see, the understanding of freedom in terms of choice or decision misses the sense in which the deeds most proper to who we are take their direction from the very world in which we find ourselves. They are acts of interpretation and care rather than will-power and choice. By examining agency as a mode of attentive-ness and response, we will come to see that the capacity to fashion a coherent life is always guided by a prior understanding of the life one is already living. Only because we find ourselves in the midst of a life that has always already been unified and delimited in some provisional way can we forge a life out of new ventures and encounters.

Even those instances of personal moral conflict in which our lives seem to get pulled by external circumstances in radically different directions, one of which we must simply choose, attest subtly to a unity of self, a pregiven "whole" of commitments, lived in relation to each other, which makes possible the dilemma and prepares the choice we might make. The upshot of such a realization is that far less rides on the choices we make than we often think. What matters most and what constitutes our freedom is not the choice itself but the way in which we live out the path we take as an ongoing possibility within the circle of a life already in the works.

The Meaning of an Ideal for How to Live

It might be tempting to think of the contrast between goal-oriented striving and activity for the sake of itself as highlighting two rival alternatives, one of which we ought to replace with the other if we are to find true and lasting fulfillment. But the conception of activity for the sake of itself, as I aim to develop it, is not simply an ideal in contrast to the actual lives we are living. It is as much an account or explanation of our lives, an interpretation of what already motivates us deep down and that finds expression, subtly and implicitly, in even those ways of being that deviate from what a consistent and clear-sighted understanding of activity for the sake of itself would entail.

What I want to reveal is that activity for the sake of itself is not the mere opposite of goal-oriented striving but, paradoxically, what makes goal-oriented striving possible as a way in which we *lose* ourselves. It is only because our lives are already unified and directed by an open-ended journey that involves at least gestures toward self-possession, friendship, and engagement with nature, that we can get lost in a part of that life and fall victim to tunnel vision and obsession. But this means that if we closely examine even the most narrow focus on a goal that seems to know nothing else, we find hints of an alternative way to live. For something to appear as a goal in the first place such that we can see it and aspire to it and lose ourselves in its pursuit, it must arise from within a way of life that understands itself as more than goal-oriented striving, even if that "more" has not been consciously formulated or lived out with much consistency. The self-defeating vices into which we fall—the opposites of self-possession, friendship, and engagement with nature—are not the results of temptations or forces incompatible with activity for the sake of itself but rather ways in which such activity becomes diverted and distorted.

Because the ideal, so to speak, is already within us, or expressed, however inadequately, in the way we live, the project of recovering and justifying the ideal involves showing how it already characterizes our lives, even as we fail to see it and to live by it consistently. So in our examination of the ways in which we fall short of self-possession, friendship, and engagement with nature, even when those ways seem to deviate wildly from what the genuine virtue would require, we will find at work at least an aspiration to the real thing. Put another way, in our various ways of acting and striving that we mistakenly believe will bring us happiness—including very unfriendly, even hostile attitudes toward others, or oppositional stances toward nature—we are never entirely satisfied. Our actions, upon careful interpretation, reveal a simmering discontent that can be fulfilled only in the exercise of the genuine virtue.

In this sense, the "ideal" that I propose for how to live is also an account of what it means to live, a way of making sense of our lives as we are currently living them, including the mistakes into which we fall. The mistakes are not to be understood as merely negative ways of being, or as alternative postures at odds with the ideal, but as forms of confusion and incoherence that point the way to a truth that has been obscured. Though this may sound somewhat abstract, it will become clear, I believe, as we examine a range of concrete instances of goal-oriented striving—from the ways in which we might manipulate others as means to our ends, or appropriate nature while turning a blind eye to its meaning—and expose these ways as implicitly depending upon, or gesturing toward, genuine self-possession, friendship, and engagement with nature.

Self-Possession I

Navigating Modern Life with the Help of Aristotle

It's not easy to conjure images of self-possession in the demanding and comprehensive sense of which classical philosophy teaches. If we look to Hollywood, national politics, or the world of big business, we find many examples of self-confidence but few of self-possession. The difference between the two aligns with the distinction between a goal-oriented display of mastery or self-assertion in a particular domain and a manifestation of integrity, or wholeness, throughout every moment of one's life. To be self-confident is to know and feel one's self capable of carrying out a role or accomplishing a task—pitching a baseball game, making a business deal, giving a lecture, teaching a class, building a house, or curing a patient. To be self-possessed is to understand that above and beyond adeptness and accomplishment in a certain field is the capacity to discern and define the narrative arc of your life in which successes and failures rise to equal dignity as episodes that make you who you are.

The more we look for people who illuminate the virtue of self-possession, especially when it comes to putting one's goals in perspective, avoiding obsession and tunnel vision, or confronting resistance with poise and a spirit of redemption, the more we find ourselves identifying friends, teachers, mentors, and family members who live outside the limelight.

On the one hand, we all strive for self-possession and admire it in others. We don't need philosophy to teach us that it's a significant virtue. On the other hand, we find self-possession difficult to maintain and easy to misinterpret. Let us consider several reasons why.

The Pressure to Produce and to Accomplish

It's easy to lose possession of one's self in the hustle and bustle of the workday, to become obsessed with planning and checking boxes on the way to certain milestones—like promotions and finished projects. Even as the completion of our goals leaves us longing for a happiness that lasts, we have a way of suppressing our dissatisfaction and falling back into goal-oriented striving.

The tension between goal-oriented striving and activity for the sake of itself is something I experience acutely in the context of athletic training. The sense in which I genuinely love being in the midst of a pull-up workout, quite apart from any result that may come of it, has many dimensions. One has to do with a joy that I believe is common to a wide range of physical activities but that is easily diminished and degraded by an understanding of exercise simply in terms of health, weight loss, strength, or some other desired outcome. This is the exuberance of coming to understand one's powers as they work their force on a world and respond to its resistance. It has to do with a certain freedom of movement—the concerted negotiation with one's surroundings, such as the pull-up bar, the forces of gravity, or, if one is on a run or a walk, the sun, wind, rain, and rolling landscape—which, at its highest, is an appropriation and befriending of what at first seems alien and external. Here one might imagine a sailor's attentiveness and response to the wind, at first a force of its own, which is gradually coaxed into becoming a partner in powering the boat through the ocean. Such freedom represents an oasis from the idle conformity of movement that characterizes much of our everyday lives, as we find ourselves boxed in and contorted in various ways by precisely the devices meant to make life easy (think of elevators, subway cars, office cubicles, desks and chairs, and other "conveniences" or "efficient layouts" that direct us to move and position ourselves in ways we hardly question).

But the intrinsic joy of training is not something that I experience without effort. Many times I catch myself judging the worth of a session by whether I reached the numbers I set for myself or by how close I am to reclaiming a record. How easy it is to fall into this goal-oriented mindset when we are surrounded by technology and advertising that encourages us to focus on progress and to quantify our gains obsessively, by the step and the second as measured on our Fitbits and other such gadgets. This achievement-oriented approach leads me to quickly forget that each time I set the record— for the first time in 2016, then in 2017, then twice in 2018—the joy of the accomplishment itself faded quickly, forcing me to consider the way of life I had forged and brought to expression in training for these milestones. I also lose sight of the simple fact that records will always be broken, or worse (from the perspective of renown), lost upon a world that may one day no longer value, in any sense, the activity of hanging from a bar and then raising yourself until your chin is over it. What lasts and continues to live and grow, I remind myself, is the narrative to which victories and defeats both attest. So I tell myself to approach each repetition as a challenge in its own right, as part of a journey that is open-ended—that I don't *want* to end.

I tell myself the same thing as I sit down at my desk and write— that being done with a book is not the most important thing. Part of me wants to finish the manuscript ASAP, especially as I feel the fall semester closing in. But more meaningful than completion is the activity itself, which includes the self-clarity I might gain, and the new horizons I might open, through struggling to express my ideas on the page.

When I get caught up in looking ahead to the finished product, I recall what the nineteenth-century philosopher Friedrich Nietzsche says so evocatively at the end of *Beyond Good and Evil*, when he speaks of his written, now-established thoughts as having lost something of their initial charm: "Alas, what are you after all, my written and painted thoughts! It was not long ago that you were still so colorful, young, and malicious, full of thorns and secret spices—you made me sneeze and laugh—and now? You have already taken off your novelty . . . but nobody will guess from that how you looked in your morning, you sudden sparks and wonders of my solitude."[1]

Nietzsche's words are reminiscent of Socrates's critique of writing: As soon as one begins to put words on the page, one runs the risk of reducing the journey of thought to the production of knowledge. One can easily lose a sense for the exhilarating openness of philosophy, the sense in which even the most hard-fought, best-expressed insight is but a suggestion, an invitation, a spark to keep going. Reflecting on the journey of the project with the help of Nietzsche and Socrates helps me put the end in perspective. At the very least, I realize, I should welcome the simple opportunity to sit at my desk, in an air-conditioned study after a hard run on the baking-hot track, and attempt to clarify, in some small way, the inchoate ideas that motivate me. That's a great summer day. Why would I want the project to end?

Maintaining joy in the unfolding of an activity by understanding the journey it represents is no easy matter. What makes it so hard are the self-imposed pressure of deadlines and the temptations of success and acclaim, even in small forms, that lead us away from the intrinsic significance of the activity itself. To some extent these pressures are cultural. They arise of a goal-oriented society in which career advancement looms large. But in any society at any time, the danger of defining experience in terms of success and failure inevitably arises, even if the things one seeks to achieve are not work-related. This has to do with the very nature of human action, which, even in its apparently non-goal-oriented modes—singing, dancing, chatting with friends, taking an evening walk—can easily be reinterpreted in terms of some goal or other—performing well, making an impression, catching the sunset or missing it by a few minutes.

The Underappreciation and Disparagement of Self-Possession

Making the pursuit of self-possession doubly difficult is a lack of acknowledgment and encouragement for the virtue. Acts of self-possession typically don't elicit the noise and fanfare of great feats. Knowing one's self in one's commitments, acting out of a sense of the whole of one's life, remaining grounded in the face of adversity, gathering one's self when things fall apart: These aspects of self-possession that we will examine are far less conspicuous than the display of talents. Though self-possession and accomplishment can certainly go together, they often do not. And in a society that prizes accomplishment, people of self-possession but little to their name tend to fly under the radar.

Socrates is a case in point. Although he had immense influence on a small number of students, including Plato, he produced nothing of consequence. Until Plato wrote about Socrates and helped make him a world historical figure, Socrates was far overshadowed in public significance by great orators and statesmen such as Pericles. The prevailing ethic of Athens was to strive for public heroism that would be remembered, like that of the mythic Achilles. But though Achilles displayed tremendous bravery in the Trojan War, he was perpetually peeved, plagued by vengeance, and tormented by the fear of death—though he faced it with incredible fortitude. Achilles certainly exhibited an impressive self-confidence on the battlefield; but he lacked the self-possession of Socrates, and suffered for it.

Not only is self-possession overlooked, it is also misunderstood and disparaged. The low-key, imperturbable, sometimes lighthearted demeanor characteristic of self-possession is easily mistaken for in-difference or frivolity. When those who are self-possessed encounter misfortune—say, a car accident, or a missed flight—they don't get too worked up about it, especially if it was beyond their control, or a matter of honest human error. And such tranquility can disturb those who are absorbed in conventions that dictate gravity, anger, pity, or extreme remorse in such situations. To make the cultiva-tion of self-possession a foremost mission in one's life is to expose one's self to the common misinterpretation of being "irrespon-sible," "callous," or lacking in concern for "the things that matter."

The twentieth-century philosopher Hannah Arendt, a Jewish émigré to the United States before World War II, faced criticisms of this kind when she remarked, in the course of her coverage of the Eichmann trial after the war, that she found the Nazi mass-murderer to be, in many ways, a comically absurd figure. Some were offended that Arendt didn't speak in an exclusively grave, condemnatory tone of Eichmann but rather laughed in jest at what she took to be a thoroughly unremarkable, rather dumb and pathetic bureaucratic bearing, which she encapsulated in her now-famous phrase "the ba-nality of evil." In defending herself, Arendt said that she couldn't help the tone of her reporting. It was simply an expression of who she was—someone who prided herself on finding the absurd in the terrible, and who would laugh in the face of certain death. There was something Socratic in her response. As Socrates's sobbing friends gather around him before he is to be executed, and his friend Crito asks him how he'd like to be buried, Socrates responds with a characteristically wry sense of humor: "However you like, if you can lay hold of me and I do not escape you."[2] Socrates's point is that as soon as he dies, his real self will no longer be manifest in the body that lies lifeless in front of his friends. Crito therefore shouldn't make such a big deal of the burial. Socrates refused to allow the shadow of death to derail the levity and joy with which he lived.

He and Arendt were hardly insensitive people who belittled suffering out of a cynical indifference to life. Quite the opposite: They took suffering seriously as essential to human existence, and as an immense challenge and opportunity to redeem life in its darkest moments. What they strove to overcome was self-pity in the face of even grave misfortune. And just as they refused to take pity on themselves, they refused to let pity overwhelm them when it came to interpreting the suffering of others. Instead, they fought long and hard to understand suffering as integral to life and to the joy of redemption. But self-possession of this high and difficult order is vulnerable to disparagement by those who mistake the good life for one free of pain, and who mistakenly valorize pity as sympathy.

The Temptation of Empty Pleasure, and Theories of Happiness That Fuel It

As much as I love the feeling of my weight digging into the pavement with each stride as I jog to the park on a cool summer morning to embrace the pull-up bar before the sun gets too high, I often face the age-old dilemma of whether to roll out of bed for the training session or hit the snooze button. Though I know that the training session will be a more life-affirming experience than tossing around in bed half-awake, there's something very alluring about the soft pillow and the easy comfort it represents. I don't mean to suggest that rest is a bad thing. Against the backdrop of our goal-oriented striving, rest, and especially the kind of deep sleep that takes us out of our daily routines and allows us to dream things for which we may never have made space in our daytime reflections, might very well be regarded a *higher* mode of activity than our efforts to attain and accomplish. What I mean to get at in the allure of the pillow is our tendency to shirk the kinds of challenges through which we develop character and bring our personalities to expression, instead turning to the easy but insubstantial pleasures of a conventional lifestyle.

Instead of holding firm to a commitment to get outside and engage with nature, or to catch up with friends in a way unmediated by Facebook or Instagram, we distract ourselves with forms of mindless enjoyment that allow us simply to check out of a frenzied way of life. We find ourselves caught in the vicious cycle of highly disciplined striving and frivolous escapism. The latter can range from the innocent to the harmful, from kicking back to a junk television show at the end of the day to abusing prescription drugs in hopes of deadening the seemingly ineradicable stress of goal-oriented striving. Common to such indulgences is that they give us easy and momentary pleasure but leave us longing for action in which to take pride.

The notion of a career followed by retirement could be seen as the unholy alliance of striving and indulgence writ large. The career is spent in frenzied pursuit of accomplishment and anxious ministry to the so-called necessities of life, which are really, more often than not, conveniences and status symbols. Retirement is spent in the care-free passage of time devoid of adventure, risk, or personal growth. Of course, retirement can in principle free one for activity that is genuinely meaningful; but we should note that the very use of the word "retirement" to denote a postcareer life, though meant to be a *good* thing, evokes the image of someone tired, exhausted, ready to fold. It's striking that in just about every other context "retired" is a pejorative term or at least one that carries the sense of retreat or capitulation to circumstances. If you're a baseball team and "retired one-two-three in the ninth inning," that's bad. So why should retirement be good when it comes to one's career? The term implies that one's career is a source of anxiety, and that care-free withdrawal is the way out.

We might very well subject the term "vacation" to a similar critique. The longing for "vacant" time, in contrast to time spent in pursuit of a different kind or quality of activity, as a "holiday" (holy-day) suggests, makes sense only in reference to time spent in the anxious anticipation from which one wishes simply to escape.

Aiding and abetting our tendency to seek refuge in easy but insubstantial comforts is much of the popular self-help literature on how to be happy, or to make better decisions, which leads us to conceive of happiness as a mental state to be attained rather than a way of being to be cultivated. Such literature, typically written by professional psychologists, indulges both our obsession with discipline and planning (in its suggestion that we can *engineer* our happiness by correcting the supposed biases of the mind) and our haste to find an easy escape from the pressures of goal-oriented work.

A telling example of how we are taught to view happiness as a state of mind and encouraged to avoid the risk and adventure that cultivates self-possession can be found in the advice of psychologist and world-famous rational choice theorist Daniel Kahneman for how to pick your next vacation spot. When deciding where to go, he suggests, we are prone to the "cognitive bias" of the "remembering self." The remembering self tends to distort the amount of pleasure it actually experienced on some previous trip. It especially tends to accord undue weight to the pleasure or pain it experiences at the end of the event.[3] For example, if our last vacation—let's say, to the beach—ended badly in that we had to contend with stormy weather, we tend to harp on that ending even though we experienced much pleasure on the previous six days. Biased by the "remembering self," which represents pleasure and pain very inaccurately, we might be inclined to go somewhere else on our next trip—say, to the mountains—when really we'd be happier at the beach again.

The premise of Kahneman's whole approach is that what constitutes a good vacation, or a good experience of any kind, is the mental state that accompanies it. We are supposed to arrive at some overall calculation of how happy we *really were* by adding together an unbiased assessment of the amount of pleasure we experienced in each moment. Happiness, he assumes, is ultimately "in our head"—a condition, or state, of which we can be consciously aware and assess more or less accurately in "real time" as we experience it. Missing from this picture is any sense of the relation of happiness to meaning and meaning to struggle.

When I consider the most significant travels of my life, ones that are integral, in at least a small way, to the sense in which I can call myself happy today, they are typically ones that were not easy. Some involved frustrating miscommunications that taxed my powers of expression, wrong turns from which I had to find my way back, and unwanted invitations that required either some tact and diplomacy to decline, or bravery to accept. Even the vacations that I might casually refer to as tranquil or relaxing were tranquil only in the sense that they opened a space for activities, conversations, and outings that took me out of the humdrum routine of the workweek and presented opportunities for me to confront new forms of subtle resistance, whether it was the difficulty of searching for a special type of local seashell or the challenge of making sense of a cultural practice. In the midst of such experiences, pleasure and pain cannot be neatly separated, as the joy of a discovery is inseparable from the struggle in its pursuit.

At the time of many of the most significant experiences in my life, my mental state was far from tranquil. If I were hooked up to one of those brain-imaging machines in which certain psychologists today put much stock, the so-called stress regions of my brain would have surely been lighting up. Yet those experiences, accompanied as they were by psychological stress, are ones that, in retrospect, I would much rather seek again, in new forms, than moments of passive and fleeting enjoyment that I can barely remember because of their insignificance.

Kahneman might reply that I simply have a "preference" for adventure and storytelling over pleasure, and that his framework of the "remembering" and "experiencing" self can be applied to that new preference. But to accept the "preference," so to speak, for adventure and storytelling is to undermine the very distinction between a self that experiences and a self that remembers. For the sense in which an experience is a worthwhile adventure emerges only in retrospect, after we come home, reflect upon it, share it with friends, get their reaction, and encounter new, analogous situations that we are now better equipped to handle.

The remembering self, so to speak, may be *wiser* than the experiencing self precisely *because* it discounts or forgets the mental state of "back then" and has a clear view of the lessons learned since. From the perspective of the journey, there is only one self—not a remembering aspect of our identity that is prone to distort what "really happened." (Contemporary psychologists also readily forget the insight of older schools of psychology, not least Freudian analysis, according to which we are prone to misinterpret an experience *in the moment* just as much as we may do so in retrospect.) The notion of a remembering self that is inherently biased is the outgrowth of resigned spirit, submerged in a shallow utilitarianism, that has lost sight of life as a journey.

In contrast to the assumptions of rational choice theory, we should consider that often enough, the most meaningful events are ones that, at the time, are accompanied by doubt, anxiety, discomfort, and even pain, as we are not yet able, or ready, to place them within a story of struggle, redemption, and self-knowledge. Were we to judge such experiences at a discrete moment based solely on our mental state, we might denounce them as situations we'd rather escape or as events we'd hopefully forget. But in retrospect, in light of their place in a narrative that has unfolded, we may come to embrace them as essential to the meaning and direction of our lives. Sometimes we may even be unaware that we are in the midst of a significant experience, so apparently fragmentary and inconsequential is a given gesture or encounter that it doesn't even register as an event or rise to the level of our conscious awareness. Only much later, once events have unfolded and we are liberated from certain distractions that gripped us at the time can we look back and recognize something as the beginning of a commitment or passion that has since come to be part of who we are. Whatever our mental state might have been at a given moment—happy, sad, anxious, relaxed, fearful, bold—turns out to be utterly inconsequential by comparison to the happiness that was implicit *in the activity itself* but awaited a long process of self-discovery to emerge.

So often in life, we feel bad because we believe we should feel differently. We believe we should feel happier while in the company of friends, more relaxed on vacation, more at ease while giving a public speech than we actually do. In these moments it is worth turning a critical eye on the conception of happiness that leads us to expect a certain feeling from our experiences. It is only when happiness gets constructed as a mental state to be attained that the question of how we *should feel* can arise. Against this goal-oriented outlook, we may remind ourselves that what we do has intrinsic significance as an unfolding event within the larger context of a personal narrative, and that the feeling of satisfaction we may derive from it may be hours, days, or even years to come. What matters from this perspective is not how we feel in doing something but our sense of its importance as an attempt, a proposition, a moment of self-presentation whose significance goes far beyond what we may be able to understand, appreciate, or feel good about in the moment.

The conception of happiness as activity, and the corresponding demotion of state of mind to the somewhat fickle and never fully adequate register of the meaning or sense expressed in the way we live, is neatly expressed by the ancient Greek term *eudaimonia*, today translated almost uniformly as "happiness" but actually meaning "good fortune" or, literally, "having a good *daemon* [by your side]." Daemons, for the ancient Greeks, were not devilish creatures who haunt us but benevolent demigods who serve as our guardian spirits, shepherding us from birth to death to the afterlife. Thus, happiness, in the ancient Greek sense, is inseparable from activity, from being on the right path, guided by the daemon.

Furthermore, happiness is bound up with fortune. According to the popular lore at the time that Plato and Aristotle wrote, our guardian spirits are allotted at birth, suggesting that the source of our happiness is beyond our control. Though we can listen to the daemon or ignore it—and thus exercise a significant kind of agency (that of attention and response)—we cannot choose the one we get. Happiness, as expressed by eudaimonia, is something that happens to us, not something we can bring about through methods of positive thinking. The old English root of happiness—happenstance, or chance—preserves the ancient Greek sensibility and speaks against our contemporary aspirations to attain happiness by mastering the quirks and hang-ups of the mind.

It was not until early modern times that the ancient Greek conception of eudaimonia and Christian modifications of it in terms of good works and blessedness gave way on a large scale to the notion of happiness as a state of mind that we might attain through mastering the conditions of our misery. The reason for that shift ought to make us suspicious of it.

Though today we regard the pursuit of happiness as integral to freedom, enshrining it in the Declaration of Independence alongside liberty as a self-evident truth, such a pursuit was actually born of a project of social control. It was the seventeenth-century philosopher Thomas Hobbes who invented happiness as a state of mind, or at least inflated it to proportions unheard of in earlier times, for the sake of political order. Confronted by raging wars of religion, which Hobbes attributed to stubborn dogmatism and overblown confidence in one's convictions on ultimate things, he sought to provide a political philosophy of peace and order. His radical solution was to launch a wholesale condemnation of pride and to replace it with an ideal of happiness devoid of judgment and agency.

For the sake of peace and psychological repose, Hobbes suggested, we ought to surrender not only our arms but also our moral and political judgment to a unitary sovereign, what he called the "leviathan" state. It was quite a bargain that Hobbes proposed: judgment for comfort. But he felt a radical solution was needed. He therefore doubled down on his insistence that peace, and not power, or self-assertion, is what humanity really wants. He knew that this was fiction as much as fact, recognizing in one telling passage a human impulse to seek "power after power that ceaseth only in death."[4] He also remarked that laughter is derisive: People laugh as they make fun of weaknesses they perceive in others.[5]

But Hobbes made an immense effort to promote tranquility as the foremost human aspiration. He went so far as to invent a science according to which self-preservation is not only a condition of happiness but also a natural instinct of life. Humanity, Hobbes claimed, fears death as the stone moves downward.[6] He knew this was untrue, as he was all too familiar with those whose foremost instinct was to face death for their beliefs rather than surrender their arms. But Hobbes believed people could be educated into this new "science" of self-preservation. In a sense, he was right. The alacrity with which we today posit survival as the primary instinct of all forms of life, accepting Darwinian theories of animal behavior and even of human action as if they were the only "rational" accounts, attests to the long shadow of Hobbes. So too does the familiar belief voiced, for example, by psychologist and popular author Steven Pinker: In the face of moral conflict, the one thing we can all agree upon is that simply being alive is a good thing. From this premise, utilitarian thinkers such as Pinker build an entire ethics that is little but a rehashing of Hobbes's.

The flipside of Hobbes's promotion of happiness was his condemnation of pride. Instead of addressing fanaticism and the will to dominate, the actual problems that plagued his society, Hobbes attacked pride as such, condemning all confidence in one's own convictions and judgments as "vain glory." Of course, Hobbes's entire "scientific" project was perhaps itself an act of hubristic self-assertion, an arrogance of believing he could singlehandedly transform human nature through his rhetoric of the "natural." But his project was far-reaching in its effect, in part because it played upon a fundamental human tendency to confront hard times with resignation and even to justify one's own weakness in the face of suffering as "natural" or "moral." Today, we who posit survival as an inherent instinct, who valorize peace and happiness but are never quite happy or at ease, who enjoy security and comfort who but lack the pride of making a judgment, remain beholden to the legacy of Hobbes.

Our Tendency to Moralizing Self-Evasion

If the tendencies we have so far considered were not peril enough to self-possession, we might add a fourth obstacle at which I hinted in making sense of Hobbes's rhetorical coup: our seemingly boundless capacity for reinterpreting forms of dispossession and personal weakness as virtue. Consider, for example, the way in which we can easily convince ourselves that a kind of frenetic industriousness and obsessive planning that leaves us with little time for family and friends and without joy in the project itself is really "hard work" or "responsible self-discipline." We can even convince ourselves that we're doing it "to provide for our family" when really we're satisfying our own ambition.

Consider too how we might attempt to cover over a meek diffidence aimed at making a good impression and being liked with the gloss of "being a nice person" and how we might even deride frank speech as arrogance. Moralism of this kind represents a form of self-delusion whereby we fall toward what Nietzsche calls "the last man," the person on the verge of becoming a thoughtless, enervated creature no longer able to recognize his own weakness.

Nietzsche notes that for the "last man," even happiness becomes a kind of moral imperative *to be happy,* and thus to display the appreciation for the comforts of modern life that is expected of the "enlightened" individual. The last men, says Nietzsche, constantly brag about how they've "invented happiness."[7] Of course, if they were truly fulfilled, they would not need to brag about it.

Echoes of the kind of prescriptive happiness to which Nietzsche alludes abound in our society today. A comic portrayal can be found in an episode of the television series *Curb Your Enthusiasm,* in which we find Larry David, the protagonist, and his best friend, Jeff Green, eating together at a somewhat upscale but rather generic Santa Monica establishment. As they munch at their food without genuine joy in the outing, Larry asks, in the midst of finishing a bite, "How much are you loving this?" It's more of a demand for an affirmative response than a question—a need to be reassured that one *is* loving it precisely because one senses its emptiness. Exclamatory phrases such as "unbelievable," "so good," and "I'm loving this" are frequent throughout the show. They typically arise in situations that are supposed to bring happiness but issue in fleeting pleasures at best.

A ubiquitous example of prescriptive happiness is the imperative to smile for the camera. It stood out to me after traveling to countries where people routinely take photos but do not typically smile when posing. It's not that they're unfriendly or taciturn. They just don't feel the need to project happiness on cue. Instead, they simply look earnestly at the photographer, as if they were listening to him.

To these quotidian examples, we might add more theorized conceptions of "be happy" that bespeak a certain moral superiority, as when we try to put in perspective the suffering of today by contrasting it to the supposed barbarism or violence of past ages. To say nothing of how barbarism has arguably taken on new and insidious forms, there is something pathetic in a happiness that can be enjoyed only in derision of other places and times. The need to proclaim and deride speaks to the shallowness of our happiness.

Given the strong forces at work against self-possession—the pressure to produce and to accomplish, the dearth of support for the virtue, the misguided ideal of happiness as a state of mind, and our tendency to moralizing self-evasion—it's no wonder that self-possession is a virtue difficult to maintain and to even see clearly. At the same time, we have a sense that self-possession is essential to our happiness, especially when we find ourselves confronting resistance and hardship. To better understand self-possession and its significance for the good life, let us turn to classical philosophy.

Aristotle on "Greatness of Soul"

In describing the various virtues integral to a good life, including courage, generosity, and justice, Aristotle singles out one as the highest. He calls it "greatness of soul" (*megalopsychia*). To our ears, the term sounds as if it were applicable only to the greatest spiritual leaders or heroes. But Aristotle means it to be within reach of all of us. Some translators render "greatness of soul" "magnanimity," which brings it closer to a familiar contemporary term. But "magnanimity," which suggests a lavish generosity, does not quite capture the fullness of the virtue that Aristotle has in mind. As with every word or phrase that denotes something essential to the human experience, "greatness of soul" is hard to define in the abstract. To understand it requires delving into its various dimensions and instances. But self-possession is a decent approximation.

Aristotle introduces the virtue as the proper disposition with respect to honor. The person of great soul "regards himself as worthy of great things and *is* worthy of them."[8] To regard one's self as worthy while not being worthy, by contrast, is to be arrogant, or vain. And to fail to regard one's self as worthy while *being* worthy is to be small, or meek. Interestingly, Aristotle regards smallness—what we might easily mistake for modesty—as no less a vice than

vanity. Greatness of soul is thus a "mean," as Aristotle puts it, between the extremes of vanity, on the one hand, and meekness on
the other.

As an example of Aristotle's basic idea of claiming one's due we
might consider the prideful flare of Muhammad Ali after defying the
odds of the boxing world and defeating Sonny Liston for the Heavyweight Title: "I'm the world's greatest!" he memorably shouted to
the reporters who had doubted him. "Say I'm the world's greatest!"
To the extent that Ali demanded respect as the world's best boxer
at that moment, he had a fair claim and exhibited a kind of greatness of soul, which could have easily been mistaken for vanity by
those who bore a grudge or resented his stunning coup. Had Ali,
out of an excess of modesty, downplayed his victory as a fluke or a
stroke of fortune, he would have arguably displayed a kind of
smallness, capitulating to the injustice of the fans and commenta-
tors who were reluctant to award him his due. Ali claimed what
he deserved. Sometimes, of course, he would claim more, as when
he'd boast that his feats in boxing surpassed the greatest achievements in any field ever. To that extent he could be justly accused of
vanity—though it was a tongue-in-cheek vanity.

As Aristotle first presents it, greatness of soul might seem to suggest a human longing for the esteem of others, at least the esteem
proportionate to one's accomplishment. But as he continues to describe the virtue, Aristotle makes clear that it transcends a concern
for honor. To be of great soul, writes Aristotle, is "to regard honor
as a small thing."[9] He thus challenges the honor-based ethic that was
prominent in ancient Athens and leads us to rethink the idea that
acclaim, great or small, is necessary for a good life. The person of
great soul, writes Aristotle, looks down on small honors and those
bestowed "by mere coincidence."[10] He "does not rush for the things
of widespread acclaim."[11] He "will accept honor rendered by persons of high station on the right grounds with measured satisfac-

tion only." For no matter who is conferring an honor, "he regards it as nothing but his due."[12]

Aristotle thus suggests a disposition to take pride in one's work, or activity for its own sake. The person of great soul appreciates the affirmation of others but does not depend on it. He would keep doing what he does regardless. To take such pride in one's work, Aristotle suggests, is to stand up for it by claiming honor—not because you want honor in itself, but because you deserve it. You respect your work and owe it to yourself to stand by it, including when others disparage it. If, after you've said your piece, you still don't get the honor you deserve, so be it. The point is not honor but self-respect. And part of self-respect is not harping on honor when you're unjustly denied it. For to do so would be to lower yourself to those who deny you—to grovel before people whose respect you should now hold in contempt. You simply regard the injustice you have suffered as bad luck—the dispensation of the resentful, the narrow-minded, or the benignly unappreciative who lack the capacity to recognize the worth of what you do—and resume your work as if nothing had happened. Absorbed in what you're doing, you have no time to bear a grudge: "A person of great soul is in the habit of forgetting and overlooking the wrongs he has suffered."[13] Aristotle thus presents an image of someone who is gentle but no pushover, someone who, in virtue of his or her own standard of right and wrong, does not need the validation of others, and who therefore floats above the pettiness to which human life is prone.

Beyond situations concerning the bestowal of honor, greatness of soul extends to one's bearing and mode of expression in everyday discourse. It involves speaking one's mind and accepting that others may disagree. The person of great soul "is open in expressing love and hate; for concealment is the mark of fear."[14] The source of such frankness is an abiding concern with truth over reputation: The person of great soul "cares more for the truth than for opinion."[15] Such confidence is manifest in even the subtle gestures of the body—a "slow way of moving . . . a deep voice, and a steady pace of speech." For the person who is "serious about only a few things" will not act in a harried manner.[16] To be perpetually rushing around, suggests Aristotle, is to care too much about where you're going and not enough about your own dignity in every step you take. Why get bent out of shape by your destination? Aristotle leads us to consider the many daily circumstances in which we find ourselves anxiously hurrying from appointment to appointment, as if being late were the ultimate disaster. Better sometimes to carry yourself with command than to arrive on time.

Implicit in Aristotle's critique of harried speech and an anxious gate is a critique of goal-oriented striving. The reason we find ourselves rushing from point A to point B is that we regard our lives as a series of destinations to be reached. The reason we speak at breakneck pace in a monotone pitch is that we are anxious to pack a lot of words into a single breath, as if the point of speaking were to convey information, or to create an impression of being informed. Aristotle reminds us that we ought to take a deep breath and cultivate a style in which we take pride for its own sake, a deliberate way of speaking and moving that projects a sense of self. Aristotle suggests that our everyday manners and morals say a good deal about who we are. Turns of phrase, cadence of speech, and tone of voice—aspects of bearing that we might be inclined to dismiss as superficial—reflect our character.

The gist of what Aristotle presents is a certain authenticity of expression: honest self-assertion that resists self-distorting norms of decorum and an excessive concern with political correctness. At the same time, Aristotle suggests a certain nobility of speech: In expressing himself or herself openly, the person of great soul does not speak out of spite, condemnation, or resentment, but out of concern for the truth.

Speak Up! What You Say and How You Say It Are Part of Who You Are

Aristotle's proposition that manners of speech are integral to character can help us identify and overcome the myriad forms of evasive talk that threaten to disempower us little by little every day. Consider the ways in which we substitute something vague and nice-sounding for a direct request that we are too shy or ashamed to state outright. A ubiquitous example is the use of "reach out" when we really mean "ask for advice" or "request a donation." Such corporate-speak is not only euphemistic and misleading. It's meek. Someone who believes in their project or vocation shouldn't be ashamed to ask for support.

It's an amusing and potentially rewarding exercise in self-examination to try to catch one's self in the habits of speech that Aristotle might coach us to overcome. Ones that come to mind include trailing off at the end of sentences, or concluding an opinion with "so yeah . . ." or "I dunno . . . ," as if punctuating one's view with a period would offend people. Among academics and professionals, a familiar pitfall is to speak in a rapid-fire, long-winded manner, sometimes offering and refuting a number of counterarguments in one breath, while leaving no room for any actual interjection or question. Though such speech reflects a certain fluency and erudition, it also bespeaks a subtle fear of being challenged. Along with such discourse often comes the frequent use of an assertive "right?" and "y'know . . ." at precisely the most questionable parts of one's account. Philosophy professors, I've found, are especially guilty of this, and I do not exempt myself.

When I catch myself speaking in these ways, I remind myself of not only Aristotle but also my eighth-grade math teacher, Mr. C. Though he taught us a good deal of introductory algebra, he taught us far more about self-possession. One of the things he emphasized was confidence in speech. He mostly taught us by example. But he had a few rules: Sit straight, speak up, and say "yes" instead of "yeah." Partly it was an old-school sensibility. He wanted us to speak in a respectful way befitting of students. But it was also an attempt to cultivate in us a certain self-possession at a young age: that of speaking clearly and with authority.

It's very easy to unconsciously pick up evasive forms of speech that distort what we really mean to say and that, in small ways, reflect a lack of self-possession. All of us, even the most eloquent and original speakers, are vulnerable to the largely unconscious pressures of self-distorting conformity, including forms of superficial niceness that are really forms of excessive deference—too many pleases and thank yous when making mundane requests, or effusive apologies for quotidian misunderstandings that aren't your fault. Learning to say what we mean and project who we are is a never-ending process.

A great part of the difficulty lies in simply coming to recognize certain phrases and styles of speech as questionable, which requires moving in a range of circles throughout life and acquiring bases for comparison among different modes of discourse. One of the ways in which I've learned to appreciate athletic training as integral to a journey of self-formation, and not merely as a means to an end, is how it's enabled me to find a frankness of expression that would be difficult to cultivate in academia alone. If the characteristic vice of academic speech is long-winded evasiveness that projects a certain smallness of soul, that of the gym is blunt self-assertion that projects vanity or crudeness. But there is a kind of Aristotelian balance of speech that partakes of neither vice. I've often reflected on how the shouts of advice from coach to players during a game, or the exclamations of encouragement among training partners during a hard workout, or the frank banter between sets of pull-ups gesture toward the kind of open speech that Aristotle proposes.

Time and again, I find myself returning to Aristotle's insight: To be of great soul is to avoid many words when a few will do, to state one's opinion and wait for others to respond. Perhaps they'll agree, or perhaps they'll make a point that leads you to revise your opinion. In either case, you come away the better for it. Remain focused on truth and wisdom, and stop caring so much about the impression you make. Exercise diplomacy, sure, but remain true to yourself.

Of the balance between diplomacy and honest self-expression, Aristotle proposes the following: "toward persons of modest station, the person of great soul will be mild-mannered," often speaking in "ironical self-deprecation to the many."[17] But "toward people of good fortune and high station, the person of great soul will be big [or haughty]."[18] To be exceedingly decorous and deferential toward people in positions of authority or prestige, he suggests, is to distort yourself for the sake of a good impression. Such flattery is a form of weakness. If anything, suggests Aristotle, you should make a special effort to be frank before such people, to hold yourself in high regard and show that you don't live in awe of their reputation. Often this may earn you respect; but, most importantly, it constitutes self-respect. In the company of people who are unrecognized, by contrast, you should make an effort to be modest— so as not to make them ashamed or too shy to voice their opinions when they might have something worthwhile to say. The person of great soul humbles himself before those of modest station out of the same strength that impels him to haughtiness in the company of notables.

Cultivating Your Own Judgment

Underlying great-souled openness of expression is the capacity for *judgment*. When Aristotle writes that the person of great soul cares nothing for honor offered randomly or on trivial grounds, he imagines such a person making an implicit judgment: There is a difference between mere popular acclaim and honor from a worthy figure. This judgment points to another: There is a difference between the real worth of what one does and how the world perceives it.

Today, the virtue of judgment has fallen on hard times. To be "judgmental" is considered a bad thing, something equivalent to "intolerant," "closed-minded," or "unsympathetic." And, yet, we find ourselves making judgments all the time—in deciding what company to keep, what career path to pursue, how to balance work life and family life, or whether to hit the snooze button or go for a run.

Why we deride judgment per se, rather than the specific, punitive kinds of judgment we really intend to reject, may go back to Hobbes's denouncement of fanaticism in terms of a wholesale rejection of judgment. We recall that his project of establishing peace and order amid the wars of religion involved the substitution of an ideal of undisturbed happiness for the pride of taking a stand. Hobbes sought relentlessly to convince people that their judgments were merely "subjective" and would lead only to pointless, insoluble conflict. Better to outsource judgment in significant matters to the public authority, he argued. Our skepticism of judgment may very well speak to Hobbes's rhetorical triumph.

But caution though we may against judgment, we can't escape the burden of engaging in it, above all when it comes to how we live our own lives. Holding onto judgment and cultivating it is not easy, especially in the face of the goal-oriented ethos that leads us to view action in terms of utility and accomplishment. Drawn into the goal-oriented framework, we come to view judgment in terms of choice, or decision making, which aims at a particular result, such as health, financial stability, or pleasure. Whereas judgment can be made only by *you*, in light of the self-image for which you aspire, choice and decision making can be exercised by anyone skilled in acquiring the things you want. As soon as you aim at achieving a discrete goal—health, wealth, bodily strength—you can rest assured there's an expert out there ready to sell you some method for how to do it.

As living itself becomes the goal-oriented science of calculation, another type of expert arises, a meta-expert, not someone skilled in a concrete profession (such as medicine) but someone who makes a claim to know the art of the good life as such. This expert is a certain sort of behavioral psychologist, who specializes in the methods of being a "rational decision maker" and who promises to expose the so-called cognitive biases that lead to "irrational" choices. If the psychologist were pressed on what right he has to invoke the universal terms of "reason," "irrationality," and "bias" when simply referring to decisions aimed to maximize utility, he would be compelled to admit that by "reason" he simply means what most people regard as the kind of calculation best suited to achieve their goals. But such an admission demotes the psychologist to minister of a goal-oriented, utilitarian mode of existence. It shatters the hubristic claim to know the mind as such, or to be an expert in the science of "rationality."

For who is to say that even the quirky decisions psychologists regard as irrational or biased are not thoughtful in their own ways, though from a nonutilitarian perspective? Consider someone who prefers to purchase 90% lean meat to 10% fat content, a case that behavioral psychologists cite as evidence for a "framing bias" according to which our brains, when faced with two ostensibly equivalent options, are simply more receptive to the one that sounds more positively worded. A perfectly plausible explanation for why people prefer the 90% lean has nothing to do with an ingrained bias: When consumers make purchases, they are not trying to minimize fat intake but to live up to a certain self-image. In a society that values healthy eating as if it were a fashion, consumers want to think of themselves as "the *kind of person* who eats low-fat." To confirm to themselves, and to demonstrate to those in their circle, and even to the man behind the counter, that they are hip to the latest health trends, they go for the 90% lean. Though such a self-image could be questioned as superficial or misguided (why should healthiness be such a virtue?), it is certainly not irrational or a mere quirk of the brain. It involves a nuanced self-awareness bound up with reputation and pride. But just as the doctor is liable to see everything in light of health, the behavioral psychologist is liable to view everything in terms of calculation. What appears to be a universal science of living turns out to be an approach to decision making no less narrow than any professional perspective.

There's nothing wrong with taking expert advice in particular domains. If you break your leg and want it fixed quickly and safely, you go to a doctor. To reason out a remedy on your own would seem foolish. But if you get in the habit of depending on experts to get you what you want, you can easily slide into relying on them for advice that far exceeds the scope of their competence.

Especially when an expert deals in something that many people desire and need, such as health, you might be inclined to trust that person's prescription not only as a targeted course of action for a particular aim, but also as a guide to life. You start trusting the doctor both to fix your leg and to advise you on what risks you should and shouldn't take once it's better. You easily forget that the doctor can speak only to likely health outcomes, not to whether health is the most crucial consideration in determining your course of action.

Experts have every right, and perhaps even a duty as thoughtful human beings, to offer their views on how to live. But their opinions are no substitute for one's own. All too often, we thoughtlessly adhere to the life advice of experts simply because they have authority in one significant domain. We relinquish our judgment to them out of fear of judging for ourselves. Worried that we might judge poorly and bear responsibility for the consequences, we outsource our judgment to someone else with a veneer of respectability—with a fancy title, a white coat, or a suit and tie. If things go wrong, we can at least say to ourselves, and to those who may be implicated in our failure, "well, I hired the best advice out there. What more can I do?" In this way, we attempt to salvage our pride and clear our conscience.

The experts, flattered by the deference they receive, and empowered by their mastery of a widely prized skill, take greater liberties to pontificate from the narrow perspective of their trade on matters that have nothing to do with their technical knowledge. Their confident bearing draws in more and more credulous seekers of advice, and that becomes difficult to resist, even for those with a good deal of self-possession.

The tendency of experts to overstep their bounds finds memorable expression in Socrates's account, at his trial, of how he went about questioning various Athenian citizens to see if they were wiser than he. When he gets to the technical experts (the craftsmen), he notes that they did indeed possess knowledge of which he was ignorant: They knew how to make and fix things. But they believed that in virtue of their expertise they were also wise in other matters, including the greatest ones, "and this folly eclipsed what wisdom they did have."[19]

An amusing example of Socrates's point arises in Plato's *Symposium,* in the mannerisms and speech on love (*eros*) delivered by Eryximachus, the doctor. As Socrates, Eryximachus, and other Athenian notables gather around the dinner table of Agathon, the decorated tragic poet, to celebrate his recent award for putting on a popular play, they turn to the topic of how much wine to drink. All agree that, as they've drunk to excess the night before, they will take it easy. After it's been decided, Eryximachus takes it upon himself to expostulate on drunkenness, given his expert opinion as a doctor: "Now, since in my opinion, none of those present is eager to drink a lot of wine, perhaps I should be less disagreeable were I to speak the truth of what drunkenness is. For I believe this has become quite plain to me from the art of medicine. Drunkenness is a hard thing for human beings, and as far as it is in my power, I should neither be willing to go on drinking nor advice another to do so."[20]

Eryximachus clearly speaks from the limited perspective of a doctor, oriented to health, yet claims to know "*the* truth" of what drunkenness is. He is soon made to look ridiculous, as, by the end of the dialogue, Alcibiades, the young rising star of Athenian politics and military prowess, barges in drunkenly and offers surprisingly honest praise of Socrates that he might very well have repressed if sober. The sense in which drunkenness turns out to be a bad thing from the standpoint of honest self-appraisal is at least questionable. But, for the doctor, drunkenness is simply a harm to health, therefore bad.

The folly of Eryximachus is compounded by the laughable speech on love (eros) that he offers with notable pretension. (Eros is the topic of discussion over dinner and the theme of the dialogue.) Whereas other, more thoughtful participants speak of love in terms of passionate attachment, a longing for one's lost other half (Aristophanes), or the love of beauty (Socrates), Eryximachus offers a meandering account of eros in terms of health (perhaps the most unerotic topic). Eros, he claims, is the perfect ordering of the body, brought about by the art of medicine. As if to highlight the ridiculousness of Eryximachus's confidence, Plato has him begin his speech with the high-handed remark that, although the others spoke well, he will now "put a complete end" to the discussion by offering a sufficient account of love. None of the others had made such a claim.[21] But it is the nature of experts—whether doctors, lawyers, or mechanics—to see solutions rather than mysteries.

To some extent, Eryximachus is a caricature of the expert who takes himself to be wise in all matters. And, yet, there are those who gobble up his projection of confidence hook, line, and sinker. Phaedrus, another dinner guest, is one of them. In response to Eryximachus's admonishment on drinking, Phaedrus dutifully follows the doctor's orders: "Well, as for myself, I am used to obeying you [Eryximachus], particularly in everything you say about medicine; and now the rest will do so too, if they take good counsel."[22]

Phaedrus thus represents the tendency we have to trust experts in virtue of their expertise, even when they speak on matters that have nothing to do with their technical skill, such as how much to drink at a dinner party. Clearly this is not a medical question but a question of judgment, of practical wisdom: how to balance the conviviality of drinking against the price of a hangover. But Phaedrus, enthralled by the professional credentials of Eryximachus, dutifully follows him, even admonishing the others to follow suit. Phaedrus's response is emblematic of a threat to self-possession at all times: the temptation to outsource our judgment to a technician—a doctor, a psychologist, or an economist—in a matter that is really one of personal or political judgment.

A resonant contemporary rendition of this temptation can be found in another episode of Larry David's *Curb Your Enthusiasm* entitled "The Therapists." Desperate to win back his ex-wife, Cheryl, but afraid to exercise his own judgment, Larry asks his therapist for advice. The therapist tells him to be decisive with Cheryl, to give her an ultimatum: "I want you to move back in with me. You have until *Monday* to decide. Then the offer's off the table." Before implementing his therapist's advice, Larry is enjoying a convivial lunch with Cheryl. Things seem to be moving in the right direction until the moment of truth. Compelled to follow through with what his therapist recommended, Larry makes his bid. Predictably offended by Larry's imperious stance, Cheryl recoils in disgust and storms out of the restaurant. Trailing after her in a futile attempt to rectify the gaffe, Larry yells plaintively, "The therapist told me to say that!"[23]

The episode is thought-provoking on two levels: First, it attests to how readily we trust experts in matters beyond the range of their professional competence. Though some therapists may profess to be relationship "experts," and though some, in a Socratic spirit of questioning, may happen to be very good at giving relationship advice, it is far from clear that they are able to do so in virtue of any *technical* training rather than the cultivation of common sense and attentiveness to the range of human motivations. There is no reason to assume that a relationship "expert," in virtue of learning principles from books and following a specialized method, would be more adept than a thoughtful friend or wise acquaintance at how to advise someone on how to find a meaningful relationship or to salvage a broken one. In the final analysis, when it comes to something that touches close to the human good, such as the kind or quality of relationship conducive to a flourishing life, one's advice, no matter how much professional experience one has accrued, is no better than the philosophy of life on which one implicitly or explicitly relies. And, yet, we are inclined to trust experts simply because they comfort us with their credentials, client testimonials, and (paradoxically) the high fees that they charge for their services. Instead of taking expert advice as one perspective, alongside that of friends, mentors, and family members, and then coming to our own judgment, we take it as if it were God's word.

Second, the episode leads us to consider what it means to make a judgment in the first place. Is the point to attain a result (getting your wife back) or to bring to expression a sense of self—"whether I get my wife back or not, I'm going to make an attempt that's true to who I am, that will not distort my personality for the sake of an outcome." It's not clear that the two aims can be neatly separated. For "getting one's wife back" in a meaningful and lasting sense would seem to require rekindling a relationship for which *you* are responsible. Even if the therapist's ultimatum had worked, and led Cheryl to move back in with Larry, it would not necessarily have "gotten her back" in a way liable to overcome the sources of discontent that led to the breakup in the first place. It would not have recaptured or deepened the relationship between Larry and Cheryl as an honest, personal gesture might do.

The episode ultimately helps us to understand that the very act of taking and applying expert advice is self-defeating, regardless of the outcome, if it means relinquishing our own sense of judgment, style, and moral disposition. The expert may help us get certain things. But without our personal affirmation of the course of action, what we acquire is bound to be external. What we get is not something suffused with our own character but merely something that we've been fed by someone else—a prod, not a reference point in a personal narrative.

What we learn from the accounts of Plato and Aristotle, and, by implication, from the plight of Larry David, is that the point of judgment, as opposed to mere choice, or decision making, is not to achieve some end, or to maximize some good, but to take a stand. The point is to assert our own sense of self and to bear responsibility for our actions.

Evading the Tempting Perils of Life-Sapping Technology

Exacerbating the perils to judgment that come from a naïve faith in expert knowledge are technological advances that promise to make life easier but that eliminate opportunities for adventure and the cultivation of character. From the advent of cell phones to Netflix to GPS navigation and now driverless cars, technology is increasingly streamlining our channels of communication and movement. Such innovations speak to our goal-oriented, efficiency-focused culture: They help us get the stuff we want without going through a long and difficult process to acquire it. "Hey Siri. Do everything for me"—Apple's latest pitch for its high-tech wristwatch—could very well be the motto of our time.

The problem with the seemingly miraculous ability to, as Apple puts it, "find directions, figure out what song is playing, or even get a language translation just by raising your wrist" is that the process we used to go through to achieve such things, if sometimes tedious, was often an occasion for character building and the *formation* of one's desires, not just the satisfaction of them.

Consider the experience, now quaint, of going to the video store on a Saturday night to select your evening entertainment. It required some effort. You had to get up, walk or drive to the store, and hope your rental was in stock (if you hadn't made the effort to call in advance). But it was an adventure. There was always the possibility of stumbling upon a movie that you hadn't thought of, something out of the box that caught your eye as you browsed the aisles. Sometimes you would go without a movie in mind and ask the clerk for a recommendation. You'd tell him or her what your favorite movies were and why you liked them. You'd have a conversation, developing your ability to express, interpret, and refine your preferences. Dealings with the clerk were not always easy. There was the ubiquitous shadow of late fees and the challenge of trying to talk your way out of them. But the awkwardness called forth the ability for diplomacy and quick thinking on your feet at a young age. It was the kind of stuff that made for good stories and reference points in your friendships. ("Remember the time when we cracked up in the middle of our excuse for the late return and got totally shut down by the guy behind the desk?") Going to the video store was an event, exciting and fulfilling in its own way, even before you had watched the movie.

With Netflix, you lose all of that. You gain the instant gratification of your whims but lose the journey through which your desires—and personality—are formed. There is a sense in which you can still browse on Netflix; but it's not quite the same as going to a store. For the options Netflix presents for your "browsing" are already predetermined by your previous selections. The element of surprise is deadened. So much of modern technology conforms to the "Netflix structure": It gives you easy pleasure at the expense of agency and self-command.

GPS navigation may be the starkest example. It's a technology that allows you to get from point A to point B as efficiently as possible, but it utterly deprives you of the agency of finding your way around. Of course, even before GPS, you didn't usually have to find your way around from scratch. There were maps and signage. One could say that a sign is already on the way to GPS, a form of technology that directs your drive, or hike, disburdening you of the need to navigate by looking for landmarks alone or by tracking the north star. But the use of signage still requires a good deal of agency and attentiveness. To follow a sign, you need to be on the lookout for the things to which it refers, and you need to be able to recognize them. Though the sign guides you, it also orients you in your surroundings—or forces you to orient yourself. This is clearest in the case of a map, which stands in sharp contrast to the moving blue dot or automated voice of a GPS device. In noting an intersection or a landmark on a map, you have to translate the symbol to the actual thing. For example, you have to anticipate a mountain that is a certain height, set against others, that should appear on your right as you drive west. Seeing the little triangle symbol on the map is one thing, but recognizing it in person another. The act of recognition involves the imaginative application of an image to reality. Strictly speaking, you can't follow a map. A map is itself a special kind of sign that requires interpretation. It guides you but forces you to figure things out on your own. It leaves you to envision things creatively, and to describe them as they come upon you, so that you'll be able to remember them as signposts on the way back.

In describing the landmarks on which you rely, and eliciting their features, you come to appreciate them as sources of guidance that you have brought to life. You come to see the landscape as an extension of yourself, and you thus gain a stake in protecting and cultivating it. We might consider the extent to which our disregard for the environment is connected to a lack of rapport with our surroundings that technologies such as GPS tend to foster. When we rely on an algorithm to get us from place to place, we tend to look at the things around us idly and impersonally, as things "out there" with which we have little personal connection.

Unlike a GPS device, which makes a trip thoroughly mechanical (unless the device malfunctions), a map, though it provides direction, can heighten the allure of a journey. Will the landmark as depicted on the map be as I envision? Will I be able to recognize it?

I remember in seventh and eighth grade one of the main assignments, and highlights of my social studies class, was making maps—an exercise that seems passé in the age of GPS. We had to take large sheets of Mylar, superimpose them on a given map, and trace the outlines of a region. We started with our home state of Massachusetts, and then we branched out to other countries and continents. We would have to identify cities and towns, rivers, lakes, and mountains. Some were easier to find, others harder. We'd often have to look at multiple maps to get them all right. For extra credit, we could shade by topography, or climate, or adorn the periphery of the map with depictions of local wildlife and culture.

In learning where things were, and imagining how you would guide someone from one place to another, you gained a greater appreciation for the places themselves. You loved them, in part, because they bore your mark, but also because they carried mystery. Would the actual places conform to the way you conceived them? Making the map made you want to travel to the places you located and traced. By charting the way, and imagining yourself a navigator, you gained a stake in the destination.

The experience of making maps, navigating, and developing the sense of self that comes with finding your way is threatened by the proliferation of GPS, which simply tells us where to go. I wonder how many schoolteachers even assign map-making anymore. With GPS, we simply follow a command without having to describe or interpret anything. Without a stake in our surroundings as signposts, we don't go to the trouble of describing things in the detail we would if navigating for ourselves.

We also deprive ourselves of other dimensions of the journey through which we gain an appreciation for the surrounding world and pride in ourselves. Without the attentive eye of a navigator, we are liable to overlook unexpected attractions—a distinctive rock formation, or a roadside farm stand. When an algorithm tells us where to go, we have no need to stop for directions and therefore little occasion for potentially memorable encounters. We may get to our destination faster and with less resistance. But we deprive ourselves of context that may enrich the destination. Arriving at a friend's house with an amusing story of the journey to get there can enliven the conversation and conviviality of the visit. Pulling up to a natural wonder, such as the Grand Canyon, with a contrasting image of the landscape leading up to it can heighten the majesty of the thing itself.

When I had the opportunity to travel to Australia with my family at age twelve, my first trip out of the country since I had been to Spain for a family reunion six years earlier, I distinctly remember how the journey to get there was integral to the actual experience. Long before we landed Down Under and snorkeled on the fabled Great Barrier Reef about which I had read and watched many nature documentaries in anticipation of the trip, I remember seeing the expanse of coral from high above, from the westerly window of the 747 jet, as we barreled north on the flight from Auckland to Cairns, and I tried to get my bearings. The shimmering golden expanse of barely submerged reef, flanked by turquoise ocean on either side, gave me a sense of the reef's immensity, which I could later appreciate from a different perspective as I swam directly above it.

Of course, it is not impossible to appreciate one's surroundings while using GPS. Technology enthusiasts might point out that you can even better appreciate the things around you if you don't have to worry about when and where to turn. You can just look at things. But the theory of "just look" assumes that we see things best as disinterested observers. What this misses is the sense in which perception requires a point of reference—an interest, or a concern in light of which one sees. We could certainly acquire such a perspective without taking an interest in navigation. Perhaps as we enjoy the car ride, we view the landscape in light of the beauty of an account we recently read in a poem or a novel. Or perhaps we draw on our memory of a previous trip and compare the landscape we now see to what we saw before. The perspectives from which we might observe are infinite. But the attitude toward one's route to which GPS caters—maximum efficiency in reaching the end—is liable to preclude any sort of appreciation of the way. Instead of admiring the path at all, we turn away from it to kill time. We withdraw into the confines of the car and lose ourselves in electronic distractions.

The logical extension of GPS navigation is the driverless car, which eliminates the need to play any active role in moving yourself around. The notion, however, that driverless cars will encourage us to enjoy the scenery, or to orient ourselves in the surrounding world, is naïve. It's more likely that we'll be set "free" to check email and scroll idly through social media en route to wherever it is we're going. It's hardly a stretch to imagine that what has motivated Google to pioneer the development of driverless-car technology is the assumption that if people can just ride around, they will remain fixed to their screens and conduct more Google searches.

Against the spiritual benefits of a rugged way, one could raise a number of objections. "What about being in a rush?" my students sometimes ask. Surely then GPS is helpful. It is undeniable that in circumstances of genuine urgency, GPS comes in handy. We would be willing to sacrifice the agency of navigating on our own for the sake of getting an injured person to the hospital as quickly as possible. But the question is not whether GPS is sometimes a good thing. The real question is why we find ourselves perpetually in a rush, such that the GPS is our go-to system of navigation rather than a map or our own sense of direction. Could it not be that the possibility of relying on GPS is what leads us to cut things down to the wire and to be in a rush in the first place? If we consider, on top of that, the advent of cell phones, which allow us to be reachable at all hours, and at the beck and call of a boss long after we leave the office, it is hard to see how technology has not itself exacerbated the problem of a harried pace of life.

A similar question could be raised in response to the claim that GPS is a good thing for those who have a "bad sense" of direction. To what extent is such a deficiency the product of a technology that obviates the need to cultivate navigation skills? Once we come to rely on GPS, we become helpless without it. We speak of our sense of direction as if it were a fact of nature. But if we had to rely on it, we'd practice using it and improve.

Another objection to the critique of GPS that my students have raised is that it romanticizes getting lost. But we have to ask ourselves whether "romanticizing" is not a pejorative term employed by one who is trapped in a goal-oriented framework. Why are we so fearful of making wrong turns? What is so important about our quotidian goals and destinations that we must reach them as fast as possible? Getting to the hospital is one thing. But why do you have to get everywhere on time? In Plato's *Symposium,* Socrates shows up to Agathon's party halfway through dinner because he's sidetracked by a thought that strikes him along the way. He has to stop at a neighbor's porch to reflect on it. When Socrates finally arrives at Agathon's house, he is greeted warmly, and his delay becomes a point of entry to the conversation.

The anecdote of Socrates leads us to consider whether the significance of a destination can be neatly separated from the path to reach it—and from the possibility of getting sidetracked, delayed, or lost. Imagine if Odysseus had had access to a GPS and been able to sail with relative ease from Troy to Ithaca. He would have gotten back to his wife, Penelope, faster. But he would not have returned with the same kind of devotion to her. For a wife to whom one returns speedily and without trial is not identical to a wife for whom one fights monsters, evades Scylla and Charybdis, and resists the temptation of the Sirens.

Heroes such as Odysseus speak to the sense in which we admire adventurers and navigators for the virtues they display—for their ingenuity, wit, and fortitude along a difficult path. Though we may ourselves turn to the GPS when we venture on a trip, we thrill to the survival smarts of the protagonist of the TV show *Man versus Wild,* Bear Grylls, a former Special Forces operative who gets dropped by parachute into a remote corner of the world entirely unknown to him and must find his way to civilization with only a knife and the clothes he has on his back. But if we really do find Bear Grylls admirable, we should take a leaf out of his book and apply his spirit of adventure to our own lives in at least some small way—by picking up a map or by seeking situations of resistance that compensate for the ease with which technology affords us.

The point of critically considering technologies such as Netflix and GPS is not to reject them as "having made life worse" but to treat their use as questionable and involving significant trade-offs—just as choosing a video instead of going to the movies, or a car over a horse, involved earlier trade-offs. Too often we regard such innovations as unmitigated advances, as tokens of the progress of reason and science. The notion that technology bespeaks the advent of enlightenment and human intelligence is naïve and self-defeating. It assumes that had people of old seen what we've made and developed, they would have marveled at it and kicked themselves for not thinking of it "back then." But even a cursory examination of ancient Greek thought reveals that the Greeks were well aware of the promise of technology yet reluctant to embrace it. Philosophers such as Aristotle were critical of the goal-oriented framework that prizes the ability to produce and manipulate above all else.

Whereas today we idolize inventors, ancient Athenians were more impressed with those who were oriented to politics and citizenship and who displayed virtues of character in the assembly. What the Greeks called *techne,* the knowledge on the basis of which we can make or produce something, from which we derive the word "technology," Aristotle regards as decisively lower in rank than practical wisdom (*phronesis*), the knowledge by which we can put something to good use. It was the abiding focus on practical wisdom, judgment, and character formation that constrained the ancient Greek development of technology. Or, to put it bluntly, our avid development of technology today bespeaks what the ancient Greeks would have regarded as vice: a willingness to submit to slavery to get what we want. The ultimate enslavement at issue is not to the machine that tells us what to do or where to go but to the object of our own desires. It is a kind of internal slavery whereby we let the prospect of accomplishment, acquisition, and the end of a journey control our lives.

Understanding One's Life as a Whole

The faith in one's self that characterizes greatness of soul implies a certain understanding of what it means to *be* a self to which Aristotle points his account of "practical wisdom." This he defines as the ability to deliberate about what is good, "not with respect to a part of life, such as wealth or strength, but with respect to living well as a whole."[24] In his distinction between the part and the whole, Aristotle leads us to consider the sense in which there is always more to one's self than the multiplicity of aims and roles that one might represent on a CV. This "something more" is the power to understand the various parts of one's life not simply as isolated spheres each with its own aim and standard of excellence, but as ways of being to be worked out and clarified in relation to one another, as the parts of an integrated whole.

In being a teacher, for example, I might find myself deliberating not only on matters pertaining to the limited realm of the classroom—what to assign for homework, or how to get the class clown to behave—but also on how I might draw upon the habits and dispositions of this particular vocation to inform and illuminate the spirit in which I live in all situations. Perhaps in growing accustomed to addressing the seemingly naïve but, on reflection, quite profound questions of my students, I become attentive to the world in a new way, raising questions myself where I used to see only self-evidence. Perhaps in coping with the unpleasant experience of being rudely cut off in traffic on the way home from work, I approach the encounter in a "teacherly" way, holding at bay my indignation by considering what might be going on in that driver's personal life that led him to act that way—as I might do with a difficult student. Thus I cultivate knowledge not only of a particular domain (how to be a teacher), but also of the relation of one domain to another, and thus of myself as someone capable of comparison, analogy, and an understanding of the "whole."

To cultivate such an understanding is to liberate one's self from the fear of accident, misfortune, and failure. For regardless of what may transpire in a particular domain, one is ready to draw lessons and insights to be applied wherever one goes. From this perspective, no defeat or loss is final. The effort you made, and the creative energy you expended, is still with you, ready to be redirected and strengthened in the face of a new challenge. For this reason, "the person of great soul remains balanced with respect to wealth, power, and every stroke of good fortune and bad, however it may come about, neither rejoicing overmuch in the good nor bemoaning the bad."[25]

A nice expression of this sensibility came from Red Sox superstar slugger J. D. Martinez after being selected for the 2018 All Star game and designated to hit "cleanup" (traditionally the most respected position in the batting order). J. D. appreciated the honor as "surreal" and "really cool," but he didn't get carried away by the hype of making the team. Instead, he took the honor as an occasion to reflect on and ultimately affirm his difficult path to stardom. As a young player, he had been drafted in the twentieth round. After finally making it to the big leagues, a feat that most minor league players never attain, he was released after three years. But gradually he reinvented his swing and became the greatest hitter in the game. Looking back on things, J. D. declared the following: "I wouldn't change it for anything if I could go back in time. I'm glad I failed. I'm glad I've fallen on my face. I feel like it made me who I am today."[26] The success of making the All Star game was, for J. D., not in itself a cause for great celebration. It was rather a moment that put in perspective the whole of his trajectory, that gave him an opportunity to affirm his journey. It's difficult to understand J. D.'s attitude as anything but exceedingly humble unless we consider the sense in which our own accomplishments rise to significance, and bring lasting happiness, only in virtue of the stories they carry with them.

Once in a while, I'll go online and pull up the spreadsheet of results from the World Drug-Free Powerlifting Association Championships, held in Milton Keynes, England, in 2009. This was before my days of chasing the pull-up record, when I was a member of the Oxford University Powerlifting Club in graduate school.

I scroll through the 75-kg. weight class to find my name and numbers: 175-kg. squat, 120-kg. bench, 212.5-kg. deadlift. Those were my best results in a powerlifting meet. I placed fourth in my weight class in a small but competitive league. I smile to myself as I remember the thrill of seeing the three green lights from the judges after my third and final deadlift. But what moves me now, long after the triumph of a personal best is a thing of the past, is the journey that the competition brings into focus.

I look back on the hard training sessions with my teammates in the Oxford University Powerlifting Club. On Monday, Tuesday, and Thursday evenings, we piled into the little box of a gym on Iffley Road, right next to the storied track where Roger Bannister ran the first mile under four minutes back in 1953. The little café, appended to the athletic center, where we'd often grab protein shakes after

training, was aptly named "Café Sub-four." The gym was equipped
with just the basics—bars, plates, benches, and two squat racks.
I can still smell the noxious fumes that engulfed us as my teammate Dan cracked a stick of ammonia in front of his nose for extra
energy before a big lift. If Dan was successful, he'd rack the weight
with authority, turn to us, and make sure we hadn't missed it:
"'That's how you motherf**kers bench!" The crude arrogance of the
gesture provided a welcome contrast to the formality of Oxford
University. By the end of my afternoon classes, and meetings with
professors that taxed my powers of diplomacy, I thirsted for the
brash, frank banter in the gym. And by the time the workout was
over, I sometimes longed for at least a touch of the formality at
which I bridled during the day.

I also remember having my best stretch of injury-free training
interrupted, only a month before the championships, by a bad flu.
I was in bed with a fever for a week and was too enfeebled to train
for a week more. I wondered whether I'd regain enough strength to
even compete in the championships, never mind place well. After
two weeks of laying around the house, including watching the film
Troy, starring Brad Pitt as Achilles, I was able to roust myself to hit
the gym. I remember my warmup weight of 60 kilos, which, a
month earlier, had felt as light as a feather, pressed down on me like
a ton of bricks. My head was light and my legs were shaky. But as I
gradually added weight, the months of training began to kick in and
powered me through the initial fatigue. It was at that moment I
learned a valuable lesson that I've repeated to myself many times
since: How you feel when you first begin an activity—whether its
athletic training, writing, or going to work in the morning—does
not determine how you'll feel in the midst of it or how you'll come
through in the end. Inspiration can strike when you least expect it.

Finally, I remember lying in bed the night before the competition, trying to take my mind off the next day and tame the butter-
flies churning in my stomach as I anticipated my name being called

to the bar. In an effort to put the competition in perspective, I pictured Socrates standing before the 500 citizen-jurors of Athens about to defend himself in a capital case. If Socrates could face his trial with such self-possession, I could at least cope with the disappointment of missing a third attempt the next day! I comforted myself with the aphorism of Nietzsche, "whatever does not destroy me makes me stronger." It's a slogan made popular by singer Kelly Clarkson. But it was Nietzsche who coined the phrase. It's a good example of how much of our popular advice and motivation has trickled down from philosophers who came up with these aphorisms ages ago and thought them through in much greater depth than we do today. As I thought ahead to the competition, I told myself, "Whatever happens tomorrow will at least be a test of character, a chance to redeem a loss or put a victory in perspective." The simple activity of reflecting upon the words and actions of thinkers who lived centuries before me was comforting. In some way, difficult to express, these philosophers continued to live on through me, long after their bodies and physical abilities had become a thing of the past.

I remember these things and many more—all of which are alive now as much as then, in a way that a good result is not. A result is fleeting. It's thrilling in the moment but soon becomes a thing of the past. But an insight never grows old. As soon as you return to it for counsel or inspiration in the present, it is as alive as much as when it first came to you.

Looking back at the spreadsheet of results and recalling everything that led up to that day reminds me that a goal can be taken in two ways: as a bounded pursuit at which one might succeed or fail and as a point at which some aspect of your life as a whole comes into focus.

Aristotle calls attention to this dual aspect of a goal in the opening lines of his *Ethics,* where he distinguishes between particular ends, or good things, and the good as such. Every human action, Aristotle

writes, aims at "some good." It is action "for the sake of" a particular end (*telos*). The example he gives is bridle making, which is for
the sake of horseback riding, which, in turn, is for the sake of leadership in war.[27] If our action is to have a point, however, it can't be
the case that we do everything for the sake of something else. We
must always act with a view to some highest good.[28] But the highest
good, Aristotle suggests, is not some goal further down the line
from the particular aims we pursue, such as pleasure, honor, or
knowledge. The highest good is happiness, or eudaimonia, which is
not a state of being but a way of life. Happiness is inseparable from
the ongoing practice of deliberation and judgment, which involves
making comparisons among moments and situations, balancing
competing claims, and taking a stand on the whole.

Detachment versus Integration as the Way to Independence

In confronting the fear of failure, misfortune, and loss, or in attempting to escape the grip of some obsession or source of anxiety, it is tempting to seek refuge in an aloof indifference to life, or
at least a resigned self-restraint: "Nothing I do, or even regard as
necessary, is of ultimate significance in the larger scheme of things.
Who I am is not the job I work, the country to which I may be said
to belong, or even the people to whom I find myself attached—my
family, my friends—but the capacity to step back and survey my life
from a distance, to pick things up and let them go. So enjoy things
as they come with measured enthusiasm and without becoming
too attached." It is easy to convince one's self that such dispassionate
independence constitutes a sober and mature outlook and even
the quintessence of self-possession. But from what we have considered of greatness of soul, practical wisdom, and the relation
of the "parts" of life to the "whole," we can identify the folly of
this attitude.

The real source of our fear and obsession is not an overly passionate devotion to the things we hold dear but a certain goal-oriented way of relating to them. Only when a job becomes something that I might keep or lose, a country something that may stay unified or fall apart, a person someone who is now here but may one day be absent, does the sort of fear arise on the basis of which I might talk myself into detachment from these things and locate my "true" self in the capacity to survey and assess my life from a distance. But for as long as I attend to the things that move me as sources of practical wisdom, as possibilities that continuously emerge and rise to significance as they work their force on one another, I come to possession of myself in an altogether different sense: as the power to see together, draw analogies, and carry many into one.

In contrast to the dispassionate distance from our commitments to which we might aspire in moments of frustration and anxiety, we might consider the exercise in self-examination that Nietzsche proposes: "What have you up to now truly loved, what attracted your soul, what dominated it while simultaneously making it happy? . . . Compare these objects, observe how one completes, expands, surpasses, transfigures the others, how they form a step-ladder on which until now you have climbed to yourself."[29] Seen in this way, the things you truly love are always with you as sources of support and inspiration for the journey of life.

Aristotle on Morality of Greatness and Smallness

Toward the middle of his account of greatness of soul, Aristotle makes two radical claims: The first is that greatness of soul carries within itself every other virtue. For it would be impossible, writes Aristotle, to imagine a person of great soul "frantically retreating from battle, or acting unjustly."[30] Greatness of soul, therefore, is not simply one virtue among many. It is the most comprehensive virtue, which somehow includes courage, justice, and generosity. It would seem, then, that the virtues Aristotle discusses leading up to greatness of soul are threshold virtues for the attainment of the highest one, as if one had to first establish one's self as brave, just, and generous to qualify for the next level, which is greatness of soul. But Aristotle makes a second, even bolder claim that calls into question the possibility of such a progression: Greatness of soul, he writes, is a sort of "arrangement" or "crowning ornament" to the virtues. Not only does it include them; it "makes them greater."[31] Aristotle thus suggests that greatness of soul is the source of every virtue in its truest or highest sense. Without greatness of soul, all the other virtues lose their splendor. So one couldn't be fully just or brave or generous or virtuous in any way while deficient in greatness of soul. Strictly speaking, greatness of soul is the one and only virtue, or the disposition underlying every other virtue that renders it an expression of the genuine good. The many virtues can be understood as dimensions or offshoots of greatness of soul. We ought to consider this claim with some care, as it has important implications for the relation of virtue to self-possession.

One way to think about the priority of greatness of soul to the other virtues is this: In the case of every virtue, there is a greater and lesser version—the virtue itself, that which attests to greatness of soul, and a resemblance of it, that which is tainted by a kind of smallness. Aristotle offers no elaboration of this thought-provoking suggestion. But it is worth the effort to imagine what he might have in mind.

Take the virtue of justice. There is a way of being just that bespeaks greatness of soul: living with an abiding care for giving the different people in your life what they deserve, paying your debts and following through on commitments even when it is not convenient to do so, giving credit where you have promised none but recognize that credit is due (and even when the credit you offer is to someone with whom you often disagree), relinquishing something that is technically yours by law or convention but that can be better used or appreciated by someone else. Being just in these ways bears the mark of greatness of soul. It requires exercising judgment for yourself as against conventional valuations of who deserves what. It also involves an expansive conception of what you might "owe," which goes beyond material things and may simply be your attention or engagement.

But there is another kind of justice—one that bespeaks a smallness of soul and is a form of stinginess, weakness, or resentment. This is the "tit for tat" justice that consists in the constant calculation of what is "fair"; the heartless, bureaucratic justice that invokes "the rules" at the expense of what is right in a particular case; the punitive justice that is vengeance decked out in the garb of proportionality—the retributive impulse to seek an eye for an eye as a kind of futile exertion of agency in the face of loss: "I can't redeem the harm I have suffered, but I can at least get back at the perpetrator!" A close relative of this justice (which is often unaware of itself as such) is the petty policing and moralistic scolding of others familiar to everyday life that, at bottom, is resentment in disguise.

For a glimpse of this sort of justice, I cannot help but turn once more to *Curb Your Enthusiasm* (a show of the utmost intrigue as a caricature of our cultural maladies). Larry David is waiting in line for an ice cream behind a woman who's sampling all the different flavors. Impatient and frustrated, Larry, to his friend Jeff but in earshot of the woman, accuses her of abusing her "sampling privileges." The woman whom Larry accuses gives him a dirty look and finally settles on vanilla. As she walks away, Larry vents his frustration and tries to commiserate with the woman serving the ice cream—"Vanilla! She winds up with vanilla! You gotta be kidding me!" he says. Without sharing in his indignation, the woman behind the counter awaits his order silently. After a short pause, leading us to believe that Larry will definitely request his flavor of choice, he switches his tone. With an inquisitive glance, he asks, "How *is* the vanilla?" Larry, it turns out, wants to indulge in the very taste test for which he chastised the woman. But he feels constrained by the fear of social disapproval. Larry's appeal to justice was born of resentment. He wags his finger at others for indulging in tendencies that he represses in himself out of meekness.[32]

Under the light of greatness of soul we might examine other virtues, such as honesty. Telling the truth and saying what you believe can be born of self-regard: the conviction that to speak a falsehood out of convenience or fear of consequences is a form of personal weakness. Instead of using a difficult situation as occasion to affirm what you stand for, say, by refusing to answer a sensitive question, or by answering in an ironic but truthful way, you bend yourself out of shape to fit the situation. Quite apart from whether telling a lie would be harmful or disrespectful to someone else, it is disrespectful to your own integrity.

But honesty can also be a form of weakness, a kind of compulsion to say whatever is on your mind out of excessive scruples or guilt, a need to dutifully and guilelessly answer every question asked of you. The honesty of Jim Carrey's character in the movie *Liar Liar* is a telling example of such indiscriminate, guilt-ridden openness. In response to a police officer who pulls him over for running a light and asks him if he knows what he did was wrong, Carrey's character can't help but confess to every violation of his life, including a heap of unpaid parking tickets, which burst out of his glove compartment as he opens it, unsolicited.

Perhaps the virtue most conspicuous in its potential to express either greatness or smallness of soul is generosity. Generosity can be a virtue through which you, the benefactor, find fulfillment in your gift—as when you devote resources to cultivating the talent of a student, or support a charity whose mission fulfills some dimension of your own life. But generosity can also be a form of self-depletion. There are people who feel pressure to give everything away out of guilt for those who have less than them, or out of pity for those who suffer. Some even keep giving to those who take advantage of them.

A caricature of this pitfall is the case of "Bud" Baxter, played by Jack Lemmon, in the classic film noir *The Apartment*. Browbeaten into submission by a gang of upper-management execs at his insurance firm, Baxter offers his apartment for their use as an off-the-grid hotel room where they can indulge in their affairs. Baxter dutifully vacates his apartment and comes back after his bosses have enjoyed the evening. At one point, Baxter is left sleeping on the street the whole night and comes into work the following day with a terrible cold. One could say that Baxter runs an early version of Airbnb, with the payoff being the prospect of a promotion. Though he abets the philandering of his bosses and is, in that sense, complicit in their immoral behavior, his hospitality is, in a twisted sense, generous. Baxter even goes above and beyond the call of duty, diligently stocking the drinks tray so that his "guests" will have a good time. But this is a very limited and uninspiring generosity, one born of smallness rather than greatness of soul.

Generosity and Self-Possession on the Fields of Little League Baseball

In sharp contrast to the Bud Baxter generosity of weakness is the generosity of a mentor or teacher who, in cultivating his or her student or mentee, takes pride and finds self-possession. An old mentor of mine from my days of playing Little League baseball comes to mind. But to give due credit to his virtue, I have to briefly set the scene of the unsavory competitiveness that is commonplace on the Little League ballfield. Mainly it's the parent-coaches (many of whom double as league officials), longing to relive their imagined glory days on the field, putting excessive pressure on their kids, and jockeying to win the town league championship by hook or by crook. I remember one spring back when I was twelve years old, when our team had won the first playoff game in a best of three series. When the second game in which we were leading was canceled midway by rain, one league official, who just happened to be the coach of the opposing team, suggested that to make things more "efficient," we play a single sudden-death game to determine who would advance. The same parent-coach was lobbying to have our star pitcher suspended for the entire playoffs after he had been ejected from a game by the umpire for shouting disapproval at a strike call against a teammate. Our pitcher had yelled to the umpire in reference to his wide strike zone, "Hey Shawn, is there somewhere you have to be?" In the end, a modicum of fairness prevailed over the sudden-death idea, and our pitcher got to play.

Once in a while, however, I'd meet someone who was an exception to the small-time treachery. I remember one soft-spoken father of three boys who were a little older than I was. He had been through the system with his own kids and seen it all, but he didn't let the pettiness get to him. He simply loved baseball, come victory or defeat, and was an astute analyst of pitching mechanics. I'm sure he spent a good deal of time cultivating his own kids. But instead of sweating their every move, he took time to coach me and to talk pitching with my dad. I remember his pulling me aside to a mound, and watching me throw, even while his own son was playing on the other side of the park. It was generous of him. But more than that, it was an act of giving through which he, the giver, found joy and fulfillment. It was a chance for him to hand down an activity that he loved, with its own form and integrity, and to witness its development among the next generation of ball players.

This father was not only more cultivating of others than the Little League parents who clamored for wins. He was also more confident in himself and at ease. The other parents, who were ungenerous in their adversarial attitude, remained perpetually dissatisfied. Whenever they lost, they would gripe and find excuses. Whenever they'd win, they'd brag, perhaps offer some high-handed advice, and then scheme to win some more. They were nearly incapable of taking joy in a game well played on both sides, in which the kids displayed the makings of mature ball players, turning double-plays, or throwing runners out from home to second.

They were also unable to appreciate the life lessons of the game—the meaning of team loyalty, for example. In our star pitcher's frustrated but spunky shout of disagreement with the umpire from the bench, he was backing up a teammate, not arguing about his own pitch. And although arguing balls and strikes is considered bad form, he hadn't cursed or hurled abuse at the ump, as an angry twelve-year-old might be inclined to do. There was something admirable in the way he lost his temper. But all the opposing coaches could see was an opportunity to aggrandize themselves at his expense. In their obsession with winning and losing, they remained mired in discontent. The father who took time to coach me, by contrast, was steady throughout the ups and downs of the game. He knew the activity of coaching to be intrinsically rewarding, a way of making a lasting difference, quite apart from whether any of his young pitching students would win the game or play baseball beyond high school. His generosity went together with self-possession.

In a highly competitive setting focused on rank and relative achievement, or in a society focused on production, accomplishment, and career advancement, we risk losing sight of self-affirming generosity. We risk getting caught up in the anxious, petty attitude of "everything for me," which leaves us utterly without resource when it comes to the question "why win?"

Against the backdrop of self-service as the norm, generosity takes the form of the empty and unstable virtue of altruism, the willingness to relinquish something of one's own for the sake of someone else. Though potentially helpful as a means for channeling goods to those who need them most, altruism is a scarce moral resource, as it fulfills neither the giver nor the recipient. In Aristotle's terms, altruism is generosity without greatness of soul. The giver is left depleted of time or money and can find satisfaction only in the praise of others or the moral feeling of having done a good deed at some expense. The recipient gains something useful but external, something that is now formally his own but does not speak to his virtue or ability. This is why many who receive altruistic gifts in the form of charity come to resent and reject them. What they really want is the capacity to develop powers of their own. Genuine generosity, of the kind that the Little League father displayed in coaching me, is that through which both the recipient and the giver are enhanced and empowered. The gift at issue is a shared activity or way of life.

In all of these cases—honesty, generosity, justice—there is the way of greatness and smallness of soul. Virtue in the highest sense is the first way. That, I believe, is Aristotle's point. Even so, there is something of virtue in the small-souled expressions of morality. In many cases, you do, in your dispossession, help someone or maintain a certain respect for a principle worth defending in the abstract. But such morality comes at a personal cost, sometimes an immense one. It lacks the splendor of virtue born of a great soul.

We might look at it another way: In the case of virtue born of smallness, the question of "why be virtuous" looms over every deed. Because such virtue involves self-depletion, you expect something in return. You want the world to reward you, not necessarily with money but with recognition or good fortune. The question of "why bad things happen to good people" inevitably arises and troubles you. In the case of virtue born of strength, the question doesn't arise. For your acts of morality speak to who you are. From the perspective of greatness of soul, there is no difference between your "good deeds" and everything else you do.

Self-Possession II

The Life and Death of Socrates

When I first read Aristotle's account of greatness of soul, I took him to be presenting an idealized version of the typical Athenian gentleman—someone with a strong sense of dignity and noblesse oblige. But when I returned to it for this project, I came to a somewhat different view. What stood out to me was Aristotle's focus on the concern for truth above reputation. I came to conclude that Aristotle actually has in mind a different model: the outwardly modest, often slovenly philosopher-hero of Plato's dialogues, Socrates.

By most accounts of Socrates, including Plato's, Socrates was a funny-looking, even ugly man who had none of the apparent grandeur of an Athenian aristocrat. He was known for walking the streets of Athens shoeless and for consorting with a wide range of people, foreigners and citizens alike, engaging with anyone who was willing to have a conversation with him on the meaning of justice, piety, honor, beauty, the soul, the good life, and other themes of the deepest human concern.

Unlike an Athenian aristocrat, who would consider it beneath him to engage at length with commoners or slaves, Socrates would often ask everyday people questions with no less interest than he would the luminaries of Athenian society. In Plato's dialogue *Meno*, for example, Socrates has an extended discussion with Meno's slave attendant, the upshot of which is to reveal, at least to us, the readers, that the slave is actually more capable of learning than his arrogant master. Whereas the well-born and highly educated Meno engages in discussion with Socrates primarily by parroting the views of famous poets and orators, so as to appear clever, Meno's slave, who is not so steeped in conventional wisdom, and has no reputation to preserve, honestly and straightforwardly answers Socrates's questions. Socrates thus reveals Meno's slave to be freer than Meno in the fundamental sense. Unfettered by norms of what a respectable person should say, the slave thinks for himself.

In the fashion of Aristotle's person of great soul, Socrates would ironically poke fun at the pretentious aristocrats of his society while vindicating the common sense of lesser-known figures. Throughout the Platonic dialogues, Socrates's favorite partners in conversation are young Athenian men rather than their established fathers.

Though Socrates lived a long time ago and had an unusual lifestyle of extended street conversation, I propose we study him as a model from which we can learn. At least the portrayal of Socrates that we find in Plato, which may very well be an idealized version, presents an impressive exemplar of self-possession. What interests me in Socrates is not only the content of what he proposed to his students, though many of his explicit suggestions bear upon the theme of self-possession, but also the virtue he displayed throughout his discussions in the way he carried himself and dealt with disagreement, even hostility.

A focus on Socrates's demeanor as a significant indication of who he was and what he thought is justified by Plato's dialogical form of writing. A dialogue, unlike a treatise or expository account, makes it impossible to separate the content of what is presented from the way in which is delivered. It is impossible, therefore, to separate a Socratic teaching from the spirit in which Socrates lived. To understand Socrates's proposals and assertions, we have to consider them in the context of the action and, in particular, in light of how he might be expected to contend with the particular characters with whom he converses.

If we attend to Socrates's demeanor as much as to his proposals, we find that his action conforms remarkably to Aristotle's account of greatness of soul. Throughout his discussions with established Athenian luminaries, the sons of Athenian gentleman, notable foreigners, slaves, and all those with whom he interacted, Socrates maintained an impressive immunity to familiar insecurities, such as anxiety over popularity, decorum, and esteem, and fear of looking foolish in front of those regarded as wise. As we will soon examine, he also stands as a model for overcoming misfortune.

Understanding Those with Whom We Disagree

The source of Socrates's openness to the honored and marginalized alike was his abiding concern for truth above reputation. Unlike the educated elite of his day, Socrates cared nothing for looking smart, sophisticated, or erudite. He was unafraid to broach risqué or even sacrilegious topics, such as the relation of love to sex, or whether the gods were truly all-powerful. He was equally intrigued by famous poetry, great events, and shoemakers. His sole focus was self-knowledge. He wanted to understand and live by the virtues of character that constitute a good life. Driven by that singular purpose, he was eager to hear from anyone with something interesting to say, regardless of rank, title, or reputation.

Socrates welcomed skepticism and dispute with the faith that he stood only to gain from questioning conventional wisdom. Socrates lived by the insight that when it comes to self-knowledge, there are no winners and losers. For to be corrected, or shown a new and better perspective on how to live, is a far greater good than to correct someone else. As Socrates readily concedes to the famous orator Gorgias, "I would be glad to be refuted, were I not to speak the truth, and glad to refute anyone else . . . but the former I regard the greater good, insofar as it is a greater good to be liberated from the greatest evil than to liberate someone else."[1]

Socrates's focus on self-knowledge set him apart from the famous speakers and educators of his day, the orators and the sophists, who prided themselves on being able to win arguments in the assembly, or before a jury, without regard to whether they themselves took the argument to be true. The sophists, from whom we derive the word "sophistry," were traveling teachers who went from city to city around Greece collecting fees for instructing young ambitious citizens in the art of clever discourse aimed at miring an opponent in contradictions. They were hired by wealthy Athenian fathers to educate their sons in the kind of speech that could help them prevail in public debate. It was Plato, in his portrayal of Socrates's critique of the sophists, who gave the sophists a bad name and paved the way for today's pejorative term "sophistry."

Because the sophists and orators focused exclusively on how to convince a third party, and failed to cultivate an internal standard of right and wrong, they would readily turn frustrated and angry in discussion whenever their professed mastery appeared to be challenged. Socrates, by contrast, maintained a measured and confident bearing, no matter how harshly he was confronted. For example, when Thrasymachus, a hotheaded, ambitious young orator, breaks into a conversation on the meaning of justice, berating Socrates for asking questions without giving answers, Socrates keeps his cool and responds to Thrasymachus with genuine curiosity: "Thrasymachus, don't be hard on us. If we are making any mistake in consideration of the arguments . . . know well we're making an unwilling mistake . . . So it's surely far more fitting for us to be pitied by you clever men than to be treated harshly."[2] When Thrasymachus asks Socrates what his punishment should be if he,

Thrasymachus, can offer a "better" answer to the question of the meaning of justice, Socrates replies that his "punishment" should be, simply, "to learn from the man who knows."[3]

Ignorant of the honesty in Socrates's response, Thrasymachus, who is enthralled by the love of victory and blind to any notion of learning beyond studying methods of verbal conquest, thinks Socrates is speaking sarcastically, with the confidence that he will win the argument. But it turns out that Socrates really does want to discover what Thrasymachus means. When Thrasymachus bombastically unveils his supposedly enlightened, no-nonsense understanding of justice that justice is "whatever is to the advantage of the stronger" (a view that, unbeknownst to Thrasymachus, was hardly original to him but a conventional trope among those who reveled in dispute), Socrates takes the opinion seriously: "First I must learn what you mean," he says. Instead of attempting to refute Thrasymachus, Socrates poses a simple question aimed at clarifying his opinion: Is justice what the rulers *think* is in their interest, or what is *genuinely* in their interest? For don't even the most powerful tyrants sometimes harm themselves through poor judgment? And when the citizen who is to serve the tyrant and thereby act "justly" knows that doing so would harm the tyrant, is it just that he do so nonetheless?[4] It's a good question, at once sympathetic and critical. It preserves the possibility that Thrasymachus is onto some aspect of justice but also exposes that what Thrasymachus means by "the advantage of the stronger" is very ambiguous and confused. By posing this question, Socrates opens the way to a wide-ranging discussion through which the meaning of justice comes into clearer view.

As the dialogue unfolds, Socrates reveals the sense in which Thrasymachus is not wholly mistaken. For justice, as Socrates leads his young friends to discover, is related to the good, to a certain harmony of soul, in which the love of wisdom guides the love of honor and the love of profit. So understood, justice is "to the advantage" of everyone, including the so-called stronger. Thrasymachus, despite his narrow view of "advantage," and his reduction of "the good" to honor and material possession, was not entirely off track. He recognized that justice is not simply self-sacrifice for the sake of another. Justice properly understood, is, in a sense, enriching and empowering for the person possessed of it.

By the end of the dialogue, it is clear that Socrates has managed to understand Thrasymachus better than he understands himself. Socrates presents the true and comprehensive view of justice for which Thrasymachus is grasping in his initial definition. Socrates thus overcomes the opposition of Thrasymachus—not by defeating him in the manner of an orator who wins a case in court, but by revealing the implicit common ground beneath their initial disagreement.

In the fashion of his interaction with Thrasymachus, Socrates would question in good spirit those who opposed him, earnestly attempting to reveal the implications of their most controversial opinions. Socrates would even encourage his interlocutors to state a controversial view in more elaborate and precise terms, in order to elicit its appeal. For example, he invites the two young partners in the discussion, Glaucon and Adaimantus, to embellish Thrasymachus's "might makes right" view of justice by considering an all-powerful thief who, in virtue of a magical ring that turns him invisible, can get away with any injustice he desires. Is not such a person happier than a just person who dutifully respects the rights of others but always gets the short end of the stick? This bold and thought-provoking question turns out to be the central theme of Plato's *Republic,* through which Socrates addresses the tyrant, or aspiring tyrant, on his own terms. In the context of a democratic political regime, the very premise of such an investigation—that there may be something to the life of the tyrant—would seem taboo. But Socrates was unconcerned with moralism or political correctness. He wanted to investigate every tempting impulse.

Socrates eventually leads his friends to a critique of the tyrant from the tyrant's own perspective. In getting away with injustice, and amassing wealth and women and acclaim, the tyrant merely feeds his desires with fleeting and insubstantial things, "feasting" on possessions and accolades that leave him trapped in a self-defeating cycle of gratification and emptiness. He must always, at the same time, preoccupy himself with flattering the people who empower him. True happiness, suggests Socrates, can be found only in the pursuit of philosophy, which elicits the meaning implicit in all beautiful and desirable things and holds fast to them within a vision of the good life.

But this means that the tyrant and the philosopher are not wholly different, despite their stark divergence in outward appearance. Both the tyrant and the philosopher are driven by a passionate and unlimited desire for satisfaction that transcends the bounds of the reputable and conventional. The difference between them lies in their respective attempts to fulfill the same basic need.

Socrates's guiding assumption as revealed in his mode of questioning and in his explicit statements, was that in every opinion, there is at least a glimmer of insight. Among the very few assertions that Socrates makes without reservation is that *all* human beings, even the most ignorant or vicious, desire the good.[5] Even the person tempted by the ideal of the all-powerful thief desires the good: He believes, mistakenly, that by getting the better of others and stealing their possessions, he will bring himself happiness. Because we all strive, in our own more or less effective ways for coherence and harmony of soul, even the most apparently lost and confused of us are not wholly misguided.

Because Socrates sought to understand people on their own terms, and was able to conceive of vice in terms of ignorance rather than malice, he attained a remarkable liberty from the indignation that besets most people. Even in the case of direct attacks on his philosophical way of life, Socrates would remain poised and inquisitive, reveling even, in the challenge of defending philosophy in front of others in attendance whom he might influence.

The most striking example is his response to an aspiring young orator named Callicles, who denounces philosophy as a pursuit that is "unmanly and ridiculous," endearing in children but unbecoming of a mature adult.[6] Callicles urges Socrates to move on to "greater things," the affairs of state, for which the art of rhetoric is needed. A philosopher, claims Callicles, is utterly devoid of the abilities needed to excel in private and public affairs, blind to human pleasure and pain, and without resource when it comes to sizing up men's characters. The philosopher, he adds, is consigned to a life without reputation, "whispering in a corner with three or four boys."[7] Callicles concludes his case against philosophy by foreshadowing Socrates's own fate:

> If someone should seize hold of you, or of one of your kind, and haul you off to prison, accusing you of an injustice that you hadn't committed, you wouldn't know what to do with yourself, and would be dizzy and agape not knowing what to say . . . and, coming up in court, even if your accuser were a feeble rogue, you would be forced to die if he wanted to inflict the death penalty on you. And what wisdom is there in art, Socrates, that leaves one unable to save himself or deliver himself or anyone else from the greatest dangers?[8]

The charge of Callicles represents an age-old critique of philosophy that was not unfamiliar in Socrates's own time: the idea that the philosopher devotes himself to abstract theoretical investigation, which isolates him from practical affairs, and makes him a kind of buffoon when it comes to life on the streets. Aristophanes, the famous comic poet of Socrates's day, had even playfully ridiculed Socrates in precisely these terms, depicting him as a helpless child with his head in the clouds, studying insects under a microscope in his "think-tank." Through the objection of Callicles, Plato presents what would seem to be the most significant charge against Socrates, a more thoroughgoing accusation than that levied by the city of Athens (that Socrates corrupted the youth). Whereas the charge of the city carries a high penalty, it does not strike at the core of Socrates's way of life. It targets an effect of philosophy, not philosophy itself. Plato has Callicles put Socrates to the test in the most direct and compelling terms.

In response to Callicles's scathing critique, Socrates is not in the least bit indignant. To the contrary, he thrills to the opportunity of conversing with someone who speaks his mind and who will therefore be a fitting partner in discussion on the greatest topic: how one should live his life:

> What a lucky stroke I've had in striking up with you! . . . For I conceive that whoever would sufficiently test a soul as to the rectitude of life or the reverse should go to work with three things, all of which you have: knowledge, goodwill, and frankness . . . I once overheard you debating how far the cultivation of wisdom should be taken, and I know you were deciding in favor of some opinion such as [the one you've just presented] . . . so when I hear you giving me the same advice as you gave your own best friends, I have sufficient proof that you are well disposed to me . . . And on no themes could one make a more honorable inquiry, Callicles, than on those which you have reproached me with—the character one should have, and what should be one's pursuits.[9]

He then goes on to address each of Callicles's points. With respect to the philosopher's supposed ignorance of practical affairs, Socrates questions Callicles on the relation of the pleasant to the good.

Callicles had proposed that the good life consists in giving free rein to one's desires and indulging them to the fullest extent possible. For this, he claims, one needs rhetoric, so as to be able to persuade others to give you what you want. Socrates fastens upon Callicles's identification of the good with the pleasant and asks him if he really takes the two to be identical. At first Callicles holds firm to the view that there is no difference between the two. The good life is simply the life with the greatest influx of pleasure. But when Socrates presses him on the matter, he is forced to acknowledge a distinction. Attentive to what motivates Callicles, Socrates asks him a simple question to test where his commitments truly lie: "Have you not ever seen a foolish child taking pleasure?" "Yes," answers Callicles. "And have you not ever seen a foolish man taking pleasure?" "Yes, I suppose I have," says Callicles.[10] Socrates then leads Callicles to the inescapable conclusion that, by his very own admission, not all pleasures are good. Living well involves having the sense, or wisdom, to distinguish among desires and not simply indulge whatever desires one happens to have at any moment. Socrates leads Callicles to this conclusion by suggesting a claim that Callicles cannot deny based on his very accusation of Socrates. For Callicles has accused Socrates precisely of being a foolish child in pursuing philosophy. Yet Socrates, quite clearly, and in front of Callicles, takes pleasure in the activity of philosophy. To be consistent with his opinion that the life of the philosopher is worthless, Callicles must admit the very distinction he denies: that the good is different from the pleasant.

But this admission tacitly undermines Callicles's denigration of philosophy. His case for rhetoric over philosophy rested on the claim that rhetoric enables one to rule, and therefore to acquire the things he desires, whereas philosophy is weak and helpless. The philosopher, according to Callicles, is unable to indulge in the things he might want, consigned to a life of ascetic self-denial. Now, however, Socrates has shown Callicles that a good life requires some form of good sense or wisdom, which involves the critical assessment of what one wants, not simply the means to acquire it. But rhetoric, as Callicles presents it, aims simply at persuading a third party to give you what you want—as if you already knew what is good. Rhetoric neglects the all-important consideration of how to put one's own house in order.

Callicles's charge against philosophy is really a charge against philosophy conceived as an abstract discipline, or study of nature that takes no heed of virtue and the good life. Though philosophy has acquired this reputation and did, to some extent, have that reputation before Socrates came on the scene, it is not the kind of philosophy that Socrates practices. What Callicles misses in his equation of Socratic philosophy with unworldliness is the abiding need to deliberate on the right course of action and to examine the whole of one's own life to determine what is truly worth pursuing. For this ultimate task, rhetoric, which aims only at convincing another, will be of no use. Socrates thus reveals that philosophy and not rhetoric is the truly *practical* endeavor. It is the philosopher, focused on self-knowledge, and not the orator, focused on victory in court, who is truly equipped to offer wise counsel.

In response to Callicles's accusation that philosophy leaves one unpersuasive in court, unable to defend himself or his friends, and vulnerable to suffering the most terrible injustice, Socrates raises a difficult dilemma: If being persuasive means simply gratifying a third party, as one might do in saying to a jury whatever might lead to acquittal, then it comes at a cost, for to gratify a vicious jury to ensure one's safety is to distort one's soul—to commit a grave injustice against one's self. If one is to maintain the integrity of one's soul and avoid being done injustice, one must somehow attempt to sway the court without gratifying it. As we will see, this is precisely the predicament that Socrates faces at his own trial.

Socrates deals the final blow to Callicles's argument by pointing out that the greatest orators in Athenian history, the ones, such as

Pericles, whom Callicles and others now revere, were not able to save themselves when the Athenian democracy turned against them in times of turmoil. Rhetoric is not the all-powerful force that Callicles takes it to be. More powerful than rhetoric is philosophy, which is concerned with striking the proper balance between protecting one's self and taking a stand.

If Socrates could be said to have had a vice, it was not meekness or lack of persuasive power, but his tendency, in the fashion of the great-souled man, to look down on people from a height that revealed their depravity as comic, as the folly of immature children out of which he could share a laugh with a fellow philosopher.

The only time in Plato's dialogues when we see Socrates be uncharitable to a partner in conversation, when, for example, we see him attempt to trip someone up in logical contradictions, is when Socrates seeks to free the discussion from a domineering participant who would tend to silence younger, more reticent people in attendance, or leave them impressed for the wrong reasons. At a certain point in his discussion with Thrasymachus, Socrates tangles him in verbal confusions that obscure rather than clarify the meaning of justice.[11] But he does so only after Thrasymachus has recalcitrantly raised the question of why it matters that he speak the truth as he sees it rather than simply try to refute Socrates. In response, Socrates shows Thrasymachus that when it comes to abstract adversarial argument, in the fashion of the sophists, he, Socrates, can beat Thrasymachus at his own game. Through tricky shifts in terminology, and the use of the same words in different senses, Socrates proceeds to get Thrasymachus to conspicuously contradict himself. He does so not to defeat Thrasymachus in the abstract, something for which he couldn't care less, but to cut Thrasymachus down to size in front of Glaucon and Adaimantus, the two young men whose attention Socrates wants to command. As Glaucon and Adaimantus will no doubt be impressed by someone who can make a tough guy turn red in the face with embarrassment, Socrates takes the opportunity to reveal Thrasymachus as weak at his own game. He does so, strategically, however, with the larger purpose of engaging in a genuine search for wisdom with the young men. In the manner of Aristotle's man of great soul, Socrates does not cut people down "unless he has reason to deliberately offend."[12]

A further aspect of Socrates's self-possession was his honesty, in Aristotle's terms, "openness of expression." Though he often spoke indirectly, through the questions he posed, Socrates always spoke his mind. He said what he took to be true and never once, as far as I can see, told a lie. Many times, he asks leading questions that invite thoughtless assent from a particular character. But he does so for the sake of other, more attentive participants in the discussion, not least for us, the readers. (We must always remember that Socrates is Plato's protagonist and that we are Plato's public.) But a question that may lead someone down the wrong track is not a lie. It is a form of carefully presented honesty that places the burden of discernment on the person who is to respond. Socrates was not one to bear his thoughts for the world indiscriminately. His own opinion was almost always implicit in the questions he asked of others, rarely presented in assertions of his own.

When Socrates was pressured by friends and foes to state his view outright, he would often speak ironically: He would say the truth, but in terms he knew would be lost on some for his or their benefit. Through irony, Socrates was able to maintain possession of himself throughout his many conversations. He would neither succumb to the self-distortion of a lie nor indulge in careless honesty liable to abuse and misunderstanding.

A famous example of his irony was the statement he offered at his trial, the culminating event of his life that we are about to examine. There he confessed that he did not take himself to be wise either much or little.[13] On a certain level, the statement was true. Socrates never claimed to possess knowledge in the familiar sense of a sure fact or clear and distinct awareness of the truth. He reveled in the *search* for wisdom, treating every insight as a possibility to be clarified and revised in the unfolding of his life. Those who knew Socrates well would have understood the truth in his ironic statement. Those who didn't know him might assume that he was offering a straightforward account of a life devoted to a debunking skepticism that left him empty.

Socrates on Trial

At age seventy, Socrates was hauled to court by three prominent Athenians who accused him of corrupting the youth and introducing new gods unrecognized by the state. It was a serious charge, punishable by death. The circumstances surrounding Socrates's arraignment and trial highlight the misfortune into which he fell. As we learn in Plato's dialogues, Socrates had taken precautions throughout his life to practice philosophy without provoking the ire of the city. Though he avoided politics for fear of being implicated in competing power plays, he dutifully fulfilled his civic responsibilities, including military service at the battle of Delium. But at the time of his trial, he found himself in unfortunate circumstances, the context of which was the decline of Athens in the Peloponnesian War with Sparta.

It is often the case that in times of political turmoil, the powers that be are less tolerant of unorthodox opinions and ways of life than in stable circumstances. At the time of Socrates's arraignment, Athens, which had been a great power and center of culture in Greece, was on the brink of defeat. To make matters worse, Alcibiades, a decorated young general, and one of Socrates's prominent students, had launched an expedition in Sicily that turned disastrous after he defected to Sparta. The military campaign, which, at the outset, held promise to be the most glorious conquest in Athenian history, was preceded by a conspicuous act of impiety that roiled the Athenian democracy. A number of sacred statues of the god Hermes were defiled by an unknown culprit who had smashed off their phalluses. Rumor spread that it was Alcibiades, who sought to assert his own authority against the religious faith of the city. We know from Plato's *Symposium* that Socrates had tried to instill moderation in Alcibiades, to temper his infatuation with fame and glory. But the young general's ambition had consumed him at just the wrong time. When the Athenian civil authorities recalled him from the Sicilian expedition and threatened to bring charges against him (an act that by some accounts undermined the expedition), Alcibiades fled to Sparta. In the wake of his defection, the suspicion spread that Socrates was undermining the loyalty of Athens's young leaders.

At the same time, conflict raged between the Athenian democrats who wanted more power for all the freemen of Athens, and the oligarchs who wanted more for the elite and who sought to maintain their power by hiring sophists to teach their sons the art of clever speech and governance. In this atmosphere, Socrates was easily mistaken for a sophist. He consorted with the sons of wealthy aristocrats (among others) and would encourage them to question conventional wisdom. He would also engage foreigners in discussion as readily as he would Athenians.

But in reality, Socrates was no sophist. As he reminded the jury, he never charged a fee for his teaching. And he never claimed to impart virtue as if he were a pitcher of knowledge and his students empty vessels. The point of philosophy, as he practiced it, was not to pass along knowledge, to win an argument, or even to reach an endpoint, but to engage with others in a joint search for self-knowledge that would inspire further questioning.

Socrates's nuanced critique of sophistry was lost on those who saw him from afar. He came to be hated by the traditional Athenian democrats, especially in the wake of the Alcibiades fiasco. At the end of the dialogue *Meno,* in which Socrates defends the idea that teaching means eliciting from the student what he already has within himself, we see the hatred of Socrates on display in the person of Anytus, a statesman who would become one of Socrates's accusers. Anytus suddenly bursts in on the discussion and denounces Socrates's mere willingness to engage with the sophists. He becomes enraged when Socrates raises the question of whether he has ever been wronged by a sophist or even met one. When Anytus admits that he hasn't, Socrates asks him how he can condemn someone he doesn't know. Anytus responds that he knows their "kind," and he warns Socrates to tread carefully lest he be condemned as a sophist himself.[14]

For Socrates to clarify the complicated misunderstandings surrounding him, including the aura of sophistry, while facing the most severe punishment the city could levy, was no easy task, especially in front of a jury of approximately 500 citizens. But he remained steady. He found a way not only to deal with his turn of fate but also to affirm his life, and provide inspiration for his students. Without anger, fear, or self-pity, he delivers to the Athenian jury a subtle defense of philosophy, which is recounted in Plato's dialogue *The Apology of Socrates*. (By "apology," Plato means defense.) Plato thus shows that Socrates was by no means the ethereal and unworldly figure typically associated with philosophers and ridiculed in fables such as that of Thales—the thinker so engrossed in examining the sky that he falls into a well. Socrates, Plato shows, was wise in matters of human motivation and knew how to stand up for himself.

Socrates's defense, as Plato presents it, was both stalwart and prudent. Lest his students in attendance, including Plato, lose their faith in philosophy, Socrates maintains unequivocally that the "unexamined life is not worth living."[15] At the same time, he summons a rhetorical power typically unheard of in philosophers to present philosophy in a way that would protect his students from his own fate. He attempts to show that philosophy goes together with law-abiding citizenship, suggesting that the city of Athens, due to its corruption, could not tolerate the kind of discourse that would make its citizens better.

Employing turns of phrase no less deft than the famous orator Gorgias, Socrates, feigning ignorance of the ways of the court, weaves an intricate account of how philosophy encourages respect for the law. He cites two instances from his past in which he stood up for the law against the passions of the masses. By attempting to present philosophy as a bulwark of the city's integrity, rather than a disruptive force, he does everything he can to inspire and preserve his way of life. If his highest hope was to defend philosophy *and* be acquitted, a seemingly impossible coup, Socrates almost attains it. But by narrow margins (almost 50 / 50), the jury reaches a verdict of guilty.

Upon hearing the verdict, Socrates maintains his honest self-appraisal. Instead of begging for a sentence less severe than death, as the condemned in Athens were allowed to do, he brazenly declares as his "punishment" that he be rewarded by the city with public accommodations for life including free meals. For this, he claims, was his just desert for improving the character of Athens. Needless to say, the jury didn't go for it. The city of Athens sentenced Socrates to death.

Taking his sentence in stride, Socrates patiently addresses his accusers and supporters in turn, assuring the latter that he did not regard his death as an evil. Socrates maintains that with more time, he can convince his accusers of their folly.

Socrates faced a circumstance that would have led most people to disavow their way of life and fall head over heels begging for mercy. Consider how easy it would have been for Socrates to renounce philosophy, at least in Athens, or to have pleaded for banishment instead of death. But instead of distorting himself and abandoning philosophy to save his skin, he chose to face the misfortune and use it as an occasion to affirm his way of life. He thus displayed the virtue of the great-souled man who is "not a lover of danger" and who will "not rush into danger for trifling reasons" but who will "in a great matter lay down his life."[16] Socrates made the misfortune his own. In doing so, he got the better of his accusers—not by destroying them or beating them in court (though he tried) but by turning them to his advantage, by using them to convey a message to anyone moved by philosophy: Never give up. Do not fear death. For the unexamined life is not worth living. Had Socrates not taken such a compelling stand, it is doubtful whether he would have had the same influence on his students, including Plato.

The Death of Socrates: A Lesson in Redeeming Misfortune, and Being One's Self

To underscore his conviction, Socrates remained in prison, even when he had the chance to escape. It was standard practice in those days to bribe a prison guard and to gracefully escape to another city. Plato devotes an entire dialogue to Socrates's rejection of this option, which his friend Crito offers to facilitate. On the day of his execution, Socrates maintains his characteristically stalwart and cheerful demeanor. As Phaedo, a friend of Socrates, reports, "I was not filled with pity, as I might have been at the impending death of another friend; for [Socrates] seemed to me to be a happy man, both in deed and word, facing death with such fearlessness and nobility."[17] Ready to be executed at sunset, Socrates spent the day as he would have any other: in earnest, playful, and undistracted dialogue with his friends on matters of virtue and the soul.

Facing his impending death, Socrates leads an open and wide-ranging discussion on what would seem the most disturbing question in the circumstance: whether or not the soul is immortal. His young friends, including Simmias and Cebes, want to investigate the matter with Socrates. At first they are afraid to challenge Socrates's suggestion that the soul is immortal. They don't want to disturb Socrates with troubling possibilities in his final moments. But Socrates detects their hesitance and encourages them to spare no arguments. With a fatherly calmness, he invites them to present their deepest fears.

After Simmias and Cebes offer their fears in turn, Socrates questions them. Of note, according to Phaedo, who reports what Socrates did and said, is the manner in which Socrates assuaged the fears of everyone present:

> I have often marveled at Socrates, but never as much as in this moment. That he had a response to what [the young men asked about the soul] was perhaps no surprise. But what amazed me most was the manner in which he responded to them, how pleasant, gentle, and respectful he was in listening to the words of the young men; and then how quickly he sensed the effect of their words on us, and then, finally, how adeptly he cured us and recalled us from our flight and defeat and made us face about and follow him and join him in examining the arguments [about the soul].[18]

As the fateful hour nears and the dialogue comes to a close, Socrates leads Simmias and Cebes to "proof" of the soul's immortality. The gist of Socrates's line of questioning is to reveal that the fears of his young friends are based on their implicit reduction of the soul to the body. In their speaking of the soul's potential dispersal, or extinction at death, they implicitly rely on their observation of physical things such as a breath of air that can be seen momentarily on a cold day before vanishing, or embers of a fire that die out. But Socrates suggests that the question of the soul's fate requires a more thorough examination.

All the while, Socrates's unshakable calm in the face of death suggests a depth of spiritual awareness that no argument or proof can quite capture: What animates the body and gives it life is the soul, which comes to manifestation not simply in the body but in the meanings that words and actions convey. Though such meanings can go unrecognized, be misunderstood, and even be forgotten for long stretches of time, they cannot be destroyed or dispersed like a breath or puff of smoke. They continue to live in the actions of those who are moved by them, as Socrates lives in the words of Plato and in our own thought and action, as we interpret the Platonic dialogues and attempt to live by their insight.

In one of his final directions to his friend Crito, who asks if he can do anything for Socrates's children, Socrates replies with one simple request: "As I have always said Crito . . . if you take care of yourselves [by pursuing philosophy], you will serve me and mine."[19]

What Socrates wants is not to be remembered and praised but to persist as a living force for whoever recognizes the merit in his way of life. Not fully cognizant of Socrates's request, Crito asks how Socrates would like to be buried. With his familiar deadpan sense of humor, Socrates replies, with a gentle laugh, "however you like; so long as you can lay hold of me and I do not escape you."[20] The joke is that Socrates has already escaped Crito, who naively identifies Socrates the man with the body that will soon be a corpse. It is no coincidence that Crito is the one who was trying to convince Socrates to escape from prison. Crito, focused on the body and its preservation, can't understand the greater power of the soul.

As if to highlight for us the extent to which Socrates appropriated his misfortune and made it his own, Plato has Socrates orchestrate his own execution. It is Socrates who directs his friend Crito to call in the executioner. It is Socrates who cheerfully accepts the cup of hemlock as the executioner bursts into tears and leaves the room. Without trembling or bemoaning his fate, he downs the draught, as if it were a celebratory cup of wine.

In his final moments, as the poison takes effect, Socrates comforts his friends who are all sobbing. To Crito, he delivers his final request, which turns out to be the last line he utters: "We ought to offer a rooster to Asclepius; see to it that it is done."[21] Socrates's cryptic final line is often understood as a testament against life. Asclepius is the god of healing, and the offering of the rooster represents a gift. The implication of Socrates's instruction to Crito seems to be that life, which is bound to the body, is a sickness of which death cures us. We must therefore offer a sacrifice to the god who heals us of embodiment by bringing about death. But this rendition of Socrates's final statement overlooks the playful spirit in which Socrates utters it. Everything Socrates did and said on the day of his execution, during the trial, and throughout the rest of his life, was full of a love of wisdom that was as much this-worldly as other-worldly. It is plausible, therefore, to interpret the god Asclepius as a symbol of philosophy, as Socrates, many times, regards the philosopher (in this life) to be a kind of healer of the soul.

The notion that Socrates believed that true life can be attained only in liberation from the body, or from the travails of this world, is arguably a Neo-Platonist imposition on his thought, under the influence of certain Christian doctrines. Though Socrates asserts the priority of the soul over the body, he never rejects the body as a hindrance to the soul. In Plato's dialogue *The Symposium,* Socrates even identifies *eros,* the passionate love of the beautiful, as the origin and motivating force of philosophy. He there suggests that the beauty of a beautiful body arouses not only a physical longing to be with the beautiful, but an intellectual longing to make sense of beauty itself. Far from renouncing the bodily world of visible and tangible things, Socrates looks at it with wonder, tirelessly incorporating it into allegories for how to live.

A telling example of Socrates's understanding of embodiment, and of his exuberance for the life he lived, is the final myth he tells his friends right before his execution: that of "the true surface of the earth," seen from above, on which the souls of good men are said to dwell after death. The image of the earth turns out to be a model for a life motivated by philosophy. The earth, says Socrates, is not in size or in character what we take it to be. We live on only a small part of it, as ants or frogs around a pond. Although we think we dwell on the earth's surface, we live submerged in one of its many hollows filled with water, air, and mist. Our condition is like that of beings living beneath the ocean who believe that they dwell on the surface of the sea. Seeing the sun and the stars from under water, they confuse the sea for the sky. Because of laziness and weakness, they never arrive at the surface to see how much purer and more beautiful are the sun and the stars as they shine from our vantage point here. We are in the same position. Due to our laziness and weakness, we take the air to be the heavens in which the stars move. But this air is really mere sediment of the pure heavens, what many call the ether. If we could attain wings and fly out of our murky atmosphere, we could see the stars and everything else as they really are.[22]

The earth with its many layers stands for different levels of self-knowledge. That we dwell in "the hollows" is meant to inspire us to question conventional wisdom, to recognize there is more to life than the "truths" spoken in our circles. Those supposed truths are really opinions, which, if questioned thoughtfully, with a view to the good, point to insights more comprehensive than we currently have in view. The comprehensive perspective toward which our opinions point is "the earth from above," which shines forth as a connected variety of the most brilliant colors, of purple, gold, white, and many others. For "the hollows of the earth, full of water, air, and mist, shine forth in beautiful hues," glistening together "in a single differentiated image."[23]

The "connected variety" of color that Socrates imagines, in which each patch attains its beauty in relation to the others, offers a way of understanding the integrity, or wholeness, of a life possessed of itself. The image also presents a view of ignorance, consistent with Socrates's view that no opinion is entirely false: Our lack of knowledge does not consist in our mistaking the illusory for the real but in falling victim to obsession or myopia, in becoming lost in some detail of ourselves, in one of the earth's many hollows, so that we lose sight of the connected variety of color to which each hollow contributes. Seen in the right perspective, in relation to the other regions of the earth, each hollow is an indispensable part of the one shimmering image.

The beautiful dwelling place of the "good souls" is really *this* world seen in true proportion and color, illuminated by philosophy. Socrates implies that a life guided by the love of wisdom is a ceaseless journey through which one gains ever higher perspectives and clearer vantage points on the world one already knows and loves.

At the end of his defense, after he's been convicted, Socrates tells the jury that his greatest hope after death is the continuation of philosophy. If he were to meet Achilles and Odysseus in Hades (the mythical underworld), he would like nothing more than to question them on the same matters he always discusses with his friends.

Born of his love of wisdom and tireless pursuit of self-knowledge, Socrates faced his trial and execution with the very same poise that defined his life at its freest. Just as he confronted hostile interlocutors and made something of their opinions, so he faced his accusers and used his trial to affirm philosophy. Socrates understood his life as a journey. And because he did, he was able to put even death in perspective. His execution was but another event in his story, which would continue to be written in the thoughts and deeds of others.

Life Is Beautiful: A Contemporary Socratic Tale

The story of the life and death of Socrates reveals that philosophy is not simply about arguments, discourses, and speculations. Above all, it's about *being* philosophical—responding with poise to life's trials and travails. If that's right, we should be able to identify philosophers beyond the highly intellectual.

We find a compelling example in the Roberto Benigni film *Life Is Beautiful,* a modern-day story of transcending immense hardship through the redemptive power of knowing oneself in one's commitments. The film features an unlikely hero who is strikingly Socratic in that his self-possession shines through a goofy, shameless façade.

We first find the hero, Guido Orefice, in a comic circumstance. A funny-faced waiter of modest means, Guido is in pursuit of a woman far out of his league: a beautiful aristocrat, Dora, who is engaged to be married to a pompous government official. With wit, romantic flair, and an indomitable tolerance for rejection, Guido eventually wins Dora over. At her engagement dinner, Guido poses as the waiter, sneaks under the long table at which Dora is seated, taps her on the leg, and convinces her to elope with him. We next find Guido several years later, husband to Dora and father to their playful five-year-old son, Giosuè. His story seems to be an unlikely tale of success, a comedy in which everything falls into place.

But suddenly things take a tragic turn. The Nazis come to power, and we learn that Guido is Jewish. One afternoon, Dora returns home to find their apartment ransacked and her husband and son missing. She frantically tracks them down to the railway station, as they are being herded like cattle onto a train bound for a concentration camp. Though Dora is not herself Jewish, she begs her way onto the train to stick with her family.

The rest of the story is the unlikely tale of Guido's ingenious protection of his wife and son in the brutal confines of the concentration camp. The focal point is Guido's wily strategy for keeping Giosuè hidden from the Nazi authorities after the rest of the children have been murdered. Giosuè had escaped execution in the gas chamber by staying behind in the barracks while the other kids were ordered to "take a shower." With his characteristic creative turn of mind, Guido convinces Giosuè that they are participants in a grand competition with the other inmates. The most important rule of the game is to escape the notice of the prison guards. Among the other rules is no complaining that you are hungry or miss your mother. Whoever follows the rules carefully and earns the most points will win a military tank. Wide-eyed at the prospect of such a prize, Giosuè obeys his father and remains hidden.

As the story unfolds, we come to understand that it's more than an elaborate tale of survival. As the title of the film suggests, it's about the possibility of human flourishing and self-possession in conditions of extreme oppression. The game that Guido devises is not merely a means for protecting his son. It's an expression of his own spirit of levity and creative flair that has defined his life from the moment he met Dora. The game, therefore, should not be regarded as a whimsical illusion meant to fool a child for his own good. It is the way in which Guido is able to be himself, even in circumstances that would impel anyone toward self-distortion. The game is what Guido makes of his reality. And his reality—in all its terror and resistance—becomes the resource for the game. As Socrates does at his trial and execution, Guido is able to find himself in the most hostile of settings.

The self-expressive dimension of the game emerges in the way Guido first introduces it. Having been forced into the barracks after disembarking from the train, Guido and the other Italian men sit and stand quietly, awaiting orders from a stocky SS officer wearing a severe round helmet. Their situation seems to be one of utter powerlessness. With a constipated severity of voice, the officer asks if anyone is able to translate from German to Italian. Guido, not knowing a word of German but seeing an opportunity, boldly steps forward at his own peril.

To the surprise and bafflement of the other prisoners, Guido, feigning intent focus on the officer's every word, and even preserving his harsh tone in translation, begins to make up the game and to outline the rules he wants Giosuè to follow. All the while, the officer, who understands no Italian, thinks that Guido is faithfully conveying his orders. Guido's conceit is an act of resistance through which he turns the tables on the officer. Furthermore, it's a sort of repetition, in a much graver circumstance, of the prank he pulled on Dora's arrogant fiancé, and of the other antics that have defined his spirit of jest.

Guido manages to display the same resource and self-possession to express his love for Dora, even when they are separated in the camp. At the beginning of work one morning, as he pushes a wheelbarrow in which Giosuè lies hidden, Guido notices the communication control room unattended. Risking capture, which would mean certain death for him and his son, he stealthily steps out of line and takes control of the loudspeaker, beckoning Giosuè to join him. "Good morning, princess!" he announces to his wife, wherever she is. "I dreamt about you all night. We were going to the movies and you were wearing that pink suit that I really like. You're all I think about, princess!" He then lets Giosuè say a few words before they beat a hasty retreat. Dora, in the midst of hard labor with the women in another corner of the camp, hears and lights up with surprise and hope. Through his appropriation of the loudspeaker, Guido turns a tool of oppression into a way of being himself, just as he had done in "translating" for the Nazi officer.

His final act is of the same character. As the Allies approach to free the camp, the Nazi officers start rounding up the prisoners to kill them. Guido hides his son inside an abandoned furnace while he rushes off to find Dora so they can escape together. As he hurriedly searches for her, he's caught by a guard, in full view of his son who's peeping through the furnace door just several yards away. Knowing that his son can see him being held at gunpoint, he turns to where he's hiding and gives him a covert wink. As the guard forces him toward an alley where he'll be executed, Guido marches with a comically exaggerated gait—the very same way he'd walk when he was playing with his son in their days of freedom. As Guido disappears from view, we hear the machine-gun fire signifying his death. Soon after, the Allies close in and free the camp. Giosuè and Dora survive and reunite.

In Guido's life and death, there is something strikingly Socratic. On the surface, Socrates and Guido are quite different characters.

One is a philosopher who cared little for his family, the other a de-voted husband and father whose theoretical turn of mind extends only to solving riddles (one of Guido's hobbies). Yet both exemplify the same philosophical disposition. Out of a resolute sense of who they are and where their commitments lie, they are able to confront and redeem disaster. Thus Socrates transforms the trial and execu-tion into a platform to defend philosophy. Thus Guido appropriates the loudspeaker in the concentration camp to express his love for Dora. In such acts of redemption, the lives of Socrates and Guido come full circle. They are able to return to themselves out of ex-treme opposition. From a ruptured world, they salvage a life worth living. Even in their respective deaths, which are, on one level, co-erced, they bring to expression a unity of self, dying in the very spirit by which they've lived, thus freely. The lives of Socrates and Guido offer the insight that suffering is no testament against life. In even the darkest moments, life is overflowing with the possibility of re-demption and joy.

The Meaning of Genuine Sympathy in the Face of Suffering

In thinking through the meaning of suffering, whether it be political injustice, disease, or personal tragedy, we face a delicate balance be-tween acknowledging the horror of what happened and admiring the strength of those who faced it with nobility, even making a life for themselves out of the direst circumstances. Too often we focus on the pain and terror itself, taking pity on those who suffered, high-lighting the ways in which they were dehumanized by the condi-tions they faced.

One familiar reason for this is that we feel, rightly or wrongly, complicit in the suffering. Perhaps we, or our ancestors, played a role in a regime of oppression, or failed to provide aid to victims of a disaster when we could have. Out of guilt, we have a stake in recalling the pain of those we failed to help and highlighting how terrible it was. Though doing so can reflect a healthy sympathy and sense of responsibility, it can also be a form of perverse self-laceration that degrades the virtue of those who suffered and overcame.

In cases of disaster in which we are not complicit, our pity for those who suffer does little but cultivate a shallow identification based on self-pity, as we imagine how terrible it would be to suffer that way ourselves. But if all we do is bemoan how they suffered, we at once glorify our imagined inability to cope (praising it as sympathy) and degrade their strength. We overlook the crucial lesson that even in conditions of extreme deprivation, hardship, and injustice shines the possibility of redemption, and the imperative to salvage not only a mere existence but a flourishing life. To regard those who suffered as mere victims is to deny them, and to deprive ourselves, of greatness of soul. We should instead relate to them as exemplars of the highest virtue from which we can draw inspiration. Such a relation is a form of respect infinitely greater than pity-based sympathy.

A travesty of sympathy is today's politically correct tip-toeing around the suffering of others (or the historic suffering of the groups to which they may belong), often involving some disclaimer to the effect of "based on my own position, I couldn't possibly understand," which makes the reaction of pity and guilt the universally "safe" modes of expression. To focus primarily on the strength of those who suffered, and to identify ways in which they were even able to flourish amid injustice and grave hardship, is to invite a slew of condemnatory questions: "Are you saying that what happened to them was not such a bad thing? Are you saying that a grave wrong was justified?" Such familiar responses fail to recognize that an act can be unjustified in its perpetration yet redeemed, and thus in a deeper sense justified, through the creative adaptation of those who faced it. To study, appreciate, and learn from those who transformed their oppression into a life they could affirm is the highest and really the only form of genuine sympathy, which means, according to the Greek root, a "suffering together" (*syn-pathos*). If we are to suffer together with someone, we must do our best to imagine our own efforts to overcome what they suffered had we been there. Too often we foreclose upon such an exercise from the start by assuming an unbridgeable difference between us (in our supposed comfort or privilege) and them.

Life Is Beautiful came under fire from some critics for not abiding by the thoroughgoing heaviness and gravity of the typical Holocaust film. They suggested that by presenting a character whose comic sensibility transformed the horrific circumstances of a concentration camp into a game, the film made light of the Holocaust. Such criticism overlooks the tremendous insight and creative power that the hero's levity required. His levity is compelling only in proportion to the horrors above which it rises: the mass murder of children from which the hero's son narrowly escapes, the separation of families as both women and men are sentenced to backbreaking labor, the smoldering pile of bodies that the hero encounters as he loses his way one evening on the way back from serving the Nazi officers at one of their decadent parties. It is this most terrible reality out of which the hero must summon the fortitude to live.

To reject such a depiction of character strength as implausible is to deny the power of an ideal. But it is also to neglect the reality of the historical record. Among the most moving documents on display at the Holocaust Museum in Jerusalem are the carefully crafted, quite elegant personal ornaments—rings, earrings, hair combs—that some prisoners in the concentration camps made from scratch in the little time they could find. What makes these things so striking is that they are beautiful but utterly useless in circumstances of survival. They are of the same character as the love that the hero in *Life Is Beautiful* surreptitiously declares to his wife over the loudspeaker in the camp. More than any household fineries one might encounter, they give resonance to Aristotle's claim that "the person of great soul values beautiful but useless things, for they affirm his independence more."[24]

It is possible, in summary, to acknowledge an injustice while recognizing the sense in which those who suffered transformed the sources of their oppression into a life they could affirm. From the perspective of the one who struggles, rather than that of the onlooker who attempts to sympathize from afar and sees only pitiable accident, "I wouldn't have it any other way" is really the expression of the greatest strength and highest virtue.

We ought to acknowledge such strength for our own sake. For strictly speaking, we are never simply onlookers to the fate of those who suffer in shocking and horrific ways. As the seventeenth-century philosopher and theologian Blaise Pascal writes, "The final act is always bloody."[25] By this he means that death confronts us all, and that when it comes to the ultimate things, none is more or less privileged than the other. Whether the immediate cause of suffering be disease, political oppression, or simply old age, it's all a battlefield of divine accident. Our conventional sense that certain forms of death are better and worse than others serves to comfort us as we flee responsibility for confronting the passage of time at every moment. Pascal had a notoriously morbid sensibility. But we should not take his disquieting perspective on the fragility of life to imply a pessimistic outlook. It should rather inspire in us a spirit of redemption and levity, in the fashion of Socrates and the hero from *Life Is Beautiful*. Every moment is precious, as it speaks to a life for which we are responsible, a life that is beautiful, tempting, threatening, inspiring, right here and now.

3

Friendship

Sometimes at the end of the semester, my students ask me in what ways, if any, philosophy has changed the way I live. I used to give a general answer concerning the merits of reflectiveness and of casting a critical eye on conventional wisdom. But as I've thought more about the question, and considered what I'd say to my college-student self, I give a more specific answer: Philosophy has led me to a stronger appreciation of friendship.

If, from my studies of philosophy, I have a single piece of advice to give ambitious college students figuring out their paths, it's to make an effort to have friends, and not only allies. An ally is someone who shares an interest with you and will help you achieve a goal—like the person who works with you on the editorial board of the student newspaper, or who fights alongside you for a social justice cause. A friend is someone who will help you put a goal in perspective, overcome the fear of failure, and remind you that there is more to life than accomplishment.

Whereas an alliance always aspires to some finished product—an article published, a reform implemented, a victory notched—friendship aims at nothing beyond itself. The "fruit," so to speak, of friendship is an empowered sense of self born of the knowledge that someone has your back and you theirs. This is not to say that allies can't also be friends, and vice versa. Some of my closest friends are also training partners and colleagues. But as you grow older and become immersed in a career, it's easy to find yourself surrounded by people who are there for you with alacrity when it comes to making an introduction or "talking shop" but who are "too busy" to come to your wedding. It's hard not to succumb to this instrumental mode of friendship. The truth is that friendship does not sit easily with goal-oriented striving. In our haste to be over and done with things, we tend to seek allies rather than genuine friends.

The problem is not only a contemporary one. Aristotle was alive to it in his distinction between friends who seek some exchange of benefit from each other's company—"friends of utility"—and those who are drawn to each other out of shared commitment to virtue. Friends of utility do not love each other "in themselves" but only for the goods or services they provide. Such friends part ways as soon as one is no longer of use to the other.[1] As the relationship is transactional or limited by a particular goal, such friendships involve the frequent invocation of justice; in being with one another, friends of utility remain ever attentive to whether each does his part, or whether the exchange is fair.

Friends in the genuine sense, by contrast, enjoy each other's company for its own sake, quite apart from whatever it may accomplish. They are drawn to each other in appreciation of the virtue, or greatness of soul in each. While other associations dissolve as interests change, friendship for virtue lasts as long as friends are who they are. Such friendship exists on a higher plane than justice, as both spontaneously offer themselves to each other as if they were supporting themselves. The question of whether exchanges are fair never arises. "Among friends, there is no need for justice."[2]

Though we often use the general term "friendship" to designate relations of utility and relations of virtue alike, we are really speaking of two different kinds of association: one that is thoroughly goal-oriented, and "accidental," as Aristotle puts it (for one needn't have this goal or that), and another that is for the sake of itself.

Friendship for the sake of itself, Aristotle maintains, is integral happiness: "No one would choose to live without friends, even if he were to have all other good things."[3]

Friendship and Self-Possession

It's hard to even make sense of self-possession without friendship. When we consider the moments in which we stand up for ourselves, exercise judgment, or redeem misfortune, we find, more often than not, that we do so with the support of friends. True friends, Aristotle writes, "become better by engaging in activity together, and by keeping each other on course."[4]

Our greatest acts of self-possession are also often for the sake of friends (or loved ones with whom we share a relationship that could be broadly called friendly). The way in which the hero from *Life Is Beautiful* maintains his integrity and joy for life in the most forbidding circumstances is inseparable from his devotion to his wife and son. He is most himself in his proclamations of love for Dora and creative acts of defiance for the sake of Giosuè. When Socrates declares that the "unexamined life is not worth living," and refuses to apologize for his way of life, he stands up for himself and, at the same time, for his students. He makes the attempt to justify philosophy before the city of Athens to protect and inspire those who would pursue it.

Even when we do not act explicitly for the sake of a friend, the activities in which we take joy, and come to understand ourselves, often subtly attest to forms of friendship. Socrates's devotion to philosophy is one example. The dialogical character of philosophy, as Socrates understands it, could be regarded as intrinsically friendly. In contrast to the antagonistic mode of discourse characteristic of sophistry and judicial rhetoric, where one partner aims to outsmart the other, Socratic dialogue aims at mutual empowerment. It involves a shared commitment to clarifying the meaning of the good life through honest self-examination, answering and offering questions based on what one takes to be true or puzzling, and resisting the temptation to introduce hypothetical objections for the sake of mere argument. Attuned to the mutual commitment involved in genuine philosophy, Socrates often refers to philosophy as a form of friendship. Even Socrates's famous irony, which separates him from credulous interlocutors, connects him in friendship to knowing participants. The mutual appreciation of irony, which implies a shared disposition of character, is exemplary of friendship for the sake of itself.

So although self-possession may seem to imply independence, or individuality, as Aristotle suggests in the term *autarkeia,* or "self-rule," which he regards as integral to greatness of soul, such independence is compatible with friendship. To rule one's self, as Aristotle understands it, is not to live as an isolated individual but to adopt a critical disposition toward prevailing conventions, common opinions, and modes of deference. And in this a friend can surely help. It is often our friends who remind us to be ourselves despite the pressures of our social setting, or who gently point out the ways in which we might unknowingly stray from who we are.

When Aristotle writes that the person of great soul would never "live according to another," he adds a significant qualification: "unless the other is a friend."[5] Throughout his account of greatness of soul, Aristotle makes subtle references to friendship, which he later picks up on and develops in his chapters explicitly devoted to friendship. For example, the person of great soul is fond of doing good deeds and therefore needs a beneficiary. The true beneficiary, Aristotle later suggests, is a friend—someone who receives the benefit of wisdom and develops it in turn.

Even in those moments when we find ourselves alone in confronting a hardship or source of internal turmoil, we counsel ourselves through dialogue—by asking ourselves questions, repeating words of motivation, either silently or aloud—as if we were speaking to a friend. Aristotle even suggests that one can be a friend to one's self, for a human being partakes of "duality and multiplicity."[6] This somewhat cryptic statement refers to a common experience: As much as we are at one with ourselves, or possessed of harmony of soul, we cannot avoid moments of internal division. Sometimes we find ourselves torn between a course of action we know to be right and a temptation for something else. In this case, to be a friend to one's self is to find the power to act for the good—perhaps by taking a long, hard look in the mirror and saying "you got this!" or by turning to a motivational image that is pasted above the desk. Other times, we may not know the right course for ourselves. We find ourselves beset by competing commitments out of which we must struggle to find a way. As we deliberate on how to fulfill different loyalties at once, weighing one against the other in the situation at hand and the larger context of our lives, we act as friends to ourselves.

Such internal friendship implies that friendship and self-possession are really two ways of looking at the same virtue. The deliberations characteristic of friendship toward one's self are also of the essence of self-possession. It is not only that self-possession is more easily attained with the support of friends. It is that self-possession is intrinsically a kind of friendly relation among different voices within one's own person. Socrates thus speaks of the harmonious soul as one in which the parts are "friendly" toward one another, with the love of learning and wisdom presiding over the love of honor and profit. Aristotle concludes that a good person is, above all, a friend to one's self, and that such friendship is the most basic form of the virtue.[7]

What we typically call friendship, the close relation of a self to another, can be seen as an extension of the friendship we must have toward ourselves. Unless we have our own house in order, so to speak, unless we have some sense for how to balance commitments, put losses in perspective, and stand up for ourselves, we can't be good friends. For we would lack the very basis for offering the encouragement and advice from which friendship arises. Someone prone to resentment, vengeance, anger, obsession, or other forms of vice would seem incapable of providing the support constitutive of friendship.

Aristotle maintains that only the virtuous can be genuine friends to one another. And he draws the template for a good friend by reference to the disposition of a good person toward himself:

> The marks of friendship in relation to those around us, and by which friendships are defined, seem to have arisen from things pertaining to oneself. For it is said that a friend is someone who wishes for and does things that are good, or that seem to be good, for the sake of another, or as someone who wishes for his friend, for his friend's own sake, to be and live . . . But each of these [marks] pertains to the decent person in relation to himself . . . for the decent person is of like mind with himself and longs for the same things with his whole soul. Indeed, he both wishes for the good things for himself . . . and does them; and he does them for his own sake, since he acts for the thinking part of himself, which is in fact what each [person] seems to be. He also wishes that he himself live and be preserved, and especially that [part of himself] with which he is wise.[8]

We might wonder whether Aristotle is right to link self-possession and friendship so tightly. Are not some of us overly harsh or disrespectful to ourselves but still good friends? Does self-deprecation and self-doubt necessarily detract from the support we may give to someone else? Aristotle must have in mind something like the following: The very fact that we catch ourselves in moments of harsh self-criticism, and know it to be wrong, indicates at least the aspiration to be a friend to ourselves. And to have the aspiration is to be already familiar with what true self-regard involves. It is this familiarity that we implicitly channel—and strengthen—whenever we genuinely help a friend. Just because we have momentary lapses of virtue toward ourselves, and toward others, does not disqualify us from being good friends. Nobody is perfect. When we do act as good friends, we are drawing on a friendship that we cannot help but apply, in some sense, toward ourselves. Because we spend every moment of existence with ourselves, we may tend to lose sight of the friendship that prevails within us and exaggerate the extent to which we give in to self-hate. We may vividly remember the exceptional moments of aimlessness, obsession, or despair and overlook the moments of self-possession. So it can never quite be that we are friends to others while enemies to ourselves. That we are able to put things in perspective for a friend implies that the power is within us, ready to be applied to ourselves, in ways we may fail to fully appreciate.

One of the great benefits of a friend is that they may bolster our self-esteem by pointing out and reminding us of virtues we possess but are liable to forget. Aristotle presents this advantage of friendship in his response to the question of why the virtuous would seek friends given that they are virtuous already and supposedly in need of nothing more. To whatever extent one has attained virtue, a full understanding of the sense in which one is virtuous requires reflection in another. Aristotle reasons as follows:

> If being happy consists in living and being active; if the activity of a good person is serious and pleasant in itself . . . and if we are better able to contemplate those near us than ourselves, and their actions better than our own, then the actions of serious men who are friends are pleasant to those who are good . . . so the blessed person will need these sorts of friends, if indeed he chooses to contemplate actions that are decent and his own . . . and this would come to pass by living together and sharing in a community of speeches and thought.[9]

Aristotle's idea that we are better able to contemplate and appreciate those near to us than our very selves stands in striking contrast, as we will soon explore, to the claim of the Stoics, who proposed that we know ourselves first and foremost, and have an inclination to self-love that we must temper if we are to be good to others. The extent to which we can know ourselves and love ourselves in abstraction from others has significant implications, as we will see, for the relation of friendship to personal identity and also for the relation of friendship to justice.

Aristotle suggests that we only really appreciate ourselves when we see our own actions embodied in the deeds of a friend. Although we may be impressively virtuous in the way we conduct ourselves—in the sacrifices we make, the risks we take, and the way we comport ourselves in circumstances that would faze most people—we are liable to lose consciousness of our own virtue as we fall into the habit of simply being ourselves. We may even get trapped in self-doubt while manifesting to the rest of the world a conspicuous integrity in the way we live. This is where a friend comes in to help support us, to remind us of what we don't see because it's so close to us. Nietzsche, who almost never mentions Aristotle, was on to the same idea. He describes the friend as a buoy that keeps the hermit's internal dialogue from plunging him into despair: "I and me are already too deep in conversation: how could one stand that if there were no friend? For the hermit the friend is always the third person: the third is the cork that prevents the conversation of the two from sinking into the depths. Alas, there are too many depths for all hermits; therefore they long for a friend and his height."[10]

Friendship for the Sake of Itself

Think of a story that epitomizes a friendship in your life. Chances are it involves facing a hardship together, great or small. Friendship, at least as it comes to mind for me, is being stuck in bumper-to-bumper traffic together in Bangalore, India, two hours late for a wedding that we flew halfway around the world to attend, making the best of a helpless situation by seeing the humor in our driver—a hired chauffeur, well put together and apparently professional, but without the faintest clue of where to go. Friendship is battling it out together in a one-on-one, multi-event competition of athletic endurance where the winner is known only to the two of us and the real purpose is to push each other as high and as far as we can go. At the end of it all, we throw each other a cold towel, sprawl out on the grass outside the gym, and recount the battle.

Such gestures are not means to some further end; they accomplish nothing extrinsic to their enactment. In Aristotle's terms, they are deeds whose significance lies *en energeia,* "in action," and not in some further result. So understood, acts of friendship can be distinguished from acts of production, for example, shoe-making, whose value lies in the finished thing (the usable pair of shoes). The point of making light of an ill-fated traffic jam together, or of throwing each other a cold towel after the competition, is not to make or achieve anything, but simply to be one's self and to bolster another. Such moments of support, which often involve the creative redemption of hardship, define friendship. They speak to the sense in which friendship is the outgrowth of a journey. A friend is someone who partakes of the same story as I, a person in whose presence I come to self-possession as we face the twists and turns of life together. A close friend is someone without whom my life story would be difficult if not impossible to tell.

Furthermore, though acts of friendship aim at nothing but themselves, and are fulfilled, so to speak, "in the moment," they also partake of a perpetuity that a product, such as a pair of shoes, does not. Once the pair of shoes is complete, it's reached the apex of its value. From there, the shoes depreciate as they're used and worn out. A gesture of friendship, by contrast, continues to live and grow. It opens a future, standing as a reference point and source of insight for situations to come. The next time you find yourself stuck in traffic, for example, you can think back to "that one time in Bangalore . . ." and redeem your present frustration by reference to a similar episode that, as an expression of friendship, has become part of a memorable journey that is your own.

To take seriously the relation of friendship to a personal journey is to acknowledge that what makes someone a friend cannot be captured in terms of good qualities in the abstract. Plenty of people in the world are good in the senses of empathetic, generous, just, and so on. But they aren't all our friends. And we wouldn't necessarily want to be friends with all of them. Though we may admire a figure such as Nelson Mandela for his tremendous fortitude and spirit of reconciliation, we could not really be friends with him until we learned more about his way of life and its relation to our own, most readily by spending time with him, sharing stories, and engaging in deliberations together.

Friendship involves something more than appreciation of a person who is good in some general sense. It involves mutual loyalty and shared experience. The virtue at which friendship can be said to aim is not some general idea of the good, but the coherence of one's own life as actually lived.

Friendship speaks to the sense in which a virtuous life is about pursuing the good for one's self, not the good in the abstract. Though Aristotle sometimes seems to present the good life as if it were identical for everyone, he offers a more nuanced view in his account of friendship. In the context of defining a good friend, Aristotle takes into account the relation of *the* good to one's *own* good: "No one would choose to possess every good thing by becoming someone else." Even the way in which "god possesses the good" is "by being whatever sort he is."[11] This somewhat obscure remark is echoed in Aristotle's suggestion that virtue is, in a sense, relative to us. After defining virtue as a sort of mean between two extremes, as courage is a mean between recklessness and cowardice, or greatness of soul a mean between vanity and meekness, Aristotle asks whether the mean is absolute or "relative to us," and concludes the latter.[12]

What he seems to be getting at is this: Though virtue may, in all cases, conform to a general structure—which includes the striving for coherence, the capacity for deliberation and judgment, and the ability to put misfortune in perspective—the particular commitments and relations involved in any act of deliberation, judgment, or redemption, are relative to *you*. The weight you might accord, for example, to family, work, or a hobby will depend on your own circumstance, the place that each of these commitments occupies in your life as a whole. In all cases, however, virtue requires one to consider a totality of commitments, to balance them against each other in the situation at hand, and to act in a way that is true to one's self as a whole. Though the principle of "the whole," or of coherence, is the same for everyone, the particular arrangement of the whole is not. Because of our different circumstances and life stories, we will have different friends, even if we are all equally committed to virtue.

In other words, the reason one person is our friend rather than another needn't be based on relative virtue as measured against some universal standard. It could simply be that, given the particular range of commitments in which we are immersed, a given person has proven to be especially fitting to offer support and advice. Though Aristotle maintains that genuine friendship is possible only among the virtuous, he never claims that all the virtuous are identical in their virtue, or that any virtuous person will be friends with any other.

There is a further reason that goodness in the abstract cannot account for the goodness of a good friend. Though we all aim for an integral life, none of us is perfect. If we were, we would have no need to strive for self-understanding and no need to seek support and recognition from friends. Intrinsic to the activity characteristic of a good life is a certain restlessness—not the striving to achieve more things, but to gain greater possession of one's self. The ways in which we fall short of self-possession differ from person to person. Some of us are more prone to anger, others to pity, some to obsession, others to malaise. Some of us expend ourselves in service of others and leave little time for our own projects. Others remain so focused on our work that we lose the sense of being a generous soul to another. To the extent that we care for improving ourselves, we would naturally seek friends whose strengths are our weaknesses, friends in whose company we can learn and grow. We gravitate to those who are a good fit for us, not simply to those who are good in general.

A final sense in which friendship is not about virtue in the abstract has to do with the active, creative dimension to friendship. Friendship is not something given from the start but forged through acts of commitment. It is not as though two full-formed people meet, each with a commitment to virtue but with complementary strengths and weaknesses and then instantly become friends. Such an affinity might be the beginning of friendship, but it is not the thing itself. It is only through living together—facing dilemmas, having each other's back, resolving to stand by each other, asserting and reasserting commitment—that friendship comes into its own. As Aristotle puts it, true friendship "requires the passage of time, and habits formed through living together." People cannot be friends, he writes, until they have at least shared a meal together. Only through developing a history of shared experience and support does "each appear to each as lovable and trusted."[13]

The deepest love, suggests Aristotle, is not simply discovered but forged. Aristotle challenges the idea of love at first sight not merely because we must learn more about someone before embracing her as a friend, but because it is our own active stance toward the relationship—what we contribute to it through acts of commitment—that gives the relationship its character. We love most what we, in a sense, have made. Aristotle draws an analogy to craftsmen who love their works, and poets who love their poems: "We exist in activity . . . and in his activity, the maker of something somehow *is* the work. He therefore feels affection for the work because he feels affection for existence."[14] For this reason, continues Aristotle, mothers feel such a deep affection for their children—because they have contributed to their existence and undergone the pain of giving birth. Of course, we do not make or give birth to our friends. We encounter them in the course of life. But we do contribute to who they are as we get to know them—through acts of support, deliberation, and advice. It is through mutual acts of giving that friends come to love each other as extensions of themselves.

The Tension of Friendship and Justice: Holly Martins and Harry Lime in *The Third Man*

The active, committed aspect of friendship implies the possibility of difficult moral trade-offs. We really prove that we are a friend by being there for someone when we could have been elsewhere. To be a good friend may mean postponing other commitments or taking risks to help a friend in need. To be a good friend may even mean compromising a charitable project or bending the rules of society. If we are in the position of hiring someone for a job, it would arguably be wrong not to give at least some priority to a friend who needs the work. From the perspective of disinterested justice, such preference appears to be a form of corruption. But from the perspective of friendship, it may be the right thing. The same would go for taking a friend behind the scenes in a realm to which we have access but is otherwise closed to the public. Up to a certain point, friendship may even involve covering up a friend's misdeed.

The special imperative of friendship comes to the fore precisely when friendship conflicts with justice. Now, one could say that friendship and justice ought not to be opposed, at least in the case of friendship for the sake of virtue. Aristotle himself maintains that the virtuous person who would qualify to be the true friend—the person of great soul—would not commit an injustice. For the person of great soul cares little for the things over which most people compete and for which they betray each other. At one with themselves, the person of great soul is not prone to resentment or vengeance, even in the face of injury and insult. But to say that greatness of soul, or self-possession, precludes injustice and that truly good friends will always be just makes life too easy. For one, we are imperfect. Even if, for the most part, we live virtuously, we may also succumb to fear, resentment, anger, and despair. In such moments, we may treat others unjustly. And because the world is imperfect despite our best intentions, those of self-possession may be forced into acts of loyalty that are unjust. To what extent we stick by a friend who acts unjustly, and even help them evade justice, is one of the most difficult questions. But it can be a question only to the extent that we recognize friendship as a significant virtue in its own right.

A thought-provoking example of just how far the claim of friendship may extend can be found in Carol Reed's *The Third Man*. The film features a struggling young author, Holly Martins (Joseph Cotten), who travels from the United States to postwar Vienna to accept a job offer from a childhood friend, Harry Lime (Orson Welles). When Martins arrives in Vienna, he is shocked to discover that Lime is missing. He soon learns that Lime was killed in a mysterious traffic accident. Suspecting foul play, Martins sticks around to investigate. He soon comes up against a taciturn British police chief, who tells him to drop the private investigation. Lime, says the police chief, was a crook, a heartless racketeer, and the world is better off without him. Believing Lime is wrapped up in some relatively harmless scheme to smuggle tires or cigarettes, Martins decides to stick up for his friend and tenaciously investigate his death.

But after some shocking twists and turns, Martins learns a terrible truth: Harry Lime is actually alive. He faked his own death to evade arrest in a racketeering scheme even colder and more inhuman than the police chief had first let on: Lime and his associates have been stealing penicillin in bulk from local hospitals, diluting it to ineffective levels, and selling it on the black market to desperate patients who have since died—men with gangrened legs from battle wounds, women who have contracted infections after giving birth, children suffering from meningitis.

In a confrontation with Lime atop an ominous Ferris wheel in a war-torn neighborhood of Vienna, Martins learns just how ruthless his friend has become: Looking down from a rickety compartment that has reached the apex of the wheel, Lime points at the ground below at the people who appear as dots. He asks Martins whether he would really care if one of those dots stopped moving forever: "If I offered you 20,000 pounds for every dot that stopped—would you really, old man, tell me to keep my money? Or would you calculate how many dots you could afford to spare?" With that grim justification, he proposes that Martins join the scheme—or back off.

Being a righteous man, Martins is disgusted and refuses the offer. He's also crushed to learn what a ruthless cynic his friend has become. And, yet, Martins will have no part in helping the police chief bring Lime to justice.

We learn from Martins that he and Lime had grown up together back home. As children, they would go on all sorts of adventures and get into mischief. Lime would always find a way out (though even then, Martins realizes in retrospect, Lime would look out for himself first and foremost). Even now, Lime, in a perverse way, has Martins's back; he paid for his plane ticket to Vienna and had in mind that Martins might join in the nefarious scheme. In light of their entangled life-story, Martins will not betray Lime. Harry Lime may deserve to hang, agrees Martins with the police chief, "but don't expect me to tie the knot."

Lime's girlfriend, Anna Schmidt, takes a similar stand, even though Lime has betrayed her in disappearing to join the racket. In protest to Martins, who is beginning to have a change of heart and is on the brink of helping the police chief catch Lime, Anna affirms her loyalty to Lime: "I don't want him anymore. I don't want to see him or hear him, but he is still part of me, that's a fact. I couldn't do a thing to harm him." Anna is even willing to be deported to the East for Lime's sake. The police chief has learned that Anna has been living in Vienna with an illegal passport that Lime forged for her. He threatens to have her deported if she won't aid in Lime's capture.

In the end, Martins and Anna part ways. In a last-ditch effort to convince Martins to help him, the police chief brings Martins to a hospital full of children suffering permanent brain damage from the effects of Lime's diluted penicillin. Finally swayed by justice, Martins helps the police chief lure Lime out of hiding. At the end of a dramatic chase scene, Martins catches Lime, who's been shot and wounded by an officer. Without a hope of escape, Lime gives Martins a significant look, indicating "it's all over; pull the trigger." As the camera pans away from the two men, a single gunshot rings out, indicating that Martins has obliged and dealt the final blow to his wayward friend.

Anna meanwhile has remained loyal to Lime. She had even tried to tip him off to the final sting operation. The film ends with Anna and Martins both at Lime's funeral—this time his real funeral. In the final scene, Anna passes coldly by Martins, not even acknowledging his presence, as he tries to engage her and reestablish their relationship.

The conclusion leaves us, the viewers, to debate whether Martins or Anna was in the right. It's far from clear that Martins's decision, ultimately on the side of justice, was nobler than Anna's, on the side of friendship. What is clear is that both characters are burdened by a tragic awareness of the competing claims of the two virtues. Such awareness is possible only to the extent that one recognizes friendship as a significant virtue in its own right—alongside justice, not beneath it.

One test for determining how to balance friendship against justice is the extent to which a friend's deviousness or trickery spills over into the friendship itself. It is difficult to imagine that someone who always seeks to get the better of others would not eventually seek to get the better of his friends as well. Part of what leads Martins to cooperate with the police against Lime is that Lime has revealed himself to be a disloyal friend, and not simply an unjust person. In their grim meeting on the Ferris wheel, Lime threatens Martins and also reveals his utterly instrumental attitude toward Anna, who thinks Lime actually loves her. Martins comes to realize that even in their days of friendship, as children back home, Lime always prioritized his own interest.

But it is also plausible to imagine a friend whose acts of injustice are targeted and confined—infractions against "the system," or abstract norms of fairness, that would not jeopardize the friendship. Consider the *bons amis* that prevails among the thieves in *Ocean's Eleven*, or the rock-solid loyalty of Bonnie and Clyde as they rob banks together throughout the Midwest. Their injustices do not seem to corrupt the friendship. Though the friendships may not be especially elevated ones, they are, to some extent, friendships based on virtue of character. They can't be dismissed as merely utilitarian. In a paradoxical way, the acts of injustice even seem to strengthen the friendships, as they become occasions for plotting together, deliberating, backing each other up, and sharing in a way of life.

The possibility of friendship with someone who has committed a grave injustice and evaded the law comes to powerful expression in Fyodor Dostoyevsky's *Crime and Punishment*, in the love of Sonya for Raskolnikov. When Sonya learns, by Raskolnikov's own confession, that it was he who murdered the old pawnbroker and her younger half-sister, Lizaveta, Sonya forgives him. Though she is shocked and horrified by the deed, and can barely imagine it to be true, she sticks by Raskolnikov for the loyalty he has shown her. Notwithstanding his aimlessness and depravity that led him to commit the gruesome double murder as a kind of perverse test of power and independence, Raskolnikov has shown unwavering commitment to Sonya as he attempts to hold himself together in the wake of his crime. Whereas many of the ostensibly respectable members of Saint Petersburg look down on Sonya, who has turned to prostitution to support her destitute family and little sisters, Raskolnikov sees through to her purity of heart. He loves Sonya, and sympathizes with her father, Marmeledov, a former civil servant who has fallen on hard times and used up what little resource his family has through hard drinking. When Marmeledov is trampled by a horse and carriage in a terrible accident, Raskolnikov rushes to his aid and attempts to save his life. After Marmeledov dies, Raskolnikov leaves Sonya and her family what little he has to give. He also defends Sonya against the accusations of a man who attempts to impugn her reputation by falsely accusing her of theft. Given the support and love Raskolnikov has shown Sonya, a love through which Raskolnikov himself is eventually redeemed, Sonya remains loyal to him, even though one of the women he killed, Lizaveta, turns out to have been Sonya's friend.

Just as Raskolnikov sees the good in Sonya, she sees the good in him. In far greater clarity than Raskolnikov can himself recognize of his own motives, stuck as he is in crippling self-doubt, Sonya understands that he is a good man gone terribly astray. She remonstrates with Raskolnikov to repent and to "kiss the earth" that he has defiled. Even when he refuses to do so, Sonya remains stalwart in her love. In the end, Raskolnikov turns himself in of his own accord and is sentenced to eight years of hard labor. (His sentence is relatively lenient for murder, as the judge, failing to understand Raskolnikov's real motives, believes him to be insane.) Sonya moves to Siberia with Raskolnikov and visits him in prison every day. Through Sonya's love, Raskolnikov ultimately finds redemption. The story ends with Raskolnikov's rebirth in the arms of Sonya, in whose aspiration and purpose he resolves to share.

Had Sonya simply committed herself to justice, she would have turned Raskolnikov in as soon as she learned about his crime, or at least broken off ties with him as long as he fled the law. But her friendship and love for Raskolnikov prevail. To the extent that we admire Sonya for her loyalty, we cannot so readily admit that justice should take priority over friendship.

The Modern Bias against Friendship in Favor of Justice

Deep down most of us recognize the significance of friendship as a virtue in itself. But when we feel pressured by our careers and unable to make time for friendship, or when we find our hopes for friendship dashed by betrayal, we can easily convince ourselves that friendship doesn't matter so much in the larger scheme of things. Thanks to a modern philosophical tradition that generally degrades friendship in favor of supposedly more universal concerns, we have at our disposal a grab-bag of self-righteous, ostensibly enlightened cases against friendship.

I came across one in a contemporary Stoic self-help book, which proposes that friendship is a "preferred indifferent," something we'd rather have than not but that is inessential to a good life. The author went on to explain that the only thing not a "preferred indifferent" is moral character. He clearly took friendship and moral character to be entirely separate, the first but one step removed from mere egoism. In a telling passage, he writes "that there cannot be any such thing as (Stoic) friendship between criminals, as every time a criminal helps his criminal friend with, say, getting away with escaping justice, he puts friendship for the other ahead of moral integrity—precisely the reverse of the Stoic set of priorities."[15]

What the Stoic account overlooks is that moral integrity is considerably broader than justice. As Aristotle reminds us, justice can even be seen as a remedial virtue. We invoke norms of justice only after deeper bonds have been eroded. Higher than justice are greatness of soul and friendship, to say nothing of bravery and generosity, which Aristotle also discusses as virtues in their own right. Just because someone is a criminal does not make him a bad person or a bad friend. To argue that Bonnie and Clyde were not true friends because they committed injustices makes little sense unless one can show that their injustices began to corrode their mutual loyalty.

To simply assert the pursuit of justice as a criterion of "true" friendship is to miss the complexities of competing virtues. As the case of Martins and Lime powerfully suggests, aiding a friend in escaping justice may itself represent a kind of moral integrity. This is especially so in cases where it would be in a friend's interest to rat out his partner to the police. There's a reason we find ourselves rooting for criminals in films such as *The Godfather.* Though we may denounce their crimes, we admire their unshakable loyalty to family and friends. We cannot dismiss such loyalty as utilitarian or selfish. It does speak to a kind of virtue of character, to friendship for the sake of itself.

The assumption that true friendship cannot prevail among criminals fails to account for the moral claim of having each other's back. As Socrates remarks in Plato's *Republic,* there may be a certain virtue that prevails among thieves, insofar as they stick together in accomplishing their crime. Though we may deplore the crime itself, we cannot so easily dismiss the forms of loyalty maintained and forged in the process.

The denigration of friendship that we find in this Stoic author is hardly an aberration in contemporary moral philosophy. That friendship is a kind of emotional, narrow-minded affinity for those in our circle is a strikingly common view among today's philosophers. Friendship, many assume, is a kind of habitual loyalty based merely on the contingency of who you grew up with or happened to come across in your daily life. What really matters, and requires the effort of reason, they say, is disinterested justice. Whereas being a good friend, they suggest, comes almost naturally, as an instinctive disposition in favor of those near to us, being a good *person,* being good to people in general, requires effort. To attain an expansive moral consciousness, according to this view, means resisting the pull of selfish tendencies—including friendship.

Such a bias against friendship has roots that go back to Scottish enlightenment philosopher Adam Smith. He describes friendship as a "constrained sympathy" arising of an overly intense identification with the people whom you habitually see—those in your family, first and foremost, then your neighborhood, then your country.[16] Beginning from the principle of self-love, Smith follows the Stoics in tracing increasingly broad circles of concern, each defined by an increasingly attenuated "habitual sympathy," until one sheds the influence of habit altogether and arrives at the universal sympathy for strangers, which Smith regards as the highest moral feeling: "The wise and virtuous man . . . consider[s] all the misfortunes which may befall himself, his friends, his society, or his country, as necessary for the prosperity of the universe."[17] An almost identical sentiment finds expression in the French enlightenment thinker Montesquieu, who asserts that "if men were perfectly virtuous they wouldn't have friends."[18]

But to regard friendship as a narrow-minded, merely emotional disposition at odds with reason and reflection is a mistake. The very fact that we can take the claims of justice seriously yet side with friendship (as Anna Schmidt does in *The Third Man*) indicates that friendship involves profound considerations and painful trade-offs. To be a friend is to balance commitments, not to blindly adhere.

Even when friendship does not butt up against justice, giving rise to the need for reflection, but unfolds naturally, in the course of everyday life, it involves a creative, interpretive capacity. Consider mundane gestures through which friendship is expressed and forged, such as cracking a joke while being stuck in traffic together. To develop a friendship in this way is to be attentive to a situation of mutual concern in a way that is both true to your own disposition and alive to your friend's sense of humor. You have to be able to see the absurdity of a driver in neatly pressed uniform, projecting a sense of confidence, with no idea where he's going. And you have to know that such absurdity is something that your friend will appreciate in the moment. This is practical wisdom, not mere emotional affinity based on proximity. There are plenty of people who you'd like *less* after suffering with them through the ordeal of three-hour traffic in Bangalore.

Though people who eventually become friends may meet by chance—because they came from the same town, or found themselves in the same running club—the relationship they develop cannot be dismissed as merely contingent. In reducing friendship to bonds forged by proximity as we reflect upon the big wide world and imagine who might be our friends if only our paths were to cross, we overlook the obvious fact that when it comes to those nearest to us, those whom we literally see every day, we remain distant from many of them. And, in some cases, for good reason. Consider the troublesome neighbor whom you like less the more you see of him. We make a decision to stick only with certain people near to us, those who prove themselves loyal and help us rise to self-possession.

The aspect of mutual learning and recognition in friendship is what Smith's sentimental view neglects. Whereas Aristotle begins from shared activity, and the idea that we develop a sense of self only in discourse with others, Smith begins with the individual ego, which, as a matter of course, may (or may not) take up various relationships. Whereas Aristotle maintains that self-understanding and self-love are possible only in friendship, that we can't fully be ourselves and appreciate ourselves without friends, Smith starts with the principle of self-love that can be had even before the love of family. Only through the contingency of habit and custom, says Smith, do we come to love our family and friends. He interprets such love as a kind of attenuated self-love.

When Smith speaks of "friends of virtue," he simply means those who are bound by the shared sentiment of love of humanity in general. He remains blind to the kind of virtue that involves developing practical wisdom, judgment, and self-possession in each other's company.

The Claims of Friendship and of Universal Concern

The notion that universal sympathy for humanity ought to take priority over friendship overlooks the possibility that friendship defines what it is to be human in the first place. The cosmopolitan critique of friendship assumes that friendship is something accidental, something we may or may not acquire in the course of life. Who we are as human beings, by contrast, is necessary, or natural, and can be identified and understood quite apart from friendship. Whether we have friends or not, we are human and can identify other human beings as such by some basic trait, such as rationality, language, sentience, or some combination of criteria. Adam Smith speaks of the "society of all sensible and intelligible beings," implying that sensation and intelligence define what is human and worthy of respect.[19] According to his view, the human essence is prior to friendship.

But, according to Aristotle, what is human cannot be separated from shared activities though which we rise to self-possession. The virtue of self-possession, which, as we have seen, implies friendship, is not a property of a being already determined as human by some other standard. To be human *is* to strive for self-possession, which also means to be a friend—whether to one's self or to another. As Aristotle suggests, the human being cannot be defined without reference to the characteristic human activity (*ergon*), the activity of the soul in pursuit of virtue.

Aristotle implies that a human being is not a thing that could be observed in its humanity, or known objectively, but an active force intelligible only from a perspective that is engaged and committed. At the beginning of his *Ethics,* Aristotle asserts that only the reader who is already committed to an ethical life will understand the meaning of the book, with its elaborations of "virtue," "practical wisdom," and "judgment." It is only through the struggle to rise to our humanity in partnership with friends that we come to understand what it means to be human.

For this reason, all accounts that simply oppose friendship and universal love of humanity are misguided. We come to appreciate those who are distant only by imagining how they might be brought within the balancing act of claims that defines our own active life. We come to respect strangers as other human beings only by imagining how we might bring them within our circle of friends. We can begin to imagine the inclusion of strangers only to the extent that we hear their statements and consider how we might respond, thus already beginning to relate to them as near to us. It is through friendship that humanity, and respect for others, comes to light at all.

To accept that friendship is not some accidental relation among human beings but a constitutive dimension of what it means to be human is to recognize that the question of whether humanity in general should take priority over friendship makes no sense. Apart from our friends and the claims they make on us as we strive for self-possession, we have no access at all to humanity.

When Smith speaks of "the society of all sensible and intelligible beings," he implicitly assumes a conception of the human that overlooks the significance of shared activity, a conception according to which a human being is a thing that can be appreciated in virtue of some property common to members of a species, such as sentience or intelligence. Though in a formal and abstract sense Smith may be right, the criteria he invokes cannot be observed or ascertained theoretically. Reason, for example, is inseparable from the practice of exchanging reasons and attempting to reach clarity on a topic of mutual concern. Language is inseparable from the ideas that find expression in dialogue.

As soon as we raise the question so familiar today among biologists, anthropologists, and even philosophers of whether a species of animal has language, or reason, and is therefore akin to a human being, we have already lost touch with the engaged and committed stance that would grant us access to anything like language and reason in the first place. From a theoretical, or observational perspective, the language or reason we might find is, at most, a certain mode of calculation, a sense for how a certain action leads to a certain outcome, as when a chimpanzee uses a stick to extract termites from a nest, or how a certain sound triggers a certain gesture, as when the shrill cry of a monkey leads the others in the group to scatter in flight from a snake. But this is not the kind of reason or language in virtue of which we regard humanity as intrinsically worthy of respect. The human community that finds expression in language and reason resides in a shared commitment to the content of what is spoken. Apart from words of inspiration and counsel through which we rise to self-possession—discussions of the good and the bad, the just and the unjust—there can be no human bond.

The sense in which language, reason, or any other supposed criterion of the "human," evades objective analysis and empirical identification is well captured by twentieth-century philosopher Hans-Georg Gadamer, who suggests that whenever we experience or encounter language, it has already made a claim on us, presented a meaning to be questioned and worked out in the context of our striving for coherence. Disconnected from the way in which language *captivates* us, and exhorts us to question our lives, language is nothing. To have language, or to be capable of language, is to be already responding to its call.[20]

Our necessarily engaged relation to language means that it can never be turned into an object, defined in merely descriptive terms, or reduced to a system of signs that we control. It is language that speaks to us, and we who respond. But the call and response of language can be only among friends, among those who participate in a shared project of self-understanding.

Such an analysis of language suggests that humanity, in the sense to which we refer when we speak of universal concern, cannot be made the object of distant appreciation. Any trait we may regard as fundamentally human presupposes friendship, which is to say that friendship is the only possible basis for the love of humanity.

The Degradation of Friendship in Light of Providential Thinking

Influential though it may be, especially in academic circles, the cosmopolitan critique of friendship is more of an intellectual position than the real reason we neglect friendship. More powerfully opposed to friendship than the ideal of universal love in the abstract is a certain goal-oriented disposition that developed out of Enlightenment thought alongside a cosmopolitan ethic: the faith that the world is moving toward some ideal of justice, freedom, happiness, or technological progress, and that the highest human calling is to help bring that ideal into being. We could call it the goal-oriented perspective writ large, a view of divine or historical providence. It finds colloquial expression in the aspirations to "make the world a better place" and to be "on the right side of history."

Such a providential view places friendship second to alliance: Friendship, at its best, is a source of encouragement on the path to the ideal world, a form of attachment that will eventually be displaced by a "brotherhood of man." It is no coincidence that the foremost philosopher of historical providence, Karl Marx, writes volumes on working-class solidarity and the "species being" of man but nothing on friendship. Within his framework of world progress, friendship can only mean alliance for the sake of a society free of exploitation.

The rejection of friendship in favor of alliance is blind to a possibility that ancient thought, especially as portrayed in Greek tragic poetry, readily acknowledges: that oppression—in the form of disaster, calamity, and undeserved suffering—is an essential aspect of human existence, not a social accident amenable to reform.

The downfall and redemption of Oedipus is a classic example. The wisest man, able to solve the riddle of the ferocious Sphinx and save the city of Thebes, a man who, in return for his heroism, ascends to the throne and rules with the best of intentions, is plunged by fate into an abyss of unwitting murder and incest. It is precisely his exceptional wisdom and goodness that qualifies him for a tragic fall. The point of his story, and of Greek tragedy in general, is that people do not get what they deserve. In spite of his horrific series of blunders, Oedipus, the man responsible for the complete unraveling of the moral order, who, when he learns of his deeds, gouges out his own eyes and consigns himself to a life of exile, finds redemption, in the end, through the blessing he bestows upon the city of Athens, the city willing to accept him despite his cursed fate.

In a world of tragedy rather than providence, where our greatest goals end in failure and our best intentions backfire in ways beyond our limited foresight, where sudden and unfathomable upheaval is essential to life, and does not subtly attest to some ultimate purpose, friendship rises above justice. The virtue most needed in a universe riddled with suffering is that of redeeming accidents within a story that inspires us to live on. Without people who have our back and who accept us despite our failings, it is hard to maintain, or even make sense of, such redemptive capacity.

The anti-providential view of life to which tragedy attests could also be put in terms that highlight a form of agency—not that of foresight and planning but of creativity. Only in a universe where the aim of life is not already in sight does genuine creativity—the birth of the new, the dawning of a life transformed—become possible. Creativity in this sense is not a piecing together from scratch, which, however implicitly, always has before itself a form toward which it works, but the creative *response* to suffering, to the unbidden. Tragedy reveals that what we are doing as we live and strive is not simply working toward a goal already in sight, but working out the meaning of any possible goal. And it is the exuberant joy of being undetermined by a goal that impels us to seek friends, those who will receive and interpret our creations and keep the activity of creation alive.

No philosopher was more keenly attuned to the exuberant, joyful dimension of tragedy than Nietzsche. In his first book, *The Birth of Tragedy,* he argues that what scholars of his day had referred to as "Greek cheerfulness," the joy for life and apparent optimism of the ancient Greeks as reflected in their beautiful temples and marble statues of the gods, was born of a profound sense of tragedy and the need to redeem the "primordial suffering" at the heart of existence. Nietzsche arrives at this view after puzzling over how a people so attentive to order, proportion, and symmetry in their sculptures and depictions of the gods could also produce such terrifying myths as the Oedipus story, which seemed to shatter all notions of stability and harmony. Nietzsche concludes that the two dispositions were connected: The Greek "shaping power," which found paradigmatic expression in architecture, and which Nietzsche dubbed "Apollonian" after the god Apollo, was born of the need to give shape to the chaotic, eternally churning "Dionysian" force at the heart of existence. The ultimate way in which the Greeks gave shape to the Dionysian, argues Nietzsche, was to depict the Dionysian directly, so to speak, in the image of the tragic poem. By bringing the inchoate, Dionysian force, represented by the chanting chorus, to the Apollonian unity of a story, the Greeks unified chaos and order, generating a form of art that redeemed suffering and inspired further acts of creation.

From the example of the Greek tragic myth, Nietzsche draws a broader insight: Suffering is inseparable from the creative exuberance that makes life worth living. It is not simply that suffering shakes us loose from complacency and leads us to create. It is that the very creative impulse, whenever it moves us, involves internal tension and discord, a form of suffering that is, at the same time, life-affirming. As Nietzsche puts it, "One must still have chaos in one's self to give birth to a dancing star."[21] The dancing star to which one might give birth, is, in its essence, an offering to potential friends, to those who are inspired by its radiance to "give birth" in turn. "You great star," writes Nietzsche in reference to the rising sun, "what would your happiness be had you not those for whom you shine?"[22] As we will see in our investigation of time (Chapter 5), it is no coincidence that Nietzsche, attuned to the creative, tragic aspect of existence, ranks the gift-giving virtue as the highest virtue. In doing so, he implicitly agrees with Aristotle, who gives the same rank to friendship.

Redemption through Friendship: The Story of *Double Indemnity*

When things go terribly wrong, when our purposes meet with disaster, and when we lose ourselves to despair and depravity, friendship redeems life and makes it worth living. That's the moral of Billy Wilder's classic film noir *Double Indemnity*. Viewed as an affirmation of friendship, the film is an uplifting antidote to our goal-oriented conception of the good.

Double Indemnity is the tale of Walter Neff (Fred MacMurray), a dapper salesman in his mid-thirties who works for Pacific All Risk

Insurance, a large, impersonal company based in Los Angeles. Bored with his life of corporate conformity and rote sales-pitches, Neff falls for Phyllis Dietrichson (Barbara Stanwyck), the alluring young wife of a surly old client whom Neff encounters on a routine house call.

Phyllis turns out to be an archetypal femme fatale. Employing her well-practiced manipulative seduction, she ensnares Neff in a nefarious scheme: Sell her husband a life-insurance policy with a double payout clause for accidental death—and then bump him off, making it appear as though he fell off a train. Infatuated with Phyllis and eager to "crook the house" of Pacific All Risk, Neff helps her pull off the elaborate scheme.

In the end, Phyllis betrays Neff. She plans to leave him, abscond with the money, and orchestrate his murder. In a final confrontation with Neff, she pulls a pistol from under the pillow of her chair and shoots him in the chest, inflicting what turns out to be a mortal wound. But in the moment, Neff retains the strength to coolly approach Phyllis and face her down ("you better try [and shoot] again, baby"). As Phyllis can't quite bring herself to fire another bullet, Neff wrests the gun from her hands, turns it on her, and shoots her dead ("goodbye, baby!"). Thus concludes what seems to be a thoroughly grim tale.

But the real drama and depth of the film lies beyond the tawdry, mutually destructive affair between Neff and Dietrichson. It lies in the incongruous friendship that emerges between Neff and his colleague at Pacific All Risk, Barton Keyes (Edward G. Robinson), a brilliant false claims investigator with an encyclopedic knowledge of accident statistics.

At the very beginning of the film, we learn that Neff is narrating the entire saga of his entanglement with Dietrichson into a tape recorder, alone, late at night in Keyes's office. Neff is making an elaborate confession to Keyes: "You want to know who killed Dietrichson? Hold on to your cheap cigar . . . *I* killed Dietrichson." With that, he launches into the serpentine tale of murder and deceit.

At the beginning of the story, we see on display the unlikely friendship of Keyes and Neff as they banter in the office. Keyes is just about everything Neff is not, and vice versa. Neff is a tall, handsome young guy who speaks fluently in winsome, off-the-cuff remarks. Keyes is a short, stout middle-aged man with a brilliant mind for solving false claims cases. He speaks a mile a minute as he unfurls the complicated chains of logic, by which he is able to identify the fraudsters. It is precisely the contrast of Keyes and Neff that constitutes their friendship. In their frank repartee, full of lighthearted insult and witty one-upmanship, Keyes and Neff understand each other. Their being together cannot be mistaken for mere collegial diplomacy or strategic alliance. Keyes even ribs Neff for causing him headaches as a salesman: "I get darn sick of trying to pick up after a gang of fast-talking salesmen dumb enough to sell life insurance to a guy who sleeps in the same bed with four rattlesnakes."

Neff, in turn, pokes fun at Keyes for his maniacal obsession with solving cases: "You love it, only you worry about it too darn much . . . You're so darn conscientious, you're driving yourself crazy. You wouldn't even say today is Tuesday unless you looked at the calendar. Then you'd check to see if it was this year's or last year's calendar. Then you'd find out who printed the calendar."

And, yet, each appreciates the other for his distinctive way of being. Their mutual recognition is epitomized in a characteristic ritual: Keyes pulls out one of his cheap cigars to puff on while he mulls over a case. Neff lights it for him. The gesture is a moment of unalloyed friendship in which each can be himself without any further motive. Neff can extend his cool and steady hand without having to sell anything. And Keyes can display his deductive logic as a power in its own right, as something more than a means to solving the case. Each appreciates the other for the way of being he displays, not simply the things he accomplishes.

Without Neff, Keyes would be confined to a life of producing results (catching the crooks) without being able to display his brilliant process. Without Keyes, Neff would be stuck glad-handing to clients in hopes of another sale with no one to appreciate his charm.

It's only at the very end of the film, however, when things go awry, that Neff and Keyes come to fully recognize what they mean to each other. Until that moment, Neff had been preoccupied with deceiving Keyes, who was hot on the trial of the mysterious Dietrichson killer. Keyes had figured out that Dietrichson's death was no accident. He had even deduced that Dietrichson must have been killed before he boarded the train, and that a pair of conspirators, not a lone wolf, had done the deed. But Keyes can't entertain the thought that Neff, his long-standing friend, is involved even though it was Neff who sold Mr. Dietrichson the insurance policy.

Betrayed by Phyllis Dietrichson, Neff makes a move that defies all calculation and ensures that he'll be caught: Bleeding from the gunshot wound, he summons the energy to drive into the office and record a late-night confession to Keyes. The confession is a reclamation of self-possession in the face of disaster. It's also an acknowledgment of what mattered to him all along but got lost in his obsession with the Dietrichson affair: his friendship with Keyes.

As Neff narrates the saga into the microphone, he pays respect to Keyes in a striking reversal of roles: It is Neff who reveals the twists and turns of the case to Keyes, just as Keyes would routinely do for Neff.

As Neff is coming to the conclusion of the saga, Keyes appears at the threshold of his office. He hears enough to quickly grasp what has transpired. Before him stands the elusive criminal—the Dietrichson murderer whom he had doggedly sought; the shocking twist is that it's his best friend. Keyes has for once failed to apprehend the crook with his own wits. But in his failure, he too comes to a deeper realization: All the actuarial science and forensic power in the world met their limits in friendship. The reason Keyes couldn't crack the case is that the perpetrator was someone he trusted. Keyes knows that Neff has come to confess to him for a reason—to redeem their friendship and to acknowledge that he, Keyes, solved the case with impressive acumen, save for the final twist.

Neff makes his purpose clear to Keyes in his final words, which he delivers with labored breath: "You know why you didn't figure this one, Keyes? Let me tell you. The guy you were looking for was too close. He was right across the desk from you." "Closer than that, Walter," Keyes replies. The eyes of the two men meet, and Neff reconciles with the friend whom he had deceived: "I love you too, Keyes." Acknowledging the sincerity and depth of Neff's characteristically succinct response, Keyes completes the reversal of roles with a silent gesture: As Neff collapses from blood loss and struggles to pull out a cigarette, Keyes lights it for him. The reversal brings to clarity the genuine appreciation that each has for the other.

In the end, neither Neff nor Keyes finds satisfaction in his projects. As Neff says at the beginning of his confession, "I killed Dietrichson. I did it for money and for a woman. And I didn't get the money . . . And I didn't get the woman." Keyes, for his part, fails to solve the case. He discovers the mysterious killer only when Neff appears in a crushing revelation. From a goal-oriented perspective, *Double Indemnity* is indeed the epitome of film noir. But its deeper message is that success or failure is not what really matters in life. What matters are deeds that accomplish nothing but that embody self-possession and friendship.

Double Indemnity is really a warning against obsession and infatuation, quite apart from whether such vices lead down the path to murder, deceit, or injustice. In a way, we all risk becoming Walter Neff and are never wholly free from his predicament. Maybe we don't fall for Ms. Dietrichson. But as long as we live and strive, we find ourselves tempted by alluring goals, "getting the money or the woman," so to speak, whether that takes the form of a mystery solved, a dream job landed, or a milestone attained. The fate of Walter Neff, and of Keyes, implores us to steer clear of these sources of infatuation and to remain attentive to what is so close and essential to us that we often fail to appreciate it.

The Relation of Friendship to Competition

Another lesson to be learned from the friendship of Neff and Keyes is the sense in which the equality that pertains among true friends is not a mere sameness but a form of mutually empowering difference, even opposition. Neff and Keyes came to appreciate each other, and to recognize themselves, in their good-natured exchange of quips, which reflects the distinctive style and disposition of each. This oppositional aspect of friendship is something I have come to appreciate in the realm of sports, in considering the relationship among respectful competitors.

At first glance it might seem as though friendship and competition are diametrically opposed. Competition, we assume, aims at victory and domination. Friendship, by contrast, aims at mutual support. At best, we often think, competition is a healthy version of unfriendliness: a contained outlet for the aggressive instincts that find their ultimate expression in violence and war. As Sigmund Freud might say, sports are a way of sublimating a destructive "death instinct" basic to the human psyche. According to this view of competition, what human beings really want is to dominate others. Sports let us indulge that urge without going too far.

Plausible though this account may seem, especially when we consider contact sports such as boxing and American football, or witness brawls on the baseball field, I've come to see it as superficial. Competition in its highest form is not about mutual destruction but joint cultivation.

Within all sports lies a tension between the desire to win—to destroy or to stop one's opponent, which is the imperative of war, and the desire to elicit the game at its best. This tension finds memorable voice in the famous battle cry of Muhammad Ali: "Float like a butterfly, sting like a bee. Rumble young man, rumble. Waaaaaaaaaah!" Whereas "rumble" and the bellowing cry suggest heavy hitting and a knockout victory, "float like a butterfly" implies grace, levity, and beauty—a synchronized dance in which each tries to outdo the other in artistry. "Sting like a bee" seems to be somewhere in between. It evokes Ali's quick and precise jab, which he was miraculously able to land while backing up.

Though Ali was known for what many took to be his killer instinct, captured in the iconic image of his towering over Sonny Liston after knocking him out in the first round of their rematch for the heavyweight title, he insisted that destroying his opponent was not his primary goal. What he really wanted was to put on a show: to engage with a fighter who would elicit in him the reflexes, technical precision, and endurance of a new, artistic form of fighting:

> When I first came into boxing . . . fighters were not supposed to be human or intelligent. Just brutes that exist to entertain and to satisfy a crowd's thirst for blood. Two animals to tear each other's skin, break each other's noses . . . I would change the image of the fighter in the eyes of the world . . . I hated the sight on TV of two big, clumsy, lumbering heavyweights plodding, stalking each other like two Frankenstein monsters, clinching, slugging toe to toe. I knew I could do it better. I would be as fast as a lightweight, circle, dance, shuffle, hit and move, zip-zip-pop-pop, hit and move back and dance again and make an art out of it.[23]

Ali's attitude demonstrates that even in the most brutal and warlike of sports, a true athlete aspires not simply for victory in the sense of destruction (the knockout) but for a fight in which opponents push each other to the limit, forcing each other to display the beauty of a joint activity. At their best, competitive sports are about mutual empowerment, not destruction. They are, in this sense, arenas of friendship. The question is not who will fall but who will display the sport at its highest level, bringing to light new and unforeseen forms of subtlety and grace.

For a serious athlete, and for a true lover of the game, there is nothing more dissatisfying than a blowout victory, except for a blowout loss or, even worse, a forfeit. The most fulfilling win is that in which two sides battle it out in extra innings, extended tie-breakers, or overtime minutes, each attempting to one-up the other in the excellence of the game.

Such victory is fulfilled, paradoxically, in the unfolding of the action and not in the result. At the height of competition, the players want to play on. The end—whether a loss or a win—is ridden with longing as much as relief and satisfaction. As tennis superstar Roger Federer once revealed in a postgame interview after a hard-fought victory over his archrival Rafael Nadal, he wished the match didn't have to end. True athletes want each other to go higher and farther so that both can exhibit the game at its best. When Federer and Nadal exchange blistering forehands, Nadal with his characteristic topspin, Federer with his flat precision, each hitting his shot harder and at a sharper angle than the other, back and forth, they engage in a battle among equals, each with his own style and complementary skill. Each comes into his own in responding to the other's challenge.

This oppositional character of friendship is something to which Nietzsche was attentive: "How divinely vault and arches break through each other in a wrestling match," he writes of ancient Greek architecture—"how they strive against each other with light and shade, the godlike strivers—with such assurance and beauty, let us be enemies too, my friends."[24] Nietzsche thus concludes that there is "war" in all beauty and friendship. He clearly understands the essence of war to be mutual empowerment—not zero-sum opposition.

We might ask whether in using the term "war" Nietzsche is speaking loosely and hyperbolically. After all, the hostile and self-destructive opposition that plays out on the battlefield—what we are inclined to regard as "real" war—seems about the most distant thing from friendship, even when friendship involves a certain intensity of competition. But with the relation of friendship to competition in view, we might conceive of "real" war in a new light. Perhaps what Nietzsche wants us to see is that "real" war, so to speak, is, on examination, a crude and inadequate striving for the recognition that prevails among friendly competitors in the wrestling arena or on the tennis court. Perhaps our familiar view that sport gestures toward the full-blown aggression of war has matters reversed. Perhaps the aggressive instincts that find expression in war implicitly aspire to the friendly competition of sports.

As Hegel, one of Nietzsche's philosophical predecessors, brings to light in his analysis of the origin of slavery in the ancient world, there is something insatiable and unsatisfying in a life oriented to the mere destruction or negation of one's opponent. Even the most ruthless conqueror, Hegel points out, feels compelled, eventually, to spare the vanquished so as to preserve a reality capable of recognizing his superiority. Thus arises the practice of slavery: as a way in which the conqueror attempts to break out of the vicious cycle of destruction and emptiness by asserting his prowess before someone who will survive to honor it: "I defeated you! Now, in recognition of my superiority, and in exchange for your life, you must serve me!" Instead of destroying the vanquished, the conqueror makes him a slave. The problem, however, is that coerced recognition, wrested from someone you regard as an inferior, is no recognition at all. By subordinating someone to minister to your desires—reducing them to a mere thing, or tool at your disposal, and by thus depriving them of personhood in your very own eyes, you undermine the value of any respect they may offer you. Whatever respect the slave does display, moreover, is always, from the master's perspective, suspect, for the master cannot be sure whether such respect is not a mere charade for the sake of survival. Thus, the master, who seeks to affirm himself through domination of another, loses his very personhood and certainty of self in the process.

Genuine recognition, teaches Hegel, can only come to be in a way of life that involves the complementary striving among equals, in which each displays a distinctive excellence that bolsters and inspires the other. Hegel proposes that such recognition prevails in a form of economic life in which each member of society belongs to a particular profession with its own equal dignity within a system of interdependence.

A striking illustration of how the longing for friendship lies implicit in even the most hostile opposition can be found in the Coen Brothers' television series *Fargo*. The antagonist, Lorne Malvo (Billy Bob Thornton), a gun-for-hire who "has no friends," and revels in sowing chaos throughout his decaying community of middle-class suburban Minnesota, has just defeated two rival hitmen who had tried to kill him. One of them he ambushes and stabs to death in the midst of a shootout; the other is shot and apprehended by the cops, sending him to the hospital under law enforcement surveillance. To finish the job, so we think, Malvo sneaks into the hospital and stealthily strangles the police officer guarding the room where the rival hitman is recovering. Malvo approaches the bed and menacingly sits down beside his vanquished opponent. We assume he's about to deal him the final blow. But, instead, Malvo produces a pair of keys that he stole from the officer—the keys to the handcuffs that chain his rival to his hospital bed. Malvo tosses him the keys with a curt acknowledgment: "You got close [to killing me]. Closer than anybody else. I don't know if it was you or your partner, but look, if you still feel raw about things when you heal up, come see me." With that, he exits the room.

Even Malvo, who despises humanity and takes a certain pleasure in manipulation and murder, cannot bear a life of mere destruction. He wants recognition and thus a partner in crime. He can't quite silence the allure of a kind of friendship. The misery of his life consists in his inability to make good on the desire for recognition that is perpetually thwarted by his attempts at dominion over others.

In contrast to Malvo, *Fargo* presents an unlikely hero who can be seen to embody the self-possession, born of genuine friendship, for which Malvo strives but fails to attain. This is the young female detective, Deputy Solverson (Allison Tolman), who doggedly pursues Malvo throughout the show. Different though they appear, Solverson and Malvo, hero and antihero, are not mere opposites. They both see through the shallowness of everyday manners and morals that prevail among the good citizens to the repressed wolfishness that lurks beneath them. (The show is rife with subtle instances of pettiness, hostility, and indifference that break through the veneer of wholesome Midwestern life.) They both strive to be themselves in the face of a world from which they find themselves alienated. But whereas Malvo assumes that there is no alternative to a life of sheepish conformity but the predatory domination of society, Solverson has faith in the possibility of genuine community. Her faith derives from oases of stalwart loyalty, including, above all, the love and mentorship of her father, a world-wizened ex-cop who now owns a local diner in which he cooks and serves. In the company of her father, her adoring colleague from Duluth, and her colleague's spunky teenage daughter, Solverson summons the motivation to protect a community in which she never quite fits and can barely even recognize herself. From the perspective of her inner circle, she is able to look outward with the hope that such loyalty and friendship may find expression in the lives of others. Solverson's hope, born of those close to her, elevates her power above Malvo's. Whereas Malvo seeks autonomy from the world he despises by opposing it with a resounding "no!," expressed in acts of manipulation and murder, and remains stuck in the self-defeating alternation of destruction and emptiness, Solverson gains possession of herself through discerning in her surroundings the glimmer of a way of life that that she has a stake in promoting.

Opposites Attract? Or Like to Like?

The back and forth among competitors devoted to bringing a game out at its best reveals the sense in which kinship and opposition go together in friendship. Federer and Nadal are alike in that both are devoted to eliciting the beauty of the game of tennis. This they prize even above wins and losses. But they are different with respect to the particular ways in which they play, and the distinctive forms of grace and strategic intelligence they embody in their movements on the court. It seems there is something of such unity and opposition, identity and difference, in all friendship, whether conspicuously competitive or not.

Both Aristotle and Plato emphasize the sense in which friends must be akin. Socrates, quoting Homer's *Odyssey*, suggests that "God always leads like to like," which he interprets as the good to the good.[25] As against the view that opposites attract, Aristotle invokes the distinctions among friendship of utility, of pleasure, and of virtue. If all we are after is utility or pleasure, "opposites attract" makes a good deal of sense. When it comes to allies and business partners, you want someone who brings something different to the table, who makes up for what you lack. In friendships for pleasure, you, as a shy and restrained person, may revel in the company of a prankster. But when it comes to friendship of virtue, "opposites attract" loses its force. If you want a friend who will bolster you in greatness of soul, you would not be attracted to someone who is the opposite, who is small, cowardly, susceptible to resentment, or quick to anger. You might try to help such a person if they came under your guidance. But you wouldn't seek them out. You would want to surround yourself with people with the same commitment to virtue and track record of solid character.

But even in friendship of virtue lies an implicit opposition, or difference, in a sense analogous to that between Federer and Nadal. For the reason we seek such friendship is not simply to have our virtue echoed in a word of praise—"beautiful deed," "you acted well"—but to highlight for us the very meaning and significance of the virtue we display. A friend is someone capable of finding words to understand and appreciate our virtue better than we could on our own. A friend is someone who can thus motivate us to continue to be ourselves in moments that threaten weakness, confusion, myopia, or obsession. Most of all, a friend is someone who, in appreciation for the character we display, helps guide us and call us back to ourselves when we lose our way. There is some truth, then, to the idea that "opposites attract," as expressed in a passage from Heraclitus that Aristotle offers for consideration: "From that which differs the most beautiful harmony arises."[26] When friends, both with a commitment to the good but each with a distinctive strength of character, encourage and teach each other to grow stronger, they bring to expression a unity out of that which differs.

4

Engagement with Nature

At the end of graduate school, I decided to bid farewell to the world of competitive powerlifting for two reasons: My hips and pectoral muscles were strained from years of squats and bench press, and I missed playing sports outdoors. One could say that nature issued me a warning and an invitation. My chronically aching body urged me to consider a new physical challenge more suited to my build. And the blue sky, summer breeze, and freshly cut grass of the athletic fields beckoned me out of the gym.

Of course, I could have resisted these promptings of nature. When it comes to how to live one's life, nature never simply has the final say. It can urge and implore, but not compel. I was reminded of this when I witnessed the defiant response of a powerlifting teammate to a freak accident that befell him during a competition. In the midst of his first attempt at a deadlift (an exercise that involves lifting a very heavy barbell off the ground until one is standing upright), his biceps tendon on the arm he used for the underhand grip suddenly ruptured. The harrowing sight of his biceps muscle detaching from the bone and jumping up his arm into a tight little ball at the base of his shoulder accompanied by the horrible sound of Velcro being torn apart is something that no one present will easily forget. If that wasn't nature sending him a message to drop everything and go to the hospital, I don't know what was. But my teammate had devoted everything to this competition, even putting his degree program on pause to devote full attention to powerlifting. In an act of supreme determination, he wrapped his injured arm as tightly as he could with an Ace bandage, switched his grip, completed his second deadlift attempt, and won the competition.

I do not mean to suggest that my teammate's action was advisable or exemplary of the kind of engagement with nature I propose. I relay this story only to illustrate the extent to which we may push back against nature, even if to our detriment. This is what I mean in suggesting that nature never simply has the final say. (As we will investigate in Chapter 5, even death, which we are inclined to regard as the ultimate natural barrier to our striving, is not a phenomenon in the face of which we are powerless. The way in which we interpret death participates in constituting what death is.)

Ultimately if we are to live well, and to discover where our true passions lie, we have to listen to nature and negotiate with it. Even my defiant teammate had to concede a bit to nature by wrapping his injured biceps muscle and switching the grip on his deadlift. In the face of my own relatively minor but nagging injuries, I could have driven a hard bargain with nature. I could have doubled down on my powerlifting routine and insisted on reaching the vaunted 405-lb. squat and 315-lb. bench press. In return, I'd have to concede extra mobility work and stretching before and after each training session. It would have been conceivable. But I decided that's not what I wanted. Nature, I believed, was leading me in another, more promising direction: toward a new challenge to combine strength, endurance, and contention with the outdoors.

So I decided to make a new experiment in my athletic journey: I would keep training the powerlifts, but for less weight and more reps. And I would get outdoors and run. My new aim was to lower my mile time to under five minutes while being as strong as I could for twenty reps (short for repetitions) at squats, bench press, and power cleans. Along the way, I'd toughen up by running in any condition, rain or shine.

Before long, I was learning to endure the extreme fatigue of a hard workout on the track and to handle relatively heavy weight for an extended period of exertion. Although I didn't realize it at first, I was developing the abilities that would soon lead me into a new sphere of life: that of competitive pull-ups and calisthenics.

More significantly, I was also gaining a new appreciation for the outdoors. In the grueling third and fourth laps of the mile, I was learning to contend with the wind, to use it for support by leaning into it without distorting my form. I was starting to notice features of the natural world that before I would have either ignored on my way to work or treated as a mere nuisance. Never had I been more grateful for a sudden burst of rain on a hot summer day. What before I would have regarded as a blight on the afternoon I welcomed as a blessed source of cool in the tenth mile of a long run.

Coming to terms with the limits of my body after years of powerlifting taught me an important lesson about human striving and the forces of nature: Though we often view the two as locked in a perpetual battle for dominion, we should regard them as partners in a shared activity. We should come to see nature not as a mere adversary but as a friend in dialogue—or at least as an opponent with whom we can negotiate and attempt to persuade. In my turn from powerlifting to strength and endurance, I was engaged in a kind of conversation with nature. My nagging injuries were not insults or barriers that nature was hurling in my path. Like the abrasive opinions of a troublesome character from a Platonic dialogue, they were starting points for reflection on my capacities and aims, opportunities for soul-searching and self-knowledge.

The Concept of "Nature"

Before proceeding in our exploration of an engagement with nature, we might pause to reflect on a difficulty: What exactly do we mean by "nature"? In recounting my shift from powerlifting to other athletic adventures, I have used "nature" in a somewhat loose sense that spans a range of meanings: the limitations of the body, the strengths and weaknesses to which a person is predisposed, and the phenomena of the outdoors—the sun, wind, and rain. To these familiar understandings of nature, we may add more. The nature to which we refer in the term "natural sciences," for example, is not simply the outdoors, or the things of the earth and sky, but, in a sense, everything that "is" and can be known. The physicist deals no more with trees and rocks than with radios and airplanes. This very broad sense of nature hearkens back to the ancient Greek *phusis,* from which our word "physics" arises. *Phusis,* according to one common usage that we find in Plato and Aristotle, means, simply, "everything that is." In this sense, it is almost interchangeable with "being," in Greek, *to on.*

Beyond the nature that is the object of physics, we speak of "the nature" of this or that topic—the nature of justice, the nature of law, the nature of physics as a field of study. "Nature" in this sense means something like "character," or "essence," and can apply to an idea as much as to a material thing.

Thus we are confronted by such a remarkable diversity in the single term "nature" that any attempt to lay hold of nature *as such* seems futile. And, yet, there is something common to our many usages. In all the cases we have considered, nature refers, in some sense, to that which confronts or comes upon us, whether we want it to or not. Nature refers to what is *given.*

Nowhere is this more evident than in our ascription of nature to the path of the sun and the change of the weather. Though we can try to predict these phenomena and adjust to them in various ways, we do not bring them into being. They do not bend to our will. Even in the case of nonmaterial things such as justice, or law, which we often regard as products of human artifice in contrast to nature, the moment we attempt to understand them with respect to what they *are* ("what *is* justice?," "what *is* law?"), we deal with something that confronts us as puzzling, something *from which* our investigation will proceed. Thus we still speak of examining the nature of such things.

"Nature," in all these senses, answers to the condition of being limited, or finite, rather than omnipotent. "Nature" reflects the sense in which we are always in the midst of things, forced to find our way around. The counterpoint to nature is artifice, or that which comes to be through an act of will. To be a thoroughly artistic or creative being is to bring about one's surroundings from scratch and thus to face no nature.

The question that I want to investigate in this chapter can be stated as follows: How are we to understand the given and relate to it? Is the given entirely external to ourselves, a force that acts on us and constitutes the "way things are" quite apart from the life we live? Or is the given in some paradoxical sense *self-given*—at once a source and product of our interpretive capacity?

Another way to put the question is whether there is such a thing as nature apart from the way in which we understand and interpret it. The question could also be posed in the reverse: Is it possible to conceive of the self I call my own apart from the way in which I confront and come into myself in response to the promptings of nature?

The notion that nature is external to us, running its course quite apart from what we do or think, is a familiar view. As we consider the rising and setting of the sun, the path of the stars, and the change of the seasons, we are accustomed to regard these phenomena as regularities that play themselves out whether we want them to or not, and in utter indifference to whether we pay heed to them. The Stoics understood nature in precisely this way: as an order that we may come to understand, and to which we may adapt, but that in no way depends on us. Nature "is" quite apart from the ways in which we might relate to it. "Live according to nature" was the famous Stoic motto, which suggests that we should accept what nature dictates. Instead of stubbornly and futilely resisting the necessary order of things—growth and decay, birth and death—we should attend to the sense in which everything breaks and joins again, and come to appreciate nature as an infinite cycle in which we, along with all things, are swept up.

And, yet, alongside the apparently commonsensical view of nature as self-standing, independent of us, is the sense that we human beings do play a role in shaping the natural order. The awareness that carbon emissions from our industry contribute to the heating of the globe and the alteration of the seasons suggests a sense in which seemingly autonomous forces are influenced by our actions. In a deeper sense, our technological disposition to view things as given *for us,* to use in whatever way we deem fit, implies a nature that is infinitely malleable. Even the change of seasons, from the technological perspective, is something that we could alter, if only we could find a way to set into motion the chain of causes that leads to the warming and cooling of the atmosphere. Nature, so understood, is not a fixed or insurmountable order. We can dissolve and recombine things for whatever purposes we choose. Nature is external to us only temporarily and provisionally—to the extent that we are ignorant and naive. To the "enlightened" consciousness, what lies outside of us is ultimately subject to any form we may impose on it. What presents itself as seemingly beyond our control is something we can, in principle, master.

From the technological perspective, nature becomes the object of our will. Whereas the Stoic view of nature suggests an ultimately passive human stance, the technological understanding suggests a manipulative, goal-oriented disposition. Nature is not something to be understood but to be conquered.

It would seem that the technological and Stoic understandings of nature are diametrically opposed. But they are subtly connected. To view nature as our master, in the fashion of the Stoics, is to be already possessed of the desire to break free of it, if only we could.

The Stoic maxim "live according to nature" comes to mean something only against the backdrop of the temptation to fight nature—to cheat illness and death, for example. Otherwise, "live according to nature" would be redundant. It would implore us to live as we are already disposed. Implicit in Stoic passivity is an incipient activism that rises to the surface as we indulge our promethean aspirations to master our surroundings and meet with some success.

But as we become enthralled by the prospect of conquering nature, the entire world on which we look takes on a foreign and inhuman appearance; it becomes a realm of mere matter that awaits the imposition of our will to "be" anything at all. And as soon as we put our stamp on things, they become, once again, the mere objects of a potential reconstruction. We clear forest to make way for farmland, and we clear farmland to construct an airport. Each act of creation brings forth something that is itself potential fodder for an utterly new project. At no point do we take heed of what lies before us as something to be respected, preserved, or cultivated as a source of meaning and continuity in our lives. Our technological stance thus leaves us stuck in a cycle of imposition and alienation. We depend for our subsistence and for the continued exertion of our will on an external reality that we cannot but regard as intrinsically worthless. But to live in such dependence is to lose precisely the agency we seek to exert. The stance that would seem to liberate us from Stoic subservience to nature plunges us into a new form of enslavement. In appearing as the object of our will, nature remains external, in much the same way as the slave remains external to the master.

Here we may recall Hegel's critique of domination and servitude that we examined in our consideration of friendship: The attempt to affirm oneself through lording it over another leaves one dependent on a reality that one cannot but despise, resulting in a form of self-imposed slavery. True agency requires engagement with what is "other" in the mode of mutual appreciation and learning.

The only way, it would seem, to break the cycle of imposition and alienation characteristic of the technological stance would be to let nature stand, in its own right, as a potential partner in dialogue as we strive for self-possession. This relation to nature is what I aim to elaborate.

The conception of nature that I propose is meant to recover a sense in which "the given" is not external to us but *self-given*. Nature is neither beyond our power to interpret and shape nor totally within our control. As soon as nature confronts us, it presents a range of meanings to be interpreted and applied in the context of the journey of life. Though nature may at times appear as a seemingly alien force, at odds with our aspiration and indifferent to our fate, it is, on closer examination, a potential partner in dialogue as we strive for self-possession. And though we may conceive of nature as the object of our will, to be used for whatever purposes we impose on it, such an objectivizing view attests to a goal-oriented striving that has lost sight of activity for the sake of itself. The technological understanding of nature, we will see, is but one, very limited perspective on the way things are. It is no more valid or true than myriad other ways of conceiving of the universe. Our technological stance, oriented to prediction and control, has by no means solved the mystery of nature but has rather obscured it.

Critique of the Modern Oppositional Stance to Nature

In today's technological age, our predominant attitude toward nature is oppositional. We regard nature as an alien force that we either subdue and bend to our purposes or accept with temporary resignation until our technology improves. When our body screams out in injury, we bombard it with the latest medicine and therapy so that we may return, as quickly as possible, to the lifestyle that, more often than not, induced the harm in the first place. When the weather turns stormy despite the indication of our forecast app, we curse the limits of our predictive powers, grab for our umbrellas, and run for cover, scarcely taking a moment to admire the beauty of the cloud formation and the drama of the impending downpour. When we find ourselves "too tall" or "too short," we accept the condition as a barrier yet to be smashed and then search for genetic enhancements that might alter such a "regrettable" fate, all the while ignoring the sense in which such dispensations may be blessings in disguise. Thus we treat nature as an obstacle in the way of our established routines and goals. We fail to consider that nature might offer a *critique* of the goals we pursue—that injury, illness, stormy weather, and limitations of the body might be invitations to change the way we live, partners in deliberation as we strive for self-possession.

Our oppositional relation to nature is deeply engrained in modern philosophy. It goes back to seventeenth-century philosopher John Locke, who regards nature as utterly without value until human labor transforms it into something useful. According to Locke, an expanse of wilderness is worthless by comparison to land that is cleared for agriculture and rendered productive. Labor, he teaches, puts the value on everything. It is from this basic premise that Locke derives a natural right to property, before the institution of government and before the passage of laws that secure the distinction between "mine and thine." We rightfully own "by nature" that with which we have "mixed our labor." For it is our labor, and our labor alone, that gives things their worth. Nature in itself has no value.[1]

The technological view of nature that Locke introduces comes to its culmination in Marx, who regards the whole of human history as the progressive "conquest" of nature. He envisions a final stage of history at which point we will have so successfully appropriated nature through our labor power that we may provide the means of subsistence for all at the pull of a lever. But the real human achievement, and the hallmark of modernity, for Marx, is a certain metaphysical insight: the conscious awareness that everything of the earth and sky is in itself nothing but unformed matter to be shaped by human hands and mobilized for the reproduction of the species. To see nature as meaningful in itself and as making a claim to be respected is, according to Marx, to be in the thrall of a backward, prescientific way of seeing things.

The problem with the aspiration to conquer nature is not simply that our technology meets its limit in events that seemingly can't be mastered—natural disaster, mysterious illness, death. The real problem is that in regarding nature as thoroughly amenable to our design, we overlook the promptings and suggestions that nature offers *to us*. In mobilizing nature for our goal-oriented striving, we overlook its beauty and sublimity in the presence of which we may reconceive the way of life in which we strive for certain goals in the first place.

The promptings of nature that I have in mind are not self-evident truths, as if nature were a text that spoke unequivocally. They are rather suggestions to be considered, interpreted, and tested in our quest for self-possession. My suggestion is that we adopt an inquisitive, interpretive stance to nature in its many facets, a stance that we might call "Socratic" in contrast to oppositional. Just as Socrates sought to derive insight from every opinion, no matter how narrow-minded or contentious, so we may approach nature.

People of ancient times routinely adopted such a stance, relating to nature as an infinite storehouse of symbols and signposts for the journey of life. Pick up Homer's *Odyssey*, for example, and you will find nature as both a living force of its own and as a partner in human activity on earth: "The sun had left the splendid sea: it climbed into the bronze of heaven, bringing light to the immortals and to those who die on earth, the giver of grain."[2] And, later, as Calypso accedes to releasing Odysseus from her possession so that he may return home: "She led him toward the island's rim—a stand of tall trees: alder, poplar, and the high sky-seeking fir: well-seasoned timber, dry, aged wood that would float lightly on the sea."[3] Though

Homer, in this passage, presents the trees as offering "well-seasoned timber" for sailing, which might seem to imply a quaint version of technological appropriation, he speaks, on examination, from a very different sensibility. The height of the trees, expressed in the "tall stand" and exemplified in the "sky-seeking" fir, suggests a particular purpose they of themselves are to fulfill and not merely any purpose an arrogant mortal might impose upon them. Homer implies that the sky-seeking fir, which *longs* for its partner, the sky, with which it belongs, is destined not simply for anything but to be a mast that will support a sail, which, in turn, will catch the wind and carry Odysseus on his return voyage. Homer thus presents a nature that, in its many forms, is bound together in kinship with the strivings of mortals and gods.

It should come as no surprise that Socrates engaged with nature in the same way as with his partners in dialogue—by drawing on the earth and sky to elucidate the meaning of virtue and the good. In a well-known passage from Plato's *Republic*, for example, Socrates attempts to articulate the "idea of the good" by reference to the sun. Just as the sun makes visible everything that can be seen, so the good makes knowable everything that can be thought.[4] The metaphor leads us to consider the sense in which the idea of the good—the standard by which we might live to enjoy true happiness—is not a single highest idea that can be known in independence from the many everyday opinions we might have of it, and the actions we call "good" and "bad," but is an idea somehow itself manifest, though never fully, in the many "ideas" (opinions, conceptions, actions) it makes possible. For the sun attains its majesty and splendor as light only by shining on a world and allowing it to appear in its infinite diversity. When we remark on the beauty of the sun, we have in view not simply the bright sphere overhead but the total scene it illuminates. Conceived in terms of its relation to the good, the sun, in its very *being*, is clearly more than the point of mass to which it may be reduced in modern physical understandings. The sun is an image of ourselves, and we, insofar as we draw upon the sun to make sense of ourselves, are an image of the sun.

To a modern sensibility, this metaphorical way of regarding nature, as a source of understanding for how to live, may seem naïve and fanciful. We tend to view nature in itself as neutral matter and meaning as a product of the human mind. What the sun "really is," we assume, is an empirical matter to be answered by physics; how the sun might be regarded by us is a subjective matter having nothing to do with the sun itself. Any meaning supposedly found in nature we treat as a mere projection of subjective human values onto a morally indifferent world.

But no science, no matter how advanced, can invalidate the experience of being struck by nature in its beauty or sublimity and inspired to reflect upon the *sense* in which it is, in its very appearance, beautiful or sublime. To regard such an experience as a merely subjective response to a world that is in reality meaningless matter is to overlook the way in which nature, in the manifold shapes and forms that we encounter long before we have theorized it in the terms of modern physics, puts to us, the observers, the challenge of interpreting it in *certain* ways, not just in any way we choose. It is also to ignore the possibility of learning, or coming to *new* values, in our effort to interpret the things that evoke our curiosity and awe.

I can perhaps best express this point by recounting a personal experience: an encounter with nature in the form of Iguazu Falls at the border of Brazil and Argentina. Struck by the magnificent shelves of water that crashed from different angles into the river basin below, and longing for an account that could do justice to what I saw, I got to thinking: What makes the falls so striking?

As I paced around the perimeter of the falls, I set myself to making sense of what I saw: The peaceful waters atop the cliff suddenly roar and plunge furiously into the giant basin below—and then glide serenely downstream, off into the distance, as if unscathed and oblivious to the fall. By chance, I had been reading a lot of

Greek tragedy at the time. Reflecting on the waterfall and the fate of Oedipus, I came to see that nature in this prodigious form had wisdom to convey: Beneath the security and self-evidence of everyday life—the calm river above—seethes the impending disaster, the sudden crash. As the waters return to tranquility and move gently downstream, they teach us to roll with the blows of fate, to take in stride the sudden shifts of fortune possible at any moment. So understood, the waterfall questions our self-satisfaction as we recount our achievements and make sure we are on course for a reputable career. Might we be paddling about the calm waters at the cliff's edge? After a sudden crash, will we be able to regain the repose of the waters below?

One could say that I was simply projecting my own meaning, influenced by *Oedipus,* onto the waterfall, which, in itself, is a mere value-neutral phenomenon. But that would miss the sense in which the waterfall, in its distinctive size, sound, and movement, invites a certain range of interpretation to the exclusion of many hypothetical ways of regarding it. Infinitely many descriptions would be so inappropriate to the phenomenon that we would hardly think to consider them. ("Simple serenity" is but one example; it would clearly fail to account for the waterfall's fury.) The waterfall in its *own* way longs to be "read" in terms of the Oedipus story as much as the story prepares a particular way of seeing the waterfall. This is to say that whatever insight one might have gained from *Oedipus* finds new expression in the waterfall. For nowhere on the written page of Sophocles does one encounter a river that falls of a cliff and somehow, miraculously, regains its composure. Thus, the waterfall itself, in the very way it appears, can be said to enrich the Oedipus story and vice versa. In the final analysis, the interpretation of nature is inseparable from the interpretation of ourselves.

It may be hard to shake the sense that this sort of engaged and personal understanding of nature reflects a quaint, "merely metaphorical" view of the world and falls short of the "literal," or "objective," accounts that science provides. The "real" waterfall, we might be inclined to think, is a product of geological processes and the forces of gravity. We should consider, however, that lurking beneath concepts such as "geological process," "gravity," and other supposedly impersonal ways of making sense of the world are questionable self-understandings that we leave unexamined.

The mere fact that centuries after the Copernican revolution we still say, without thinking twice, that the sun rises and sets, and have not substituted for this supposedly naïve conception a more precise shorthand for what really occurs, suggests a certain futility and folly in attempting to overcome the way in which things first appear to us, before we have learned to assume different vantage points or made the attempt to see the world without reference to our "merely human" perspective. Insofar as the rising and setting of the sun bears significance for the structure and rhythm of a day well spent, and has something to teach us of the course of life at every moment, as, in some sense, a departure and return, it expresses a truth invulnerable to refutation by any "new" science.

The insistence, so familiar to our post-Copernican world, that in reality it is the earth that revolves around the sun, and not the reverse, is a dogmatism no less narrow-minded than an unwillingness to consider things from the Copernican perspective. The truly comprehensive perspective is that from which we can consider and compare the self-understandings to which each perspective attests.

The Moral Foundations of Modern Natural Science

Of the sense in which questionable self-understandings underlie what we take to be "value-free" accounts of the world, we might consider the Newtonian explanation for a phenomenon such as the path of the moon around the earth: A less massive body, the moon, which, if left to itself, would tend to fly off at a tangent, gets pulled toward a more massive body, the earth. But the velocity of the moon's presumed linear motion is sufficient to keep it from falling straight into the earth. So, instead, its linear path gets bent around the earth into orbit. We are in the habit of regarding this explanation of the moon's motion to be rational and scientific by comparison to, for example, the Aristotelian notion that bodies that move in a circular path do so of their own accord, because they are self-sufficient, seek nothing outside themselves, and constantly return to their point of origin. But an examination of each explanation reveals that they are both based on questionable assumptions, the roots of which can be traced to divergent conceptions of how to live. Neither is more objective or true to "the way things *are*" than the other.[5]

The Newtonian explanation relies on the now-famous axiom, common to high school physics textbooks, known as the law of inertia: A body left to itself will remain in place or move in a straight line unless acted on by an outside force. Two assumptions stand out in Newton's axiom: the notion of a body "left to itself," that is, in no definite relation to any other, and the notion of linear motion as the frame of reference for all other motion. That bodies ought to be conceived in this way is hardly something that can be proved or established by any observation. The axiom itself determines how bodies will be regarded, and it lays the ground for any possible observation or experiment.[6] The term "axiom" comes from the ancient Greek *axio,* "to lay down" or "to legislate." Newton's statement can be regarded as an act of legislation. It decides what will count as a body to be observed and how experiments will proceed. Only on the basis of the body "left to itself" would it make sense, for example, to take a billiard ball and a feather, two manifestly different things, bring them together in the same experiment, drop them side by side in a chamber devoid of air, and observe that they both fall at the same rate. Only when these things are conceived as belonging nowhere in particular, and as akin in their utter homogeneity, does such an experiment become conceptually possible.

Another way of looking at it is this: As soon as we take billiard balls and feathers *together* in this way, we have implicitly shifted the sense in which they are understood. Whether we recognize it or not, we now relate to them as "bodies left to themselves," which we arrive at only through an act of abstraction, which means looking *away* as much as looking *at*. We no longer see and understand them as the feathers and billiard balls they once were when they served as quill pens or components of a table game. We look away from the sense in which they belong to a context, thus losing sight of qualities such as heaviness and texture, which relate to some way of being put to use, and bring them in relation to anything that can occupy a position in empty three-dimensional space.

What we may easily take to be laws of gravity that describe the way the world is, independent of us, turn out to rest on an interpretation of the body for which we are responsible. We could call such an interpretation poetic, in the sense that it is an imaginative construction of things on the basis of a certain disposition of the life that we, the observers, are living.

The "poetry" intrinsic to the Newtonian view becomes evident as we consider Newton's conception in relation to other plausible ones. Before Newton, people observed the natural world no less carefully and attentively. Yet, they explained motion in very different terms, on the basis of different axioms and conceptions of the body. We may return to the example of Aristotle's doctrine of motion: Bodies move according to their proper place. Those which move in circles, such as the heavenly bodies, belong with themselves. They constantly return to themselves rather than fly off in some other direction, searching for something else. Their motion attests to a certain notion of self-sufficiency. Bodies in circular motion depend on nothing outside themselves. They represent the life of self-rule, of which we are reminded whenever we look to the heavens. Things that deviate from circular motion, that move in a line, for example, are not at one with themselves but strive to be elsewhere. Fire moves upward to be with the sun. A stone falls downward to reunite with the earth.

To think that any empirical study could disprove Aristotle's theory of motion is to overlook the sense in which all observation is already oriented by a fundamental perspective. From our Newtonian-influenced perspective, we might be tempted to refute Aristotle's theory by pointing out that, on the moon, stones do not fall. But Aristotle would not be compelled by this observation to revise his basic framework of motion in terms of place. He might be led, simply, to revise his conception of the proper place *of a stone.* Or he might be led to conclude that stones on the moon are, on reflection, different beings (with correspondingly different courses of motion) than those on earth. The example is somewhat strained in that the very project of going to the moon and observing how things are up there makes little sense from Aristotle's perspective. The moon, as Aristotle understands it, is not a place to which one goes but a symbol to be understood as one strives for self-possession, here on earth. The point is that infinite evidence can be accommodated within Aristotle's framework. So long as one is committed to the spiritual imperative that animates the framework, there is no empirical limit to it.

Though we might be quick to dismiss Aristotle's doctrine of motion as quaint, we must recognize that it is no less true to "the facts" than Newton's. Oriented to the sense in which things strive for their proper place, and oriented, in a larger sense, to the idea of a harmonious order, we can offer an account no less coherent than Newton's of the way things move. We could even say that Aristotle's doctrine makes sense of the body and of motion as directly manifest in our daily lives before we are taught by textbooks to box the world into hypothetical abstractions: The train cuts effortlessly through the rolling hills on the way to its destination. Its movement is in line with its purpose: to bring the travelers from one city to another in comfort. The tree bends flexibly in the howling wind. It maintains its integrity against the storm that threatens to bring it down. If the train were to suddenly halt or swerve off course, or if the tree were to be toppled by the storm, the change would be immediately apparent as an alarming deviation from the purpose, or proper place, of the thing at issue.

For Newtonian laws of motion to become possible, there had to be a shift in the way we understand ourselves. The notion that things strive for their proper place and that circular motion embodies perfection had to be challenged. That is to say, a moral shift had to take place in conjunction with the scientific shift.

If we reexamine Newton's axiom, we can make an attempt to discern this shift. A body left to itself that can occupy any place in three-dimensional space at any time, a body that is akin to other bodies only in its utter homogeneity and lack of connection to them, is an interpretation of the body that answers to and serves to affirm the idea, characteristic of the democratic Enlightenment, that persons no longer stand in any definite relation to one another, that persons are, by birth, free and equal. The priority of linear motion represents the modern ideal of progress: the infinite conquest of nature and society. Circular motion now represents complacency. It needs to be explained as something backward, deviant. Thus, the circular path of the moon gets conceived in terms of linear motion that gets thrown off course. The apparently self-evident Newtonian framework serves to affirm and deepen a moral viewpoint no less questionable than Aristotle's. Its validity as a description of the world is entirely relative to the moral premise on which it rests. To the extent that the moral premise is questionable, so too is every law of gravity that flows from it.

In the final analysis, Newton's laws of motion are no less poetic, or laden with human aspiration, than Aristotle's. Both depend on visions of human flourishing open to question. Get down to the basic conceptions on which any theory of the universe lies, and you will find a moral perspective of one kind or another. This is to say that all ways of looking at the world and attempting to explain it are subordinate to the all-encompassing quest of coming to know ourselves.

An awareness of the moral foundation of science should be liberating. It ought to free us from a lazy acquiescence to "the way things are," which, on inspection, answers to a self-conception open to question, and restore dignity to the project of finding a human meaning in the earth and sky. It also may encourage us to take responsibility for the planet, and to care for it, for reasons that go beyond our own health and safety. We ought to protect nature and bring it to expression as a partner in our striving for self-possession.

Gravity and Human Striving

According to modern physics, there is no such thing as a weight that presses or a stone that falls. Gravity is simply a calculable force according to which the greater mass attracts the lesser. Mass is not heaviness but numerical weight. But from an earthly perspective, gravity confronts us as heavy and inexorable—the law by which all things fall. In the words of Nietzsche's philosopher-protagonist Zarathustra, as he climbs his "highest peak," "Striding silently over the mocking clatter of pebbles, crushing the rock that made it slip, my foot forced its way upward. Upward—defying the spirit of gravity that drew it downward toward the abyss, the spirit of gravity, my devil and archenemy . . . He [my enemy] whispered mockingly, syllable by syllable, 'you philosopher's stone! You threw yourself up high, but every stone that is thrown must fall.'"[7]

The mocking whisper of gravity, spoken syllable by syllable, which suggests its inhuman, mechanical character, at first confronts Zarathustra as a force beyond his control. But Zarathustra speaks not simply of gravity but of the *spirit of gravity*, which implies a heaviness within him as much as upon him. Understood as a spiritual force, gravity pulls Zarathustra down not simply to earth but "toward the abyss." The stone on which the spirit of gravity acts is not simply the rock that we might throw with all our might only to see it fall, but the "philosopher's stone," which, according to legend, is capable of turning worthless metals to gold and represents our power to restore luster and sense to the common and accidental.

Nietzsche suggests that the natural force of gravity, which, at times, seems an alien necessity to which we are subject, is really an interpretation of nature from the perspective of our despair: a view of nature from the vantage point of the end—of failure, disaster, or victory grown old.

Nietzsche makes this explicit a few lines down. On the brink of exhaustion, Zarathustra confronts the spirit of gravity: "I am the stronger of us two. You do not know my abysmal thought. *That* you could not bear."[8] The abysmal thought, as Zarathustra later presents it, has to do with spiritual atrophy, with resignation in the face of suffering, with nihilism. Wielding this "abysmal thought," Zarathustra asserts himself against the physical, bodily gravity that weighs him down as he climbs. The "earthly gravity," he suggests, is nothing but an emblem, a physical manifestation of the abysmal thought.

Gravity, so understood, never simply confronts us as a natural force in the face of which we are powerless. It is we, in our striving and resignation, who interpret gravity as a force that simply acts on us from outside. But as soon as we find gravity *within* us, or in the way we respond to suffering, we can reinterpret gravity as a life-promoting resistance.

Inspired by Nietzsche's understanding of gravity and his broader project of finding the spiritual in the earthly, I've come to a new appreciation of some of the most seemingly unphilosophical aspects of my life, including a recent athletic test: the aptly named Tabata pull-up "gravity challenge." A Tabata workout consists of twenty-second intervals of a given exercise, followed by ten seconds of rest, repeated for a total of four minutes. In this case, I was going to do as many pull-ups as I could in the allotted time.

From the perspective of the *result* for which one aims, the challenge presents itself as a brutal fight *against* gravity. By the end, your arms are screaming from shoulders to fingertips. Your back muscles struggle to find the energy for one more repetition. It seems at this point that gravity is your archenemy—an unrelenting force that in the end will take you down. But from a different standpoint, that of the *midst* of the challenge, as one swings into the cadence of the pull-up rhythm, gravity is a partner and not simply an adversary. Gravity is what enables you to fly above the bar as you press your palms into the firm metal surface and fire upward; it is what enables you to descend with quickness and ease so that you can rebound for the next repetition. Gravity and the force of your body thus work in tandem, each allowing the other to be the force that it is. Without gravity, you would have no way to propel yourself upward. Without your pull, gravity would have no counterforce on which to make itself felt. Even as you near the end and find yourself in a struggle with the heaviest pull-up, when gravity asserts itself most relentlessly, it is your own counterforce that makes this seemingly external imposition possible. As soon as you let go of the bar, and give way to the force of gravity, the force of gravity vanishes as well.

Critique of the Stoic Conception of Nature

What I have called a Socratic understanding of nature, according to which the seemingly external forces that confront us can become partners in dialogue as we strive for self-possession, may be contrasted not only to the oppositional stance toward nature predominant today but also to an older disposition that has recently seen a resurgence: the Stoic conception of nature, which teaches acquiescence rather than resistance.

According to the Stoic view, we ought to "live according to nature," which means accepting what nature delivers as part of a larger process that runs its course quite apart from our hopes and aspirations. By observing regularities in the world around us, such as the coming and going of the seasons, and the growth and decay of living things, we can come to understand nature as an eternal cycle in which everything is ultimately conserved, including ourselves, conceived as arrangements of the same matter out of which everything is composed.

In the face of injury, illness, and even death, teach the Stoics, we can comfort ourselves by coming to recognize these seemingly threatening events as but the workings of a necessary and intelligible order that itself never passes. As the Stoic philosopher Seneca writes:

> Just look at how the circuit of the universe returns upon itself. You will see that nothing in this cosmos is extinguished, but everything falls and rises by turns. The summer departs, but the year will bring another; winter falls away, but its own months will restore it. Night blocks the sun, but in an instant daylight will drive that night away. Whatever movement of the constellations has passed, repeats; one part of the sky is always rising, another part sinking below the horizon.[9]

Whenever we find ourselves fearing aspects of nature that would thwart our striving, we should remind ourselves that these aspects are integral to the eternal process of decay and renewal. In a letter to his friend, Marcia, who has just lost a son, Seneca proposes that human misfortune and even the most cataclysmic events that affect the whole of the earth are necessary to such an eternal process: "And when the time comes when the world, on its way to renewal, destroys itself, these things will strike themselves down with their own strength, and stars will crash into stars and whatever now shines in an ordered array will blaze in a single fire, all matter set aflame . . . with all things sliding into ruin, we shall be changed back to our ancient components."[10]

Some Stoics, such as the Roman emperor Marcus Aurelius, interpreted the process of nature in terms of divine providence:

> Just as the world forms a single body comprising all bodies, so fate forms a single purpose comprising all purposes . . . Look at the accomplishment of nature's plans in that light . . . and accept what happens (even if it seems hard to accept). Accept it because of what it leads to: the good health of the world, and the well-being and prosperity of Zeus himself who would not have brought this on anyone unless it brought benefit to the world as a whole.[11]

Common to Marcus's providential view of nature and Seneca's more materialistic conception is the idea that regardless of what we do or think, nature runs its own course. All efforts to control, change, or affect nature are futile. We ought instead to understand nature and to rest content with knowing how it works. What unites the various Stoic conceptions of nature is the concept of fate. In the words of Marcus, "Something happens to you. Good. It was meant for you by nature, woven into the pattern from the beginning."[12]

The appeal of this fatalistic conception of things is undeniable as a counterpoint to the futility of our goal-oriented striving. It presents the failures and losses to which such striving is destined as part of a larger plan. No wonder Stoicism held such appeal for a number of figures deeply involved in tempestuous and highly visible worldly affairs. Stoicism, for them, provided an island of serenity amid the hubbub of political life. For Marcus Aurelius, stoicism was a philosophy of self-help to which he could refer in times of need as he ran the Roman Empire. Faced with what must have been the exhausting task of coping with the flattery and deceit of those around him, and of dealing with projects gone awry for reasons quite beyond his control, Marcus thirsted for a philosophy that would liberate him from the ambition and competitiveness of human life. His writings, composed of motivational notes to self that were apparently unintended for publication but that now circulate under the title "Meditations," are replete with critiques of vanity, obsession, and the concern with accomplishment that are no less relevant today than back then.

For example, Marcus was on to the tendency to be always "too busy" to respond to a letter or to meet with a friend. In one note to himself, he issues the reminder "not to be constantly telling people (or writing them) that I'm too busy, unless I really am. Similarly, not to be always ducking my responsibilities to the people around me because of 'pressing business.'"[13]

Marcus was also keenly aware of how a concern for reputation can easily slide into a self-destructive vanity, and he sought to put appearances and popularity in perspective: "Or is it your reputation that's bothering you? But look at how soon we're all forgotten. The abyss of endless time that swallows it all. The emptiness of all those applauding hands . . . And the tiny region in which it all takes place."[14]

But although Stoicism gives powerful voice to the deficiency of goal-oriented striving, it never really breaks out of the goal-oriented perspective. It merely transposes that perspective onto nature in the form of explicit providentialism (the "prosperity of Zeus") or in that of the "health" and "renewal" of the world. It fails to imagine an alternative conception of activity that fulfills our longing for agency, or that does justice to the commitments and projects in which we come to understand the meaning of our lives. In attempting to cope with the impermanence of achievement, or of any state of the world, and to find a perspective on things from which we might enjoy a lasting happiness, Stoicism gives up on human agency altogether. It cedes agency entirely to nature. In doing so, it overlooks the possibility of a mode of activity that awaits no future for its justification and is thus invulnerable to decay "in time." Instead of attending to activity for the sake of itself, in the modes of self-possession and friendship we have explored, and making the attempt to view nature from the perspective of such virtues, Stoicism constructs nature as the antithesis of human agency: as an eternal, all-powerful force that either cares nothing for what we do or think or uses us for its own purposes. The purely theoretical contemplation of such an order is the only eternity for which we might aspire. Stoicism thus remains mired in a goal-oriented outlook. It merely turns us from agents into instruments of a grand plan. We are supposed to take comfort in knowing that whatever fate may befall us is the means by which God brings about the greater good of the world.

It is telling that the Stoics employ the phrase "human affairs" in a way that encompasses a vast range of activity—from delivering a public speech to strategizing in battle to fretting over one's reputation to caring for one's son—the whole of which gets implicitly understood in terms of the striving to accomplish or to maintain and thus takes on the appearance of a fleeting and unstable mode of existence. "All human affairs are short and transient," writes Seneca. Time "will dissolve the unity and fellowship of the human race."[15] In so loosely conceiving of human affairs, Seneca overlooks the distinction between affairs oriented to making, producing, and maintaining and those that, in Aristotle's terms, have their ends in themselves. Seneca also fails to distinguish between fellowship as alliance and fellowship as friendship. In overlooking such crucial distinctions, Stoicism is unable to consider how different modes of activity are related to time. Stoicism never even raises the question of whether it makes sense to speak of a life devoted to self-possession or friendship as something that exists or unfolds in time, or whether such a life might be temporal in an altogether different sense.

Because Stoicism fails to conceive of human activity in terms of practical wisdom and the striving for wholeness, it fails, in equal proportion, to find intimations of such activity in nature. Whatever meaning nature can be said to express is not something for which we are in any sense responsible as interpreters. "God's plan," or the "circle of nature" is simply to be discerned and accepted. "Look" and "you will see," writes Marcus in prefacing his analyses of nature. His repeated invocations of "look" and "see" throughout his reflections speak to the passive attitude that Stoicism ultimately espouses. Our relation to nature is ultimately one of reception rather than dialogue. When we look up at the stars, we are supposed to see the vast expanse of a pre-given cosmos in which our earth is but a speck of dust. In the words of Seneca, "We consider this earth, with its cities, peoples, and rivers, enclosed by a circle of sea, as a tiny dot."[16] The stars—those infinitely distant sources of light—are meant to mitigate our passion by reminding us of the ultimate insignificance of life on earth.

In the final analysis, Stoicism leaves us in search of a relation to nature that can do justice to both nature and ourselves. For what homage do we pay the stars by regarding them as testaments to a vast universe that dominates and belittles our world? Why not instead make the attempt to understand them as sources of guidance on a nighttime voyage, or as glittering sources of inspiration for the exploration of distant lands on the way to which we stand to rise to new heights of self-possession and friendship? Nietzsche, a vehement critic of Stoicism, offers a striking contrast to Seneca's view of the heavens. For Nietzsche, the heaven above is a partner in striving to constantly surmount ourselves, a friend that inspires pride:

> Oh heaven above me, pure and deep! You abyss of light. Seeing you I tremble with godlike desires . . . Together we have learned to ascend over ourselves to ourselves and to smile down cloudlessly from bright eyes and from a vast distance while constraint and contrivance and guilt steam beneath us . . . And when I climbed mountains, whom did I always seek on the mountains if not you? . . . What I want with all my will is to *fly*, to fly up into *you* . . . I am the one who can bless and say Yes, if only you are about me . . .

> I fought long and hard for that and was a fighter that I
> might one day get my hands free to bless . . . to stand over
> every single thing as its own heaven, as its round roof, its
> azure bell, and eternal security.[17]

What Nietzsche here exemplifies in the words of Zarathustra is a
mode of engagement with nature that he elsewhere formulates as
the interpretation of it for "its own self-recognition":

> All of nature's experiments are of value only insofar as the
> artist eventually divines its stammerings, meets nature
> halfway, and gives expression to what it actually intends
> with these experiments . . . Hence nature also needs the
> saint, whose ego has entirely melted away and whose life
> of suffering is no longer—or almost no longer—felt indi-
> vidually, but only as the deepest feeling of equality, com-
> munion, and oneness with all living things; the saint in
> whom the miracle of transformation occurs . . . that ulti-
> mate and supreme becoming human toward which all of
> nature presses and drives onward for its own salvation.[18]

In this conception, Nietzsche, as it were, reverses the Stoic "live according to nature" without succumbing to the mere opposite of
"use nature for whatever purpose you decide." Nature needs the
artist and the saint to express what it intends in its stammerings and
experiments. And, yet, it is nature itself that presses and drives and
must be met halfway by whoever would attempt to make good
on its promise. Ultimately the meaning of nature and the meaning
of our own lives are inseparable. Nature attains its highest dignity
only in "becoming human"; but the human, for its part, comes into
its own only in the dissolution of the ego and transformative com-
munion "with all living things."

Little League Baseball and Severe Weather

One of the few times I've been afraid for my life was in the middle of a Little League baseball practice, when I was the coach for one of my town's traveling teams. It wasn't a confrontation with a disgruntled parent that sent me running in terror—though that would have been a decent guess. It was the weather: a thunderstorm that suddenly swept in from the west out of a cloudless July afternoon.

Over the years, I've become something of a weather buff. I'm not bad at distinguishing an ordinary thunderstorm from a severe one on doppler radar, and I've learned to interpret the basic computer models that meteorologists consult in issuing forecasts. But what I pride myself on most is being able to read the sky. Usually I can see a thunderstorm coming a mile away—or, more literally, twenty or thirty miles away. The majestic deck of dense cirrus clouds, fanning outward from the top of a billowing cumulonimbus cloud, is unmistakable, especially when it cuts a razor sharp line across a blue summer sky.

But I was focused on running the baseball practice that afternoon. The trees surrounding the field obscured the horizon. And this storm came barreling in with unusual speed. No sooner did I look up at the darkening sky than rumbles of thunder, almost one every twenty seconds, then every ten, became clearly audible, even as part of the sky was still blue.

Hurriedly, I began gathering the gear and shepherding the kids into cars. I should have gotten into my own. But I decided to collect as many balls as I could to save them from the rain. Before I knew it, I was surrounded by lightning bolts darting about the base of the cloud directly overhead. Two were accompanied almost instantaneously by deafening crackles of thunder.

At that moment, I was filled with terror and awe. Suddenly the water-logged balls and wet bags seemed utterly insignificant, as did the practice itself, for which I had studiously planned the night before. Even winning and losing seemed utterly petty—though our team had a great record that I wanted to preserve. As the bolts shot out in all directions, a thought came to me: "There is no necessity . . . No necessity that there be a baseball practice today, or even that I be alive to run one tomorrow." For a brief moment at least, the significance of every one of my goals was held in suspension. It was a terrifying but empowering feeling. "A higher power," I thought to myself: not simply the prodigious storm, but your power—the fullness of your life here and now, in this moment.

Suddenly instinct and some distant knowledge kicked in: The batting cage—just a few paces away—a complete enclosure, would be the safest place during an electrical storm. I had learned this at the Museum of Science as a kid, where my parents would often bring me: Electricity will run only along the outermost surface of a metal enclosure and then plunge harmlessly into the ground. One can even touch the metal of an enclosure from the inside as it's conducting electricity and be miraculously unaffected. As I dashed for the cage, the image came to me of the man at the Museum of Science operating the Van de Graaff generator—a massive machine for simulating bolts of lightning generated by static electricity. The man in the cage touched the metal from the inside with his finger as vicious bolts struck the outside. Remembering all this in a split second, I dashed inside the chain-link enclosure of the batting cage, gratuitously shutting the small door behind me.

Safely sheltered, I returned to the thought to which the storm had given rise in me: the higher power. Not the storm, but the proverbial life that flashes before one's eyes in a moment of terror. What life was it? Not my list of successes and failures, and not my goals. The storm had negated those things in the thought of death. No, not achievement but *self*—the sudden recognition of the fullness of life here and now—a rare occasion in which the hopeful but unsure "one day I will be . . ." gets replaced by the resolute "I am!" Practices that go for the full two hours, wins, achievements, what do I want from these things? What do I expect from them? That they'll make me happier, more complete? No. The most such things can give me is an occasion for a struggle—a journey through which I gain more *of myself*—more of who (and what) I am already.

Reflecting on what I realized in that brief moment of terror, a passage from Nietzsche comes to mind: "The time is gone when mere accidents could still happen to me. What returns, what finally comes home to me, is my own self and what of myself has long been in strange lands and scattered among all things and accidents."[19]

Did the experience of that day—a practice cut short; an "accident"—not just return me to myself? The storm brought me back to my past—watching that man in the metal cage at the Museum of Science, squeezing my mom's hand in fright. In most circumstances, the man in the cage could appear only as a memory—something that happened then, not now. But in the midst of the storm, the memory came back to life in my own action. Suddenly, I had become the man in the cage; only now, it was to evade a real thunderstorm. The only thing missing from the event was a bolt of lightning to strike my makeshift enclosure.

Looking back on that event, I've learned another, more general lesson about nature, the outdoors, and the journey of life—something I tell myself often but fall woefully short in realizing. The happenings of the earth and sky, right outside your window, are replete with opportunities for adventure, full of potential stories no lesser in significance than those you might encounter at work or in the newspaper—if only you paid attention just a little more!

Though the difference between indoors and outdoors can be overstated, the outdoors has this advantage: On the whole, at least in our time, it is wilder, more chaotic, less predictable than the indoors, and therefore more conducive to adventure. The confines of an office building or a home are highly regulated—from the temperature that one can set at the press of a button, to the light available at the flip of a switch. Just about everything indoors is

predictable and at our disposal. To find adventure indoors, we typically have to wait for something to break and disrupt our routine.
Attempts at repair can certainly build character and make for good
stories. But for those of us who are not handy and rely on hired experts when things go wrong indoors, we would do well to turn
our sights outside—to step out and face the elements.

Outdoor sports, like baseball, and track, make engagements with
nature inevitable. But simply opening the door in the evening to
greet a peaceful sunset does so too. It can encourage us to recognize a meaning higher than our achievements and goals. In the
crimson sphere of light descending beneath the horizon, in the
golden clouds moving quietly toward us, we may encounter the brilliance of a life whose final outpouring is for us, the survivors, to
receive and carry on. Or we may meet the end of today's journey,
whose last rays, carried our way by the drifting clouds, remind us
silently that "tomorrow begins the next chapter!"

In reference to such moments, I remind myself: The potential
for adventure and new life is right there in front of you. Appreciate
what lies outside your door and make something of it. Run, walk,
climb the highest hill in town and look out onto the horizon. And
if that's not enough, run up as fast as you can. Do pushups till your
arms scream, swim in the ocean, go as far as you can until you're
too terrified to go further, or just lie on the grass and look up at
the stars. No one is stopping you. "There are a thousand paths than
have never yet been trodden—a thousand . . . hidden isles of life.
Even now, man and man's earth are unexhausted and undiscov-
ered."[20] A flourishing life is within your reach every day—provided
you are willing to step out of your routines and allow the world to
announce itself. The lack of such willingness is the real enemy. Its
source is almost always your own ambition, however small. It's the
submission to the imperative of the workday that leads you to wake
up at 6 AM and not even cast a glance outside to see the sunrise.

Such an engagement with nature doesn't take much. Take ten minutes to step outside and tend to the garden or watch the clouds while you sip a cup of coffee in the morning. Describe to yourself what you see as if you had to report it to a friend in the evening. Chances are you'll find something that pulls you out of your hum-drum routine and that justifies in advance whatever the day may bring. Perhaps you come to a sudden insight that hours and days of thinking had failed to unearth. Awakenings can happen in a flash.

Searching for Seashells: How Path and Destination Are One

Nature has produced few things more beautiful than a certain type of seashell called the junonia. It's a popular collector shell of the volute family that inhabits the deep waters of the Gulf of Mexico and the Caribbean. Only on rare occasions, typically after violent storms, does it wash ashore along the coast of South Florida. I've been searching for the junonia and other seashells with my brother since we were six and eight years old. We found our first when I was in high school and have found five more since. That makes six junonias in twenty-four years—a ratio of which we are proud.

As I was surveying our collection this past winter, I got to pondering a question that's struck me after each of our finds: What accounts for the junonia's beauty? A familiar but superficial answer is convention. We find it beautiful simply because other people do. Having learned that the junonia is a popular collector item, we can't help but find it attractive. But in itself, the junonia is no more or less beautiful than other less prized varieties. This kind of explanation goes back to Adam Smith, who invoked it in reference to certain styles of dress. We find particular arrangements attractive, he suggests, simply because we are used to seeing them together, like trousers and a belt. We find the absence of a belt disheveled and unattractive only because we are conditioned by habit and custom to believe so.

Such accounts of beauty in terms of convention hold a certain appeal. They suggest the possibility of liberating ourselves from the thrall of common opinion and allowing ourselves to choose what we like for ourselves. But this conventionalism, and the subjective conception of beauty to which it points, overlooks the possibility that what we claim to like for ourselves, or "according to our own taste," is possessed of an *intrinsic* beauty, a beauty that makes a claim on *us* and longs for interpretation. Accounts of beauty in terms of subjective taste alone support a self-defeating lassitude: They fore-close on the project of attempting to articulate the meaning of what strikes us as beautiful, thereby depriving us of the potential insight and self-knowledge to which the interpretation of beautiful things may lead.

Of the sense in which apparently conventional beauty may actu-ally attest to a meaning *proper* to a given aspect of nature, Nietz-sche's account of gold is a wonderful example: "Tell me: how did gold attain the highest value? Because it is uncommon and useless and gleaming and gentle in its splendor; it always gives itself. Only as the image of the highest virtue did gold attain the highest value. Goldlike gleam the eyes of the giver. Golden splendor makes peace between moon and sun. Uncommon is the highest virtue and use-less; it is gleaming and gentle in its splendor: a gift-giving virtue is the highest virtue."[21] In Nietzsche's account, we learn at the same time of gold and of virtue. The "value" of gold lies in the way it "gives itself"—just as the sun gives its light to the moon. Such an offering is a form of sharing in which the giver is preserved, not depleted by what it presents. By lending its light to the moon and allowing it to come into its own as ruler of the nighttime sky, the sun itself is able to shine after setting. Nietzsche thus finds in gold an image, a metaphor, for the kind of giving to which a life might aspire: a giving through which benefactor and recipient are empowered alike. Insofar as gold, in the way that it shines, awakens and enriches our understanding of self, we can no longer regard its value as merely conventional. There is a splendor proper to gold that finds expression in the gift-giving virtue.

In the case of the junonia, I know that its beauty has something to do with its striking shape and patterning. About three to five inches in length, the junonia takes the form of an elegant spire, about three times as long as it is wide, colored in a very pure off-white and adorned with rows of circular markings of a dark, earthy hue. One can begin to understand the special significance of this arrangement in contrast to the patterning of the alphabet cone, another popular shell, which is similar in looks but somewhat more common. Conical in shape, save for a tight spire that constitutes the top, or "nose" of the shell, and protrudes from what would be the base of the cone, the alphabet cone derives its name from the tightly packed orange-brown speckles that resemble hieroglyphs. Of all the inanimate things of nature that I've encountered, the alphabet cone offers itself to be understood most conspicuously. The markings ask to be interpreted—as if they were letters comprising a mystical note from a distant land. One could say that the alphabet cone embodies a "meta-meaning" of sorts: Its message is that nature presents itself to be read. Even in its less suggestive aspects, nature is ours to interpret for potential insights, if only we look attentively enough. That's one thing the alphabet cone teaches us.

The junonia is arguably a subtler version of the alphabet cone. Its spire is softer, more elongated, and continuous with the entire body of the shell, which thus takes on a smooth rhomboid aspect, fattest at the middle, tapered at each end. The greater symmetry of the junonia (which, unlike the cone, is roughly symmetrical if cut widthwise at the middle) suggests a comprehensive insight, one that is, so to speak, developed evenly in all directions. The markings of the junonia are clearer and more distinct than those of the alphabet cone, demanding to be interpreted all the more. Nature, it seems, took one step toward revealing the distinctive significance of the alphabet cone and thus gave birth to the junonia. This, I believe, contributes greatly to the shell's intrigue.

Gazing upon one of these little marvels that now rests in a display case in the front hallway of my home, I can't help but try to say something of the meaning that those suggestive circular letters encourage me to interpret. But to do so, I have to return to the shell as I first encountered it, beneath about a foot of water, wedged in the sand at the outer edge of a tidal pool at around five in the morning.

In the beam of my LED flashlight, the telltale pattern of brown on white flickered brilliantly as the subtle waves, deadened by the sandbar behind me, undulated over the surface of the pool and broke gently at the edge of the beach. Suddenly the tantalizing image vanished into a blur as the stiff northwesterly wind whipped the water into a frenzy of ripples, preventing my high-powered beam from cutting through to the bottom. On, off, on, off, the brown-on-white pattern appeared and disappeared on cue with the wind, a reminder of the squall that had blown through the day before summoning a relentless onslaught of whitecaps that hurled ashore the seashells now exposed by the early morning low tide.

As I waited for the latest gust of wind to subside and for the image of the seashell to reappear, my heartbeat quickened as if I were about to grab the pull-up bar for a world record attempt. The dull ache in my legs and lower back, an effect of wading through ankle-deep water for over a mile and pausing to stoop many times as I examined different seashells, suddenly vanished. This was the moment of truth. The only question would be the shell's condition, whether it was whole and intact or beaten by years of rolling in the surf. With a deep breath and sharp exhale, I reached down and unearthed it without effort.

Unlike other desirable shells, the junonia typically comes straight out of the ocean without grime, seaweed, or barnacles to scrub off.

The only cleaning it needs is a quick shake on the surface of the water to wash off the sand. I didn't need the flashlight anymore. The full moon blazing out of the crystal clear sky was sufficient to reveal the smooth, unblemished surface of the shell. But I couldn't resist inspecting it once more under the flashlight, just to confirm. Satisfied, I thrust the prize deep into my pocket and looked up at the expanse of beach to clear my head and regroup for the rest of the search. (After finding a junonia, "quit while you're ahead" means nothing. Like all beautiful things, the junonia inspires as much as it satisfies. One is impelled to keep looking for another, which always comes with its own luster and story.) Only then, as I gazed inland, did I notice the long shadows of the coconut palms and Australian pines reaching menacingly toward the ocean where I was standing. Their branches swayed and hissed in the wind. Had it not been for the soft glow of night lights emanating from the low-lying condominiums just beyond the trees, the surroundings would have taken on a rather haunting character.

My brother and I kept strolling, picking up the occasional banded tulip or lightning whelk that lay in our path until the dim light of the impending dawn began to appear on the horizon. Soon the distant smell of scrambled eggs and coffee wafted invitingly in our direction from a low-lying hotel just up the beach. And the steam rising from the hot tub, unguarded by the hotel staff, beckoned us to a trespassory Jacuzzi break to revitalize our chilled toes and watch the sunrise. The sublime adventure of the predawn hours gave way to the comforting and thoroughly domestic scene of early morning beachgoers strolling along the shore and the sounds of the glistening palm fronts rattling gently in the breeze.

As I look down today at the shell in my collection resting peacefully alongside others, so apparently self-contained and stable, I realize that the meaning suggested by its resonant patterning lies in the play of forces that it gathered when I first lay eyes on it. Shimmering in the tidal pool, the seashell drew together the rippling

waves, the gusts of wind, the storms of the day before, and my negotiation with these forces alongside my brother. In its mysterious
splendor, the shell that sits so quietly on the palm of my hand is
really the standing embodiment of a quest, the token of an adventure and the entire way of life in which that adventure could arise.

The same could be said of trophies, rankings, and accomplishments of any kinds. Their significance lies in the journeys to attain
them. They continue to shimmer and inspire only as reminders of
those struggles through which one's life as a whole comes to expression. Otherwise they just collect dust, or become old and boring,
or become the topic of bragging rights that people will soon grow
tired of recognizing.

If only we could keep this in mind as we strive for our goals: *The
journey constitutes the thing we seek.* Eager to claim victories and accolades, it's easy to get impatient and to lose the joy of being in the
midst of things. In these moments, I pause to remind myself of the
search for the evasive junonia in which each day, each hour, each
stoop, is equally full of life. Even the heartbreaking encounter with
the sunray venus clam, which, to tired eyes squinting through murky
water, has markings vaguely similar to those of the junonia, resonates with meaning. Such a moment of frustration is inseparable
from the joy of finding the real thing. Path and destination are one.

Happiness and Fortune

Philosophy, or at least the beginning of philosophy, is everywhere.
We can find it in books only because it has already made its claim
on us in the course of our daily occupations and concerns. Even
where some conception of life has "first" appeared to us on the
written page, its meaning is never simply there, before us in that
moment, or in our thoughts as we make the attempt to interpret
what we have just encountered; it is as much expressed in features
of the world that leap out at us in moments when we least expect it.

The very thought I am attempting to present in this book, that of happiness and its relation to a journey, something I had long considered from books I've read over the years, came to me, as if for the first time, after a brutal running workout one mid-summer evening. I had given it my all (or so I believed). But the heat and inexplicable laziness of my afternoon legs had issued in a subpar performance of "positive splits," meaning that you finish the workout slower than you started. As I lay sprawled out on my back, chest heaving, but otherwise motionless with exhaustion and receding nausea, I somehow sensed that happiness was near. Suddenly it met me, as I was jogging home down the street I walk every day, expecting nothing, thinking about nothing, feeling a strange mixture of the pride that comes with making one's best attempt and the disappointment of failing to hit one's times. Before me, along the road, lay the stump of a large tree, freshly cut, sawed clean at the base. From its many-ringed surface arose bright green shoots with their leaves reaching for the sun. Clearly the base and roots of the ancient tree were still strong and life-promoting—as if the tree had, of its *own* accord, given way for its children and a new chapter.

The tree had been struck down by arrogant human hands, or probably by someone commissioned by the town, just doing their job, not thinking twice about clearing the way for a new bike lane. And, yet, the tree was still full of life, old and new. It had reclaimed disaster for *itself* and now stood as inspiration for everything in its midst. Had the tranquility of dashed hopes and nothing more to anticipate or achieve not slackened my pace of life, I would have passed by that scene in the hurry of my day. But now I was stopped in my tracks, filled with admiration and fresh spirit.

Suddenly I was carried back to an evening in Athens, Greece, when I embraced the outdoors by sheer chance, after discovering to my dismay that the local gym was closed for a two-week holiday. Frustrated over my thwarted plans and itching for a workout, I made a spur-of-the-moment decision to start running and not to stop until I reached the summit of a steep hill on the outskirts of town. At that point, I had not run much more than twenty minutes on a treadmill in my life. Well over a half an hour later, having several times broken into a sprint to evade the occasional stray dog that barked and lunged in my direction (perhaps these were playful gestures, but I couldn't be sure), I reached the top. With the white rooftops of Athens spread out below me, and the sparkling expanse of the Aegean Sea just beyond, I grabbed two of the largest stones in sight, each the size of a coconut with the husk still on, and performed a set of biceps curls, lifting each to the level of my shoulder and slowly letting them back down while keeping my muscles under tension. The joy of each repetition could perhaps be compared to the celebratory fist-pump and "come on!" of an athlete who, after hitting a three-point shot from half court, or winning a fifty-shot rally, wants nothing more than the opportunity for another one. The same joy had come upon me, years later, in the presence of the tree stump. I had nothing to celebrate, but I felt like shouting from a mountaintop.

And then, all at once, I came to understand the lesson that the ill-fated workout, the jog home, and the giant tree trunk conveyed: involuntary bliss, happiness occasioned by hardship and frustration, unplanned and unexpected—happiness, happenstance, chance— they go together. The ancient Greeks, in their word for happiness, *eudaimonia,* with its reference to the "good demon," knew a truth that we have since forgotten: Happiness is fortune, and fortune the partner of a journey.

5

Contending with Time

At the center of the contrast between goal-oriented striving and activity for the sake of itself is a contrast between two understandings of time. We have touched upon this contrast already in considering the sense in which the goal-oriented life is plagued by an anxious looking ahead to what needs to be accomplished or attained at the expense of appreciating the journey of life, here and now, as an opportunity for self-possession, friendship, and engagement with nature.

It is tempting to characterize the contrast as between a narrow-minded future orientation that is never fully present, on the one hand, and a joyful "living in the moment" on the other. Though this account is certainly right in a sense, it doesn't quite get at the heart of the difference. For as we have seen, what it means to be in the moment of a journey is to be coming into one's self through a confrontation with the unbidden. The "present" of a journey is therefore an *active* present defined by what could be called a collision of future and past that is, at the same time, a mutual constitution.

The future is the open horizon out of which the unbidden can approach. It answers to the sense in which one's life is not a closed circle of meaning but an understanding toward which one is always on the way. The past is the provisional closure that has always already oriented one's journey and that propels it into the open and un-known. Without the past or the "Ithaca" from which one sets sail and to which one strives to return, one's life would be directionless—in the extreme, a disconnected array of events that would not be vul-nerable to any unforeseen disruption precisely because it is already in pieces, thus the life of nobody at all. Without the future, one's past would be a life frozen over, devoid of love, longing, or vivacity. Thus, in the moment of a journey, the future and past are always at work together.

But they come together only through one's own attentiveness and resolve. One can have before one's self the possibility of an open horizon—the "next moment" as a test and opportunity for bound-less self-discovery—only insofar as one holds fast to the commit-ments that draw together the whole of one's life and constitute the person one is. Were Odysseus not motivated at every turn of his voyage by a resolute devotion to his wife, son, and homeland—by his past—he would not have faced an open horizon in which new and unfathomable challenges could come his way. And without the opportunity to confront such challenges he would not come into his own as a person so committed. For it is one thing to set out with the intention of returning home to the people one loves and quite another to withstand the call of the Sirens and steer clear of Scylla and Charybdis for the sake of a return.

Thus, the genuine "being in the moment" that constitutes a meaningful life and that liberates us from the anxious looking ahead to what may or may not come to pass is never simply a focused gaze on what lies at hand in contrast to what may come along later. Nor is it the passive reception of one's surroundings, as one might strive for in a state of meditation aimed at momentarily forget-ting the future on one side and the past on the other. The "pres-ence" of a journey is rather the enactment of a simultaneous de-parture and return where the beginning is understood anew in the end.

Goal-Oriented Time: That Which Is Always Running Out

The special circularity of the time that defines a journey can be more deeply understood by contrast to the temporality of goal-oriented striving. What the goal-oriented future amounts to is a state of affairs already in sight but yet to be actualized—a reform to be achieved, an impression to be made, an experience to be had, a state of the world to be preserved. In every case, the goal-oriented future is a now that has not yet arrived. In eagerly looking ahead to this future for its fulfillment, goal-oriented striving has actually closed itself off to the genuine future, in the sense of the open horizon out of which the unbidden can break onto the scene and put one's life to the test. The only uncertainty that goal-oriented striving admits, though it would like to abolish it through the mastery of the means to the end, is whether an envisioned plan will come to fruition.

What the goal-oriented past amounts to is an accomplishment, acquisition, success, or failure of yesterday, a moment that could have been this way or that as it approached but has since been decided—for better or worse—and now rolls off into the distance. "Forget about the past and move on" is the mantra of goal-oriented striving, which reminds itself that within only a few days or weeks the past will cease to be a distraction. In every case, the goal-oriented past is a now that has come and gone. In brooding for a time in the past that rolls away and then turning once more to the future that is about to arrive, goal-oriented striving has lost sight of the genuine past in the sense of the closure and directedness of life that constitutes its meaning and sense.

Thus, the goal-oriented horizon of time, even in its orientation to the future and the past, remains always the *present*. Each moment is either a now that is approaching, a now that is here, or a now that is rolling away. Time becomes an infinite train of nows, each a cart that whizzes by and barrels off into the distance. Such a life is beset by the unhappy paradox of being at once fleeting and inert. On the one hand, everything for which one waits and hopes and strives departs as fast as it comes, leaving one without anything of which to lay hold. On the other hand, everything that comes to be takes on the empty uniformity of something that one already had in sight. Missing from such a life is both coherence and adventure.

As one becomes trapped in goal-oriented striving and accustomed to the cycle of anticipation and emptiness, time even begins to appear as an alien force to which one is subject. Thus we speak of the "passage of time" as if time moved itself and carried us along with it. "Time waits for no one," says the one who is feverishly on the way to finishing some project but is then interrupted by the dinner hour or by some intervening task. "There simply aren't enough hours in a day." Of course it is the disposition of goal-oriented striving itself, which would like to leap ahead to the finished project but finds itself diverted, that allows time to pass in this way.

But for one who has lost sight of the journey of life and is therefore without an alternative to goal-oriented striving, one's own responsibility for time's passage gets obscured. Time instead appears as a sort of allotment, a scarce resource in need of being managed and calculated for fear that it will run out.

The advent of the clock as a so-called objective measure of time is a natural outgrowth of goal-oriented striving and completely relative to its means-ends scheme. For it makes sense to measure time or, rather, to conceive of time as something measurable, only from the perspective of an activity that has its aim outside itself. To the extent that one is engaged in activity for its own sake, as an opportunity for adventure and self-discovery, the question of how much time has passed never even arises.

Wherever we find the anxious dismay that time is running out, we find a life that has lost itself in goal-oriented striving and forgotten the intrinsic meaning of the way. Even the phenomenon of growing old, which we are inclined to regard as an inevitable process from which we would like to escape, is thoroughly determined by a goal-oriented outlook, which has its sights on certain aims at which we will no longer be able to succeed. I know I'm aging because I now have to warm up and stretch more before working out. In time I will be "too old" to compete at a sport, to have children, or to reach some milestone at which I believe my life will be fulfilled.

Whenever we understand ourselves as aging we have already restricted the meaning of self to the capacity to accomplish a particular task, or range of tasks, which serves as the standard by which our age is to be determined. We have lost sight of the self that comes to expression in taking a stand, being a friend, or rising to self-possession in the interpretation of nature. For these activities, we are never too old. It is only to the extent that the goal-oriented perspective crowds out our vision of an alternative way of being that we come to believe in growing old as an inevitable state of affairs.

Being on the Way to One's Past, or Becoming Younger in Maturity

As long as we remain attentive to the journey of life, embracing every encounter as a chance to affirm a commitment that draws together the whole of who we are, time will never be a mere succession of moments, and life never a mere march from youth to old age. For the future, whatever it brings, can do no more than offer a chance to understand anew the life we are already living.

Consider once more the trajectory of Odysseus. Is he older when he returns to Ithaca than when he sets out for Troy? Of course, says our common sense, which immediately points to his greyer beard and to his face more creased with wrinkles. But as we place ourselves in his position and imagine ourselves with him on the voyage, our seemingly obvious judgment loses its self-evidence. From the perspective of the one who seeks Ithaca as a devoted husband, father, and ruler, there is a sense in which he can be said, paradoxically, to become *younger* as his journey unfolds. For in each episode of his voyage, the moment that supposedly defines his relative youth by comparison to now—his past or point of departure—comes into its own. As Odysseus contends with high seas and strange lands, everything that has been established of himself and thus can be said to belong to his past is hardly a moment that once was here but has since been displaced by a present that came barreling in from out of the future. His past is rather a force that propels him on his journey, a self-image in light of which he finds the resolve to steer clear of Scylla and Charybdis, to withstand the call of the sirens, and to escape the desirous clutches of Calypso. And as Odysseus braves the onslaught of the future, his past is itself perpetually reborn, each rebirth getting taken up into the next.

The past so understood has the paradoxical status of being both behind Odysseus and ahead of him. It is behind him as a moment to which he stays committed with absolute certainty and that pushes him onward. It is ahead of him as a moment yet to be determined in the confrontation with whatever the future next throws his way. In the end (so to speak), the home to which Odysseus was always devoted becomes a home for which he has withstood unimaginable trials and temptations—a home that is the very one he left but also infinitely more, as it resonates with the entire struggle involved to reach it.

One could interpret such a trajectory as either a becoming older in the sense of more mature, wiser, more self-possessed, or as a becoming younger, finally arriving at the implicit meaning of one's earlier days, a meaning that awaited the future to emerge. From whichever angle one looks, one sees that the temporality of the journey defies the unidirectional conception of time that answers to the goal-oriented perspective and finds expression on résumés and timelines. Time does not flow in one direction but circles back on itself, though always to a point that has never yet been traversed.

That There Is No Such Time as a Past or a Future "Without Me"

Here it is worth contrasting the temporality of a journey not only to the linear conception of time associated with goal-oriented striving, but also to the circular conception proposed by the Stoics. We recall that the Stoics, who were keenly attuned to the fragility of human affairs and the fleetingness of achievement, proposed that we take refuge in the contemplation of nature understood in terms of the comings and goings of the seasons, and, in a larger cosmic sense, the perpetual combination and dissolution of atoms out of which all things can be seen to be composed. From such a perspective, teach the Stoics, we find a time that always circles back to the same point. We can therefore appreciate a certain eternity in this world. Though our own lives as beings who live and strive are fleeting, we can take an alternative perspective on ourselves as parts of the great eternal cycle.

We may now juxtapose the Stoic solution to the more life-affirming conception of time that pertains to a journey. The eternity we seek is not to be found in the infinite cycles of an impersonal nature but in the way in which a life that knows itself in its commitments is a constant setting out and return to one's self with new eyes. Eternity so understood is neither a circle that repetitively turns back on itself nor a line indefinitely extended but a gyre, an upward spiral, that represents the perpetual knowing of ourselves again and anew in each adventure.

That the life I am living now, understood as a journey, includes every "before" as something that lies ahead (and above) holds true, no matter how broad a scope of time I consider. I may even consider the "before" to mean long before I was born, for example, the time of Homeric Greece or of ancient Athens. Only in a superficial sense do these moments lie behind me. Inasmuch as the life of Odysseus or of Socrates remains a question—a potential source of insight while confronting challenges in my own time—their lives surely lie ahead of me as much as behind. I might even say that their lives lie so far ahead that I have scarcely reached them in even my best interpretations.

The same conclusion follows if we expand the scope of time even wider to a "prehistoric" past before human beings walked the face of the earth, a past of tremendous volcanic eruptions that gave rise to ocean and land as we know it, or the age of the dinosaurs, or any epoch in the distant past. These moments too lie ahead of us as much as behind. For as we conceptualize such pasts and try to get them within our grasp, we cannot help but understand them by placing ourselves there, imagining how we would have coped, whether life might have even been better or easier in some ways back then. We thereby encounter the past in a manner that cannot escape a relation to the present and even a potential way to the future.

Even when we do not consciously place ourselves in such a setting, as in fanciful portrayals such as the film *Jurassic Park,* we have already implicitly placed ourselves there in the very terms and distinctions we draw to "objectively" characterize the conditions "back then." For this reason, there is always something short-sighted in theories of evolution that posit a time before human life—whether such a time goes back to the Neolithic age or to the big bang. Such theories always depend on having objectivized humanity as a species in relation to others, or placed humanity within the order of physical things that can be observed with regard to their generation and growth. What such theories overlook is the living force that has before itself an object in the first place and that constitutes the object in terms such as "big bang" and "human species," which bear certain meanings and make any sense at all only in reference to the engaged and committed life of the researcher, a life that takes the form of the simultaneous closure and openness of a journey. Ultimately all earlier times answer to the unity of past and future that defines the now to which we are committed.

The same could be said of all future times. Just as there is no past that does not invite my interpretive power and bear my mark, so too there is no future. When I envision some state of affairs in the distant future, long after I am, so to speak, gone, I am already there and very much present as an interpreter, no less than I am present here and now. For how I characterize that world without me, and make it intelligible in discourse with others, bears the mark of my own ideas, conceptions, and implicit understandings of how to live. The future thus belongs to me, and I to it, even as I imagine it without my consciousness.

Let us envision the terrible state of affairs conjured up by the Stoics to supposedly demonstrate the futility of human life on earth—the cataclysmic moment of "stars crashing into stars," as Seneca puts it, or, as we might say, the implosion of the sun that will engulf the earth in flames. Such an event appears as the end of the world only to the extent that the world gets preconceived as a product or instance of formed matter that persists for a time before falling apart. It is the detached, goal-oriented gaze of the craftsman who looks upon his finished work and wants it to last that sees in such disruption only the end or a point of termination. But such an event admits of a very different interpretation for the one who understands every moment as the potential dispersion of an integral life that must constantly redeem itself in the face of disaster. From this perspective, the so-called end of the world is not an end at all but a state of disarray that invites a reunification yet to be determined, just as the life of Oedipus, when it falls to pieces, holds open the possibility of redemption. Thus the life to which one is committed *now,* the stance one takes on what it means to be, draws into itself whatever may lie ahead.

That Every Succession Answers to the Temporality of a Journey

Lest we be tempted, still, to regard the paradoxical circularity to time as a subjective perception at odds with "real," or "objective" time, we might examine the way in which it makes possible the most seemingly obvious instances of succession that occur over a matter of mere seconds and that ground our empirical experience of the world. We see a flash of lightning and then, just moments later, hear a crackle of thunder. We believe and say that one follows the other, and on that basis arrive at the conclusion that the first is the cause and the second the effect. But the succession, and with it the distinction of cause and effect, is hardly the full picture of what actually appears and what we experience. The succession can appear as such only because the first moment, as soon as it comes, heralds the arrival of the second, which, in turn, makes good on the first. As soon as we see lightning for what it is, we hear thunder along with it, even as the thunder is not yet audible or even consciously thought alongside the lightning. And as soon as we hear thunder, we recognize it as that which belongs to lightning as a continuation and unfolding of the same phenomenon. Integral to the experience of lightning as a distinctive event that breaks onto the scene in its own imposing and formidable way is the anticipation of the thunder to follow. But this means that the thunder does not simply follow but is always with lightning as a partner in revealing what it is. And the thunder comes into its own only in partnership with lightning as its co-conspirator. Thus, the second moment is not simply after the first but its horizon from the start. And the first moment is not simply before the second but its ever-present counterpart that gets retained and transfigured by what it anticipates. The "two" moments are never simply two—first one, then the other—but a single moment that consists in a mutually reinforcing difference.

Without this mutual constitution, the before and after would make no sense and we would be unable to perform the abstraction of regarding one event as the cause and the other the effect. For, upon seeing lightning without any contemporaneous sense of its anticipated complement in thunder, or in some yet-to-be-determined event that shares with lightning a certain sublimity and prominence, we would simply be awash in the infinite variety of other things that could be said to happen after the flash of light has come and gone. Out of that infinite variety we would have no basis for fastening upon thunder as in any connection with what we previously perceived. Only because lightning opens its own somewhat definite horizon of what is to come but also holds the mystery of "perhaps something else this time" can we discover or confirm thunder as that which in fact does follow. And only because the flash of lightning is retained and reinterpreted by the thunder can we in retrospect recognize lightning as that which occurred before.

We arrive at the same conclusion if we take up the position of the person who now hears thunder and must relate it back to the lightning that was just perceived. Were we to rely on brute memory alone to recall what had just occurred before the thunder we now hear, such that we might subsequently connect the two events, we would be utterly at a loss as to what our memory should fasten upon. And there is the further difficulty that if somehow our memory were to stumble upon lightning and reproduce the experience in an attempt to connect it to the thunder we now hear, we would run the risk, the more vivid our power of memory, of confusing our mental reproduction for the actual event happening again, thereby losing any basis for knowing whether it came before or after the thunder. What is missing in the naked operation of memory to recover the contents of a moment now past and to subsequently link it up to what we just perceived is a sense of the past as *that which was but now is not*. But this historical sense for the singularity of a moment now withdrawn and irreplaceable is possible only when the past is recalled *as that which heralded a future* that now, in coming to meet us, has, in turn, indelibly marked the past such that it can never simply return.

Thus, in our everyday experience of the most seemingly self-evident instances of succession, there is always a reciprocal relation of moments that makes the succession possible. We would be able to get neither up nor down in our most basic scientific understandings of the world were the understanding of succession, which is absolutely necessary for the conception of causality, not underwritten by a more basic experience of time characterized by the openness and closure of a journey.

The sense in which the active self, in its openness and closure, reaches out and back across all times has significant implications for how we conceive of life and death. What has begun to emerge is that death cannot simply be the end, or negation, of life. To the extent that it appears as the end, we have preconceived life in terms of the presence in the world of a consciousness that will one day be absent. In such a conception we overlook the sense in which the world—in the way it solicits one's interpretive power and longs to be brought to expression—is the very basis of consciousness, and how consciousness always finds itself engaged in the world in the mode of attentiveness and response.

To think of one's consciousness as something that arrives at the world at birth, stays for a time, and then departs is to place one's self within the train of moments that appears to constitute time as one becomes lost in the goal-oriented parade of one thing after the next. But if one's own life is, in essence, an interplay of self and world that takes the form of a simultaneous openness and closure, then there can be no time at which one simply ceases to be. Death cannot be an endpoint for the simple reason that a life oriented to the journey has no end outside itself. But here it is worth exploring anew the relation of consciousness to self, self to world, and activity to time. We now do so from the perspective of the "end" and the meaning of death.

Rethinking the Meaning of Death

It is often accepted without question that death is the end of life, the moment at which one's existence here on earth comes to a close. On the basis of this assumption arises the question of what may be after death—whether the self, or soul, will be extinguished or continue to exist somewhere else and, if so, what fate it may suffer. In the face of the disquieting uncertainty of such possibilities, we fear death, and, out of an attachment to the lives we are living, we attempt to find ways of guarding against "the end," postponing it to the extent that we can, as if death later or in old age, when we assume we will have lived more fully, is more desirable than an untimely death before one's life has ripened. All the while, we leave the question of the meaning of the end unexamined. We fail to recognize that in speaking of an end that may come sooner or later, before one's life has taken shape, or after, we have preconceived life in thoroughly goal-oriented terms: as the continuation of a certain state, namely, the presence of a consciousness in the world, which is supposed to be a necessary condition for the acquisition of experiences through which one's life is gradually filled up. Such a conception of life, and of death as its end, has lost sight of activity for the sake of itself.

Understood in terms of activity for the sake of itself, life is always already at its end in the sense of its point of culmination, that for which it aims, but also in the sense of its limit, its extremity—the end of what can be expected and known. Is not this dual sense of "end" not also the meaning of death?

When we speak of the death that will befall us one day, what more can we possibly mean than a confrontation with the ultimate unbidden, through which the entirety of who we are is on the line? By "death" we can mean nothing more—or less—than the open horizon and unfathomable mystery that encircles the life we are already living.

So understood, death is not the opposite or negation of life. It is not something that comes upon life from the outside as we sometimes depict in the image of the grim reaper ominously approaching with a scythe. Such ghoulish personifications of death actually serve to render death familiar, to liken it to a threatening presence we might encounter within the world. In placing death within the world, we pass over the sense in which death pertains to the world itself—to the meaning of the world, and of ourselves as beings who come into our own through the interpretation of the world.

We likewise render death familiar as "the extinction of consciousness," a conception of death that takes its bearings from the things we can see, touch, and experience directly—such as embers of a fire that die out or a breath or puff of smoke that lingers momentarily in the air before dispersing. By reference to such phenomena that appear to our consciousness, we imagine that our consciousnesses itself may suffer a similar fate. We further conceive of this fate as the "experience" of nothing, which we imagine by subtracting, as it were, all the entities that may stand before our gaze until we arrive at an empty darkness—a "nothing" that is the mere absence of the things we know, posing no mystery at all.

Missing from such a conception is the sense in which death somehow implicates the meaning of everything I know, the sense in which death is not simply a presence or absence from a world that itself, in some form, remains, but the transformation of everything I can see, touch, and consider with regard to its meaning and significance, a disruption through which my very identity as well as that of the world hangs in the balance. Death in this sense—and really the only sense that can measure up to our divinations that death is "inevitable," "irreversible," "total," and "mysterious"—can be understood only from the engaged and committed perspective of an open-ended journey, from the perspective of a life that "is" *not* but becomes and, in becoming, aims for no end external to itself.

Though in thinking about death and attempting to conceptualize it, we sometimes acknowledge that death implicates the whole of who we are, and that it involves, in some sense, a disruption of the *meaning* of things (and not simply their physical constitution) we fall back on an understanding of "meaning" in terms of things that can be said to rise and fall in time, such as physical entities that confront us in their temporary persistence but ultimate fragility. Correspondingly, we understand disruption as the breaking apart of something present, such as the shattering of a glass that falls to the ground. We thus end up speaking about death in an utterly confused manner.

What I have in mind by such confusion is not hard to find. In a book devoted to the meaning of death, one author offers the following thought experiment intended to capture the relation of death to the meaning of life:

> I taught a seminar on death once, to a group of upper-level undergraduate students. The first day I asked them to put their books aside and take out a piece of paper and a pencil. Then I asked them to write four or five of the most important things in their lives on the piece of paper, and fold it up. I promised them that nobody would see what they had written. When they were done, I asked them to pass the papers to me, folded over so that they couldn't be seen. I assured them that I wasn't interested in what they'd written. What mattered was that each of them knew what he or she had on the paper, that what each of them had

was before their minds. When they had all passed the papers to me, I gathered them in a small pile. I asked them to focus on the paper, and on what they had written. Then I took the pile and slowly tore it to little shreds. That I told them, is what each of them—each of us—needed to confront. That is what we had to understand, as best we could.[1]

What stands out in this depiction of death is not so much its nihilism—that death is the destruction of meaning rather than somehow meaningful in itself—but its utter banality. The so-called important things that death is said to negate are likened to mere entities that lie before our gaze—pieces of paper—that simply get torn up; one moment they are here, the next gone. Death in its mystery and totality is thus reduced to a thoroughly known possibility of what may befall anything that can be seen and touched. Meaning, for its part, or "the things that matter," gets understood on the basis of a goal or a state of existence: something to be acquired, kept, or maintained from one moment to the next but that is ever vulnerable to destruction in time. Entirely neglected is the relation of meaning to activity, interpretation, and dialogue, and the special temporality that might pertain to such activity.

Indicative of this oversight is the professor's disinterest in what his students had written. He asked them only to have "before their minds" whatever it was they wrote—a request that reflects the familiar prejudice that meaning can be adequately represented as a mental state. But what if instead of the things the professor no doubt assumed his students might jot down—"my family," "my friends," "my pet dog," things that are indeed meaningful when viewed in terms of *activity* but that are easily misconstrued in terms of entities that come and go—a student had written a stanza from his or her favorite poem, or a question, or simply the word "philosophy," or, better yet, the assertion of Socrates that the "unexamined life is not worth living"? The relation of such things to time is something we will continue to examine in the rest of the chapter, as we examine the temporality of matters of interpretation and self-understanding. But from what we have already considered, it should be clear that such things are related to time in a very different sense from goals, finished products, and states of the world that may persist or depart. That we so readily and thoughtlessly equate meaning with goal-oriented striving speaks to just how submerged we are in a worldview that obscures the ongoing journey of life and the sense in which it is temporal.

The conception of death as an event that befalls us in time, not now but later (hopefully much later), does justice neither to the mystery of death nor, as we will now explore, to the boundlessness of life. For when we examine the familiar ways in which we conceive of the end that is to come—the demise of the body, the extinction of consciousness—we find that such death cannot contain or encompass the active, interpretive force of a life that is, at every moment, in the stance it takes and the understanding it projects, *more* than the bodily presence of an individual "in" the world or the existence of a subjective consciousness that is now here to perceive and report on things but may someday be absent. To examine this "something more" that not only survives the demise of the body but also may, in facing such an end, come to affirm itself anew, let us begin by exploring the insufficiency of consciousness as a way of access to the self.

Consciousness as an Outgrowth of the Enacted Journey of Life

If death is to be primarily regarded as the extinction of consciousness, then it must be consciousness that defines life. But the more we examine consciousness, the more we discover that it is but one possibility of life and often a superficial one at that.

We might first note that the more we are truly living, in the sense of thoroughly and passionately engaging in activity that speaks to who we are, the less we are conscious of ourselves as beings separate from what we do. To the extent that we find ourselves conscious of something, the content of that consciousness is often trivial by comparison to the understanding of self that lies implicit in what we *are doing* without explicitly reflecting upon it. Consider a baseball player subtly positioning himself in center field as the pitch is about to come in. His conscious attention may be directed idly to the lyrics of some inane popular song, or to what he had for lunch. But his subtle movement, quite beneath the range of his conscious attention, speaks to a practical, embodied knowledge of how to play the game—a knowledge of an aspect of the world (the game of baseball) that is, at the same time, a form of self-knowledge—a "knowing one's way around" the game as a player but also as someone engaged in a way of life, a journey, in which baseball has a place.

Or consider tennis great Rafael Nadal, who, even after a crushing loss in the finals of a major tournament, takes time to sign autographs for fans as he walks off court. One could readily imagine that as he scrawls his signature across the big yellow balls held out eagerly by his loyal fans, his mind is elsewhere, reflecting perhaps on the heartbreaking defeat, or simply looking forward to a moment of silent repose in the locker room before the media descends upon him. But his actions in the circumstance, which may entirely evade his conscious attention, speak to a virtue and wisdom that is undeniably his own. And in being his own, they are equally available for all who are there with him to understand, interpret, and apply to their own lives.

Though we are in the habit of regarding explicit, focused attention on something—whether on the game of baseball, or on the sense in which we may be acting virtuously or otherwise—as the highest, most thoughtful way of accessing it, and even the quintessence of reason, we ought to consider that matters are quite to the contrary: We understand things first and foremost by dealing with them and engaging with them rather than reflecting upon them. And rarely does our reflection on the things in which we are immersed—our conscious awareness of them—begin to do justice to their significance.

We can of course bring to consciousness features of the way of life that are essential to who we are and that typically lie beneath the range of our explicit attention. To reduce consciousness to a silly song stuck in one's head is not quite fair to the way in which explicit awareness and self-reflection can, in moments, lead to greater self-possession. Thinking things through, explicitly and deliberately, may lead to an insightful, motivating, or liberating account of what we are doing and who we are. We may be impelled to such conscious self-reflection when someone asks us why we acted a certain way when we could have done otherwise, or praises or criticizes us for an action to which we gave no thought. But in bringing to expression our action in words, we offer it to be interpreted and developed by anyone there with us. In giving an account of our actions, we are not, in other words, exposing the contents of our minds for all to see for the first time. We are offering a certain perspective on a life already manifest, open to interpretation from many angles. Consciousness, however illuminating, is thus an outgrowth of the enacted meaning of life that we are always in the process of interpreting.

Focusing on the way in which action, storytelling, and interpretation defines life, Nietzsche makes a striking comparison: Our *consciousness* of our own significance is no greater than that of soldiers depicted on canvas of the battle they are fighting.[2] The painted soldiers obviously have no conscious awareness of themselves or what they are doing. Nevertheless, their action as rendered in the painting embodies a meaning to be interpreted by whoever cares to look. Not consciousness but activity and narrative, suggests Nietzsche, defines a person.

More precisely, consciousness is itself a form of activity—an engagement with the matter of which you are conscious—the idea that captivates and moves you to think, the dilemma that confronts you and leads you to deliberate. But this means that consciousness is never really "one's own" in the sense of "mine and not yours." Consciousness is always shared consciousness inasmuch as so-called others are themselves defined in relation to the same ideas and dilemmas that motivate me. As soon as we are aware of ourselves and our world in any respect at all, we are aware that we are interpreters of a meaning that is not limited to a subjective representation that is simply "our own."

It is said by some that shared experience meets its limit in certain forms of awareness, such as pain, that are utterly subjective. No one else but I can feel the pain in my stubbed toe. But this very way of speaking of pain—of locating it in my toe, or in my mind—overlooks the significance of shared activity for determining just what it *is* I feel and how I might respond to it. The subjectivist notion of pain, or of any feeling, assumes that it is a brute sensation experienced passively rather than a prompting to be articulated, dealt with, and acted upon. It can't account for the sense in which we don't really feel pain as the pain it is until we have implicitly understood it with respect to some activity for which it is relevant. The pain one can be said to feel in the midst of a hard mile race, for example—lungs burning, legs heavy with extreme fatigue—is an instigation to keep pushing and fight through the discomfort, or perhaps a sign to back off just a bit to save energy for the final "kick" down the home stretch. Pain in this sense is a form of resistance to be expected and overcome. It is different in quality, and not simply intensity, from the sudden, imbalanced pain that signifies an injury. Though the pain of injury may, in many cases, be less intense than the healthy fatigue of exertion, the former is deadening rather than inspiring. Injury pain impels one to stop, so as to recover and avoid damage. Pain is thus determined by the situation in which it arises.

But this means that pain is not private and subjective—something that only I, the one who experiences the pain, can feel. For the situation of pain involves a shared understanding. It is quite possible to misunderstand the situation and therefore to misinterpret one's own pain. This happens often to beginners in a sport, who confuse the feeling of healthy maximum-effort exertion for a kind of pain for the bad and back off when they should forge ahead, or who dismiss injury-induced pain as "no big deal" and barrel onward when they should stop. It is only in light of a coach's interpretation of the sensation in context that the athlete is able to begin to recognize the pain for what it is. The locus of pain turns out to be a shared activity.

That consciousness is rooted in shared activity, and not an autonomous phenomenon, has profound implications for how we conceive of life and death. If life were merely a stretch of time in which a distinct subject, or center of consciousness, underwent experiences (pleasures, pains, victories, and defeats), then it might make sense to conceive of death as the moment at which life comes to an end. It is possible to imagine a mere state of existence—the presence of a consciousness that takes things in and accrues "experience"—suddenly being disrupted or cut off. But if life is defined by the striving for coherence, death cannot be such a point of termination. For a story, whether written on paper or enacted in a way of being, has its own integrity and force, whether or not its protagonist is directly manifest on earth or conscious of its meaning.

If we take death to mean the demise of the body or the extinction of consciousness, we must consider that a life comes to an end at death no more than a story comes to an end with the destruction of the paper on which it is written. Both continue to offer inspiration and insight to whoever is involved in the story—either directly, as we might say of the survivors, or implicitly, in the case of devoted interpreters who may have never met the living, breathing person, but who are moved by his or her example.

Even where there are no obvious survivors in the sense of those who remember a particular name attached to a story, a condition almost inevitable after generations have passed, the story itself—the stance one takes on what it means to be—can always, in principle, return in the action of those who in their own way, and in their own time, take a similar stand. Had Plato not written the story of Socrates, and we had no direct awareness of the precise circumstances of the virtue he displayed in pursuing philosophy, his life, which is to say the activity that defined his life, would still have found expression in the union of levity and commitment displayed by the protagonist in *Life Is Beautiful,* and so too in the lives of others who, without any explicit knowledge of a man named Socrates, display something Socratic in the way they live. To live a life oriented to virtue and integrity of self is to participate in a project that exceeds the bounds of consciousness and that transcends the comings and goings of embodied existence.

As Socrates and the hero from *Life Is Beautiful* demonstrate, death, in the sense of the demise of the body, can even be integral to life conceived as a narrative. When death brings to expression that for which one stands, when death represents a self-possessed exuberance for life, it is a moment of culmination rather than rupture. The Greek word for dying, *teleutein,* preserves the sense of culmination, as it signifies "coming to one's *telos,*" or "purpose." In articulating *who* Socrates is and attempting to live by his example, we couldn't possibly leave out the way in which he faced death for the sake of philosophy. His trial and execution is essential to his story.

Not every death is so resonant and personal. Even the death of Socrates may well be highly stylized by Plato. But the many instances of death that are mundane or accidental rather than heroic remind us that who someone is transcends their physical presence on earth. As soon as someone "departs," as we say, and is no longer directly manifest in the body we used to call their "person," we realize that what we miss in their presence is not simply their physical proximity but their characteristic gestures that no longer radiate before us—a charming wink or smile, a distinctive gait, a comforting cadence of voice. But such gestures embody meanings to be interpreted. We come to appreciate them only as we understand them, which often leads us to even close our eyes. Though manifest through the body, the gestures of a person go beyond what the body alone can convey.

Long before we might eulogize a person after death by reference to their characteristic gestures and expressions, we do so, in a way, while they are living. As we narrate, recount, and interpret the gestures of a person, perhaps in describing them to someone else in the course of telling a story, or perhaps in simply making sense of them to ourselves in appreciation, we articulate a way of life that exceeds its manifestation at a particular time and place.

What's Wrong with the Life-Extension Craze

The sense in which the active self transcends what is manifest of a person at any given moment ought to shake us loose of our intense focus on extending life in the physical, biological sense. For the meaning, or sense that one projects while living, has nothing to do with a long or a short stretch of time. One can live an infinitely long life yet be plagued throughout by self-fragmentation, each moment of one's life a mere novelty or accident that gets pushed away by the next. Such a life is always in need of more time to replenish the things that are flowing away. In contrast, one can live a short life but, at every moment, integrate what arrives, and hold fast to it as a point at which the whole of one's life resonates anew. Such a life is always at once at its end and beginning and therefore needs no more time.

There is nothing inconsistent between a long life and a coherent one. But a focus on length can come at the expense of coherence. For there will always be situations that force us to choose between mere life and a life we can affirm, between crouching safely in a corner and taking a stand.

Why we so readily give ourselves over to subsistence at the expense of narrative coherence may go back to the influence of Hobbes and his glorification of mere survival as an instinct both natural and moral. His view is unwittingly accepted by contemporary thinkers, such as Steven Pinker, who suggest that in a world ridden with moral conflict, the one "objective" value on which we can all agree is the good of survival. Exemplars such as Socrates remind us that such apparently obvious moral claims are far from self-evident. When challenged by a young orator to give up philosophy and to pursue rhetoric, so as to protect himself from harm at the hands of potential accusers in the law courts, Socrates replies as follows: "As to living a given length of time, this is surely something to which a real man should not devote his soul . . . having resigned such matters to god . . . he should then consider in what way he will best live his allotted time."[3] Socrates goes on to explain that he will not sell his soul to the city by catering to it as the orators do.

In stark contrast to Hobbes and his modern followers, Nietzsche revives the ancient critique of striving to live a long life. Reversing our contemporary intuitions, Nietzsche asserts that a few die too early and "many die too late."[4] He elaborates this counterintuitive claim in the words of Zarathustra, the protagonist of his central work, *Thus Spoke Zarathustra*. (Like Plato, Nietzsche conveys much of his thought through the adventures and teachings of a stylized philosophical hero.) Zarathustra teaches that instead of aiming for a long life, one should die at the right time: "He who has a goal and an heir will want death at the right time for his goal and heir. And from reverence for his goal and heir he will hang no more dry wreaths in the sanctuary of life."[5]

At first glance, Zarathustra's speaking of dying for a goal would seem to suggest precisely the goal-oriented perspective that we have called into question. But he makes very clear that the significance of a goal lies not in the goal itself but in the journey for which it makes occasion. "What is great in man," says Zarathustra, "is that he is a bridge and not an end."[6] When Zarathustra speaks of the "right time," he means something more than the time necessary to achieve an intended outcome, whether local or grand, good or evil. The imagery he invokes to clarify "one's goal and heir" removes us from the framework of goal-oriented striving, refuting the idea that death is a mere means to hasten the arrival of some intended outcome, and pointing instead to an ongoing activity in partnership with friends: "Verily, Zarathustra had a goal; he threw his ball: now you, my friends, are the heirs of my goal; to you I throw my golden ball. More than anything, I like to see you, my friends, throwing the golden ball. And so I still linger a little on earth: forgive me for that."[7]

The golden ball signifies the calling that animates Zarathustra's life. But the ball comes to be what it is only in being thrown. It is the activity of throwing, teaches Zarathustra, not the target, that constitutes the meaning of a goal. Zarathustra leaves the destination of the golden ball unspecified. The point of the throw is not to reach some ultimate destination but to initiate a game among friends, that they may continue throwing the ball among themselves.

As a sports fan, it's hard to read the passage without imagining a series of deft passes in the final minutes of a basketball game. Though the goal of the pass can be conceived as scoring a basket, Zarathustra's teaching shifts our attention to the act of passing itself, suggesting that there is something inherent in the dexterity, harmony, and exuberance of the play that exceeds any result.

In such a play of catch, one is also reminded of Socrates, whose "goal" consisted of the ongoing activity of dialogue, who was willing to relinquish his existence on earth so that his life-defining vocation might continue with all the more force among his friends. Nietzsche's message is this: To revere your "goal and heir" is to live your life in service of those projects and commitments for which you stand. The point is to revel in their pursuit and to inspire their perpetuation in others. To the extent that you abide by them, and find yourself absorbed in them, you *will* die at the right time for them, whether or not the explicit thought of death or its timing has crossed your mind. For the person thoroughly concerned for an "heir," the question of when to die is not something first thought-out and planned for with an eye to what might be beneficial. The question of when is decided in the very activity of cultivating one's heir, ensuring that it lives and grows. For example, it is not as though the hero from *Life Is Beautiful* thought in advance "I am willing to die for the sake of protecting my wife and child." It was in the act of protecting his son, which for him was simply a way of being himself, that he met his death. But this death was hardly the end of his life. As we learn in the final words of the film, the narrator, who had appeared briefly at the beginning, now reveals himself as the hero's son, now grown: "This is my story. This is the sacrifice my father made. This was his gift to me."

Nietzsche's imagery of throwing the golden ball unites tenacious commitment with carefree play—play in the sense of activity that aims at nothing outside itself, as when children play hide-and-seek. The very title of the game attests to the action, the search, as primary, and the discovery as but an occasion to play again. Nietzsche implores us to take play seriously, to disburden ourselves of the self-imposed heaviness of checklists, deadlines, and even images of a future better world, and to direct ourselves to the fullness and possibility of life at every moment. From his perspective, our familiar saying, in reference to a sporting event, or competition among friends, that it's "only a game," in contrast to serious matters—like career advancement, political reform, or a tax audit—cannot be farther from the truth. For the spirit of play—committed, immersed, joyful, wanting only itself—sets the standard for the attitude in which we should pursue all so-called serious endeavors. It is the ideal of what we must try to restore in the face of disappointment and loss.

To live a life that seeks nothing but itself is to exist on a different plane from that which expends itself in time. In being thoroughly immersed, joyful, and at one with one's self in what one does is to have already prepared one's self to "die at the right time." For whenever death may come, it can do nothing but affirm who one is.

The golden aspect of Zarathustra's ball evokes the sun to which he refers in the conclusion of his speech on "free death": "[In dying] your spirit and virtue should still glow like a sunset around the earth . . . Thus I want to die myself that you, my friends, may love the earth more for my sake."[8] We love the earth more at sunset, as shadows grow long and the horizon lights up in color. Nietzsche suggests that the glow of a spirit at death may radiate in ways we are liable to forget when that spirit is, so to speak, at high noon, manifest in a person who lives and moves among others, and whose luminous presence we take for granted. Nietzsche implies that death may be a moment of inspiration and continuity, for one's friends and for all those who promise and hope. His point is not that we should aim to die a heroic death but that we should not allow the prospect of bodily demise to distort the playful spirit that animates the life we live.

Even as he sat in prison, awaiting his execution, Socrates conversed with his friends, cracked deadpan jokes, and engaged in philosophy, as he did every other day. When his friend Crito enters the prison cell, bearing the supposedly terrible news that "the ship from Delos has come in," meaning that the festival to Apollo is over and that Socrates will be executed at sundown, Socrates responds with a refutation that, in his characteristic way, is at once mysterious, amusing, and moving. He reports to Crito that he has just awoken from a dream in which a beautiful woman dressed in white robes came to him and said, "Socrates, on the *third* day to the land of Pthia you shall arrive."[9] The land of Pthia is the homeland of Achilles, and arriving at Pthia implies going to the afterlife. On the basis of the words of the mysterious woman, Socrates shrugs off the report from Crito, which comes directly from the messengers who have seen the ship come in. Even in a moment of apparent powerlessness and impending doom, Socrates has the wit to subtly imply that he answers to a higher authority than the human messengers. Whereas Crito's report represents the conventions of the city, the woman dressed in white, we may suppose, represents philosophy.

As constituted by the activity of throwing the golden ball, life does not come to a halt with the demise of the body or the extinction of consciousness: The activity of throwing persists among friends. The friends to whom Zarathustra refers are "those who hope and promise," not only the ones who might directly witness his death, or who know him firsthand, but friends of the future too, all those who, in their own ways, will embark upon his project, whether or not they know it as belonging to a man named Zarathustra.

Our relation to Socrates, or to any figure of the past in whom we find inspiration, illustrates Nietzsche's point: As we recognize in Socrates a model for how to live and make an attempt to realize the examined life as he did, we receive his "throw" and pass his golden ball in our own action.

Critique of the Self as "Subject" and the World as "Object": Implications for Life and Death

We may be inclined to regard the Socrates who lives through us a merely metaphorical Socrates, distorted by our hands, no longer able to speak for himself and question whatever interpretation we might read into him. We may be disposed to wonder whether, in turning to Socrates for guidance, we are really doing as *he* would do or whether we are using him to validate a course of action that he would have rejected had he actually been "here" to speak to us face-to-face. But such skepticism mistakenly assumes a wooden Socrates whose identity was sufficiently fixed and sculpted back in

399 BC (the year he was executed) so as to delimit an utterly self-contained, fully formed individual, the subjective opinions and dispositions of whom we can only guess at in hindsight. But such a distinction between the "real" Socrates and the one we interpret is a bias of a modern understanding of the self that Socrates himself would have rejected.

Socrates regarded himself not as an isolated individual with his own private thoughts and feelings but as an active philosophical adventurer whose identity found expression and definition in dialogue with others. He lived his life with an abiding orientation to ideas accessible to any person who cared to think them through. For as long as he lived back in ancient Athens, Socrates brought to manifestation who he was in questioning others and in following the inner logic of the ideas he unfolded in partnership with them.

The active, dialogical conception of the self that Socrates presents in his words and deeds is easily obscured by the contemporary predominance of the distinction between subject and object, according to which the self is first and foremost a private sphere of consciousness capable of accessing the "external world" only through subjective representations (perceptions, ideas) that may not align with things as they really are. To establish community with the world requires aligning our subjective representations with reality, thus attaining "objectivity," or perceiving the object correctly. We imply such a subject-object distinction whether we interpret the way in which things might not be as they seem in terms of a potential "subjective delusion," or hallucination, and not what is "really there in the world." This subject-object conception of the self underlies the dramatic conceits of popular films such as *The Matrix*, *The Truman Show*, and *Inception*, all of which play with the possibility that our consciousness of what we take to be real may be utterly mistaken, or that we may be dreaming when we take ourselves to be awake. The implication is that we may have no rapport

with reality until we have undergone a long, self-reflective process
of overcoming delusion.

Such an understanding of the self could only become possible
on the basis of an abstraction from an engaged and committed relation to things in the mode of dealing with them, caring for them,
responding to their promptings, and drawing lessons from them for
how to live. To an adventurer who approaches life as a journey of
self-discovery, there is no such thing as an "apparent world" apart
from a real world. For the appearance of things presents itself to
be discerned and interpreted in the quest for self-knowledge and
thus belongs to the things themselves. A tree that bends in the wind
is an exemplar of resistance and self-possession. A soaring flock of
birds, a sign of freedom. From this perspective, the question of
whether the tree or the flock of birds is real or illusory is senseless
and irrelevant. It doesn't even arise. Equally irrelevant is the question of whether one is awake or asleep. For an insight or a source
of inspiration is the same whether discovered in a dream or in "real"
life. As Nietzsche puts it: "What we experience in a dream, provided
we experience it frequently, finally is as much a part of the collec-
tive household of our souls as anything 'truly' experienced. Thanks
to this, we are richer or poorer, have one more need or one less,
and finally in the bright light of day and even in the happiest moments of our waking spirit we are ordered around a little by the
habits of our dreams."[10]

Even phenomena that, from a subject-object perspective, we are
inclined to regard as illusions are, from the perspective of the quest
for self-knowledge, things in their own right. Consider the experience of driving on a hot afternoon and seeing before you what looks
to be a puddle in the middle of the road only to soon confirm, upon
your approach, that your eyes deceived you and that what you
thought you saw was simply the mirage of a puddle generated (so
science teaches us) by heat rising from the pavement. Schooled as
we are in viewing things as objects that may be obscured by our

faulty subjective disposition (our perception from afar or from the wrong angle, the weakness of our sight, conditions such as color-blindness, hallucination, and so on) we fail to consider the meaning and sense of things as they first appear, even after we have confirmed their so-called nonexistence. We fail to adequately reflect on the fact that water can appear in the first place as even potentially on the road only because it bears a certain meaning, which, in this context, might be described in relation to a road that can be wet and therefore risky to drive upon, at least if one hits the brakes hard. The experience of first seeing water and then realizing it isn't there is not, for the concerned driver, primarily that of an illusion dispelled but that of a way of adapting to the road—first proceeding with caution, then going ahead. The illusion, so to speak, belongs just as much to the total understanding of the situation, expressed in the way one steers the car, as the "real" state of affair. Or, from a more poetical perspective, the experience has nothing to do with illusion at all but is, quite literally, that of water withdrawing and evaporating before one's very eyes, an expression of the dashed hopes of the one "hiking through the desert" (metaphorically speaking). The idea that the world presents a field of things that we can come to know "objectively," in the sense of liberated from our subjective bias, overlooks the prior relationship, and inextricable connection, of self and world that characterizes life as a journey.

But even the foremost theorist of the modern subject-object worldview, René Descartes, who famously proposed that everything we see and touch might be the phantom of our own mind, implanted in us by an evil demon and corresponding to nothing real, gestured toward something "Socratic" in his conception of the subject. For Descartes, the activity of thinking, the paradigm of which, on his view, is the contemplation of geometrical relations, points to a self defined in what we might call a certain community with others, thus beyond the merely subjective. In considering the same geometric relations (for example, the side length necessary to create a square with double the area of a given square) and coming to the same conclusion by the necessity of our own reason (that the line we seek is the diagonal of the given square) we relate ourselves to a truth that is common to us all and not peculiar to the idiosyncratic subjective sphere that each of us (by Descartes's account) is. In thinking the same thought, we are in community with one another, defined, in the moment of relating to the geometrical insight, by an idea that we all possess, an idea that reaches beyond whatever subjective viewpoint we may have and that connects us to something with its own structure and integrity, which, unlike things of the bodily world or psychical domain, is invulnerable to decay in time.

Socrates himself would often draw on geometrical examples to illustrate what is common to the soul in each of us and connects us to an order of things beyond the visible-tangible realm. What distinguishes his view, however, from what would be Descartes's position is his far more expansive conception of what is common to us all. For the contemplation of *moral* conceptions and relations ("values" as we might say today) also, according to Socrates, cannot be reduced to the merely subjective or conventional. The statement, for example, that "justice is giving to each his due" would seem no less certain, Socrates alerts us, than the statement "two plus two is four." Though we might disagree on the precise meaning of justice, and thus appear to have two "subjective opinions" in conflict, our disagreement, Socrates shows, arises from our catching different aspects of the same thing. Our disagreements, in other words, are always on the basis of a common ground—for example, that justice is a virtue, that it is to be distinguished from injustice, that it involves the proper distribution of things, and so on. In the heat of dispute over divergent conceptions, we miss the overwhelming agreement that makes all divergence possible. The contestable opinions of right and wrong that we are inclined to regard as merely subjective, such as "might makes right," or justice is "paying one's debts," are really matters of interpretation to be developed and clarified through dialogue. And by engaging in dialogue, with friends, or within ourselves, we participate in an activity that transcends the bounds of our consciousness and the limits of embodied existence.

The flip side to Socrates's expansion of what we might call a community of understanding to the moral sphere was his critical assessment of the kind of truth at issue in mathematics. Whereas today we tend to regard mathematics as dealing with formal relations among abstract entities (numbers, lines, figures), and as arriving at truths that are always and everywhere the same, Socrates suggests that mathematics is both far more concrete and open to interpretation than we might think. Socrates would demonstrate to his interlocutors that the supposedly fixed and self-evident truths of mathematics are, on examination, open to question just as ethical matters. Socrates was in the habit of pointing out that even the most basic arithmetic equations, such as "one plus one is two," imply profound questions, which, earnestly pursued, even lead in the direction of articulating a conception of the good.[11] For example, can the "two" that we supposedly perceive so clearly and distinctly in the statement "one plus one is two" really be derived from taking two separate units together? Is "two" really reducible to one, here, another there, thus two? Is two a quantity of units? Or does "two" have its own special integrity as a unity unto itself, a term that cannot be reduced to "one plus one." For "two" can be taken as "the first even number" and as "the first prime number." But evenness and primeness cannot be ascribed to either of the units that comprise the number two. We grasp the evenness and the primeness of the number "two" only by understanding "two" within a series of numbers, which can be grouped in infinite, creative ways. Thus the "two" itself, which can be taken as a whole irreducible to the sum of its units, can be seen to partake of the greater whole of the series of numbers. But this series has the mysterious character of being an open-ended whole, open-ended in proportion to the interpretive creativity of the mathematician.

Whether "one plus one equals two" is far more questionable than first appears. It may seem perfectly clear only because we have already decided, to the exclusion of other possibilities, what "two" will mean—namely, one unit here, another there, indifferently thrown together as a quantity. If we take a broader perspective on the meaning of "two," considering its being even and prime alongside other numbers in a series, we are led, ultimately, to the problem of the "one and the many" as such, which can be adequately handled only in the broader horizon of the way of life in which mathematics figures as a field of study. Only when we grasp the idea of an articulated whole of relations, at once bounded (by a certain lived understanding of the good) and infinite in the ways it might be developed, do we arrive at the sense of "a series delimited in various ways yet infinite in scope." The mathematical and the moral thus converge as matters for interpretation to be clarified through dialogue. As such, they transcend the subjective consciousness, offering themselves to be thought through at any time and place.

As we attempt to reach clarity on such matters through dialogue, we develop, at the same time, an understanding of self. For the self is inseparable from the virtues for which it strives. Socrates suggests that at every moment of life, one's identity is defined not by the fixed bounds of a subjective consciousness but by the openness and closure of a question, the orientation to shared activities, and the strength of taking a stand.

It was for this reason that Socrates didn't write books. He believed that to put one's thoughts on the page was to give them a certain finality and authority that undermined their very significance as invitations for discussion.[12] The point of voicing a thought, or an opinion, according to Socrates, was not to present some aspect of one's identity to be recorded and stored away as a piece of data on the views of a unique subject. Nor was it to assert a truth that others could take up and store in their warehouse of knowledge. It was rather to open one's self to question, dispute, and the possibility of newfound common ground.

To live, Socrates suggests, is not simply to stake out an identity but to confront one's own being as a question. Or, what it means to stake out an identity is not simply to construct a self-image out of various views, opinions, mannerisms, and tropes, but to develop a character to test.

Plato's solution to the deficiency of the written word, and the necessarily wooden form of the self to which it gives rise, was to write dialogues. By putting ideas in the words of others, and bringing them to light through dialogues, Plato guarded against the facility of ascribing to him any particular view. Whenever we say, "Plato said this or thought that," what we really mean is that "out of the dialogues that Plato portrays between Socrates and his interlocutors, we can *infer* that he must have identified with this or that." We can infer only on the basis of joining the dialogue ourselves, considering the questions that Socrates raises, and coming to our own best understandings of justice, virtue, and the good life. Plato allows us access to himself only insofar as we look into ourselves and make him our own. Through the dialogical form of his writings, Plato takes all precaution to ensure that we take him not as a peculiar subject with ideas we might like or dislike but as a way of being that works its power on us.

Plato thus conveys the Socratic insight that we are perpetually in the process of coming into ourselves in partnership with others—whether they are friends with whom we speak face-to-face, thinkers of old with whom we converse through books, or anonymous voices that debate silently within us as we consider different courses of action in key moments. Because life in every moment is defined by questioning, movement, and the possibility of transformation, it makes little sense to draw a sharp distinction between life while directly manifest on earth and life after death, in the hands of devoted interpreters. It could even be said that one comes into one's own only in the hands of others. For what one means to express and to make clear to one's self (in words and deeds) may find new and unforeseen elaboration in the words and deeds of future generations.

In all interpretation, whether of a life, a novel, or an event, there is the risk of imposing a meaning improper to what we interpret. But we must consider whether this risk is any greater when a devoted friend or admirer interprets one's life and attempts to carry it on in their own action than when one does so "for himself." For the one who interprets his own life, even in a moment of thoughtful repose, is still a limited consciousness that speaks from the perspective of a particular moment and situation.

As long as the story of Socrates disrupts our complacency in common opinion, checks our indignation in the face of opposing views, and elicits our inquisitive charity, it exerts its own force on us. And as we react by initiating a dialogue within and among ourselves, we breathe new life into Socrates. Through such a reciprocal play of forces, the identity and difference of our lives and Socrates's emerges. The sense in which Socrates, even in our hands, maintains his own distinctive character is itself open to clarification as we live by his example and draw comparisons between his actions and our own. The same is true of any person who leaves a mark on us: We can in principle arrive at a deeper awareness of that person's life and attain a closer proximity to it long after that person is no longer directly manifest on earth.

The Eternity of the Active Self in Terms of the Gift-Giving Virtue

Immediately following his teaching on "free death," Nietzsche's Zarathustra offers another speech, on what he calls "the gift-giving virtue." The two speeches are clearly meant as a pair, connected by the theme of sacrifice. To die freely for one's "goal and heir" can be conceived as an act of sacrifice, the ultimate gift. But sacrifice, as Nietzsche presents it, is not self-negation for the sake of another. It is rather a mode of sharing in which self and other are absorbed in the same "play of catch" (recall the golden ball), as when Socrates offers philosophy for his students to take up and is willing to be executed in its pursuit. In other words, that for which, or for whom, the sacrifice is made cannot be separated from the one who makes the sacrifice. Through the sacrifice, the self comes into its own as a force that reaches beyond itself and cannot, therefore, be identified with a being who is present at this or that moment. In dying a free death, I simply let myself be absorbed in the activity that has always defined me, free of distraction, free of fear. The gift, or sacrifice, at issue is not something I lose or give away; it is rather what I offer to be enriched by those who receive it.

What characterizes a free *death,* that is, a free throwing of one's golden ball even onto one's bodily demise, that it may continue to be thrown "among friends," Zarathustra now, in his discussion of the gift-giving virtue, takes up with respect to *every moment of life* and not simply to the one we superficially call "the last." The gift-giving virtue is a way of presenting the sense in which we are never simply present and identical with ourselves but always, at all times, "with" ourselves and "outside" of ourselves at once—in the mode of self-presentation, or self-offering rather than self-consciousness.

Nietzsche introduces the gift-giving virtue not in a speech of Zarathustra but in an act of gift-giving between Zarathustra and his disciples. As Zarathustra is leaving the town to which his heart is attached, his disciples present him with a gift: a staff with a golden handle, shaped in the image of a serpent coiled around the sun. Instead of simply giving thanks to his friends and going on his way, Zarathustra offers a gift in return, what turns out to be more than what he receives: He offers a tribute to the gift-giving virtue itself. Upon receiving the staff, leaning on it, and surveying its golden splendor, he responds with a reflection on the value of gold, which we began to examine in Chapter 4: "Tell me, how did gold attain the highest value? Because it is uncommon and useless and gleaming and gentle in its splendor; it always gives itself. Only as the image of the highest virtue did gold attain the highest value. Goldlike gleam the eyes of the giver. Golden splendor makes peace between moon and sun . . . The gift-giving virtue is the highest virtue."[13]

In likening the gift-giving virtue to gold, Zarathustra introduces the sense in which the self, conceived as gift-giver, exceeds its presence at any given time and place. Like gold, the gift-giving virtue is uncommon. It gets constrained and limited by our striving for accomplishment and acclaim. In our obsession with getting things done, scoring points, advancing our careers, or making the world a better place, we become stingy to others, whom we come to see as distractions, or rivals. We say, colloquially, that our self-centeredness crowds out our generosity. Focused on ourselves, we neglect others. We offer them only so much as will win a favor in return. But self-centeredness is an imprecise account of the relevant vice. For the gift-giving self is, in its own way, self-centered, grounded in itself, and at one with itself. At issue is not self-service versus charity but the very meaning of the self. The gift-giving self comes into its own, and thus attains its centeredness, through the act of giving, as Socrates comes into his own through the questions he asks of his friends and the responses he inspires. The opposite of gift-giving is not self-focus, or self-service, but self-loss: a certain objectification of the self whereby the self becomes consumed by a particular end and diverted from the journey of life in which ends appear in the first place. Thus, in failing to live up to the gift-giving virtue, we are stingy not simply to others but to ourselves. We deplete ourselves in service of a goal to be over and done with rather than enrich ourselves in the manner of its pursuit. In doing so, we lose the spirit of play within ourselves, the spirit that revels in making an attempt and opening a horizon of unforeseeable possibilities.

Predominant though such vice may be, it is never all-consuming. Just as gold lies buried in the earth beneath layers of dirt and rock so the gift-giving virtue lies dormant beneath our goal-oriented striving. Deep down, we know that what is essential and lasting in us is the ability to bestow a gift, even as we remain fixated on getting things done. All instances of stinginess are fallings away from the gift-giving virtue, which remains latent "within the soul." As Zarathustra says in another passage, "The heart of the earth is gold."[14]

Another way of stating the rarity of gift-giving is in terms of its uselessness. Much of the time, our lives are oriented to what is useful for some purpose. To offer a genuine gift is to transcend the goal-oriented perspective from which every act of giving is for the sake of some end, and to offer something that is intrinsically valuable, like gold. To the extent that gold is useful for something else, exchangeable, it has lost its radiance and is no longer itself. The greatest gift is not useful for achieving this or that goal. It is rather a model for how to be in everything one attempts.

Such gifts are, furthermore, "gleaming and gentle" in their splendor. Like gold, which, wherever we find it, shines forth by allowing something else to appear, the gift of an act of self-possession or friendship radiates in a way that allows others to come into their own.

As useless, gleaming, and gentle, the gift-giving virtue is the giving of *one's self,* not of something extrinsic, such as money, a material possession, or a piece of technical knowledge, which, as something that can be instantly taken up and traded away by anyone else, is "one's own" only contingently and temporarily. Unlike the offering of something merely useful and tradeable, which leaves one with a little less resource and must therefore be carefully calculated so as not to deplete one's store, the giving of one's self is without reservation. In such giving, one needn't keep anything for himself, just as in shining, gold needn't keep any of its radiance.

Zarathustra's characteristic way of expressing the radiant, ec-
static nature of the gift-giving self is by comparison to sunlight:
"Golden splendor makes peace between moon and sun." It may
seem as though moon and sun are opposites: One the leader of the
day, the other of the night. But Zarathustra reminds us that both
are bound together in peace, as giver of light and as recipient. The
sun gives itself to the moon, allowing the moon to appear. But only
in giving itself to the moon can the sun continue to shine after setting. The moon as recipient of sunlight turns out to be the giver as
well: It lets the sun shine throughout the night. The sun is thus enhanced rather than diminished in giving its light to the moon. It
loses nothing of its radiance, which will shine forth again the next
morning. In the meantime, in partnership with the moon, the sun
continues to be itself even while receding from direct manifestation.
So too, Zarathustra implies, the life that has departed from earth:
It continues to be itself through those who catch its golden ball and
continue to throw it among themselves.

Live in such a way that you offer yourself as a gift—"become
sacrifices and gifts yourselves" is what Zarathustra teaches his
friends.[15] In every step of life, be an example in being yourself. Hand
yourself down—not just a piece of yourself, not just this or that skill
or resource, but the way of being that animates your life.

We sometimes speak pejoratively of those who live as if they
were "God's gift to the earth." But Nietzsche draws a sharp distinction between the true gift-givers and the pretenders. The latter
simply want copies of themselves everywhere, acolytes to whom
they can lay claim. Or they want to be recognized and remembered
as unique individuals who benefited humankind in this or that way.
In these cases, the gift-giver offers a static, sham version of the self,
a self-satisfied persona who takes their identity to be defined by
some accomplishment or state of the world to which they contributed. The true gift-givers, teaches Zarathustra, do not want to be

worshipped or remembered. For they understand their own being as a question as much as an answer. When Zarathustra's friends call themselves his disciples, Zarathustra, with a heavy heart, renounces them: "You say you believe in Zarathustra? But what matters Zarathustra? You are my believers—but what matters all believers? You had not yet sought yourselves: and you found me . . . Now I bid you lose me and find yourselves; and only when you have all denied me will I return to you."[16]

Zarathustra does not want believers who simply take his teachings as dogma, bandy them about, and report to others about their acquaintance with a marvelous man named Zarathustra who said many wise things. What Zarathustra wants are genuine friends, those who will take up his project for themselves in their own ways, in relation to their own commitments and futures. Only in such hands can the force of Zarathustra's life persist when he is no longer on earth. For as long as Zarathustra lived, he did so for his own future, discovering himself anew in each of his wanderings. So long as his friends simply revere him as a founder and mimic in an external way his words and deeds, Zarathustra will sink into oblivion: "You revere me; but what if your reverence tumbles one day? Beware lest a statue slay you."[17] Zarathustra cares nothing for graven images of himself or documents of his teachings. He wants only to persist as the anonymous, self-searching force that has defined his life on earth.

Zarathustra's metaphor of sun and moon implies a certain continuity between day and night, life and death. To elaborate this continuity, we must consider whether the sun's appearance as reflected in the moon is a special condition, pertaining only to the night, when the sun has receded, or whether it refers to something essential about the sun whenever and wherever it shines. We must ask, in short, whether the sun at high noon, or at any time of the day, is directly manifest or whether it remains, in a sense, withdrawn.

As a clue, we might consider the opening lines of *Thus Spoke Zarathustra*, in which Zarathustra steps out of his cave in the mountains and offers praise to the sun: "You great star, what would your happiness be had you not those for whom you shine? For ten years you have climbed to my cave. You would have tired of your light and of the journey had it not been for me and my eagle and my serpent. But we waited for you every morning, took your overflow from you, and blessed you for it."[18] Zarathustra's praise of the sun foretells his praise of the gift-giving virtue. Even though he has not yet spoken of it, the young Zarathustra (here forty years old) has an intimation of the gift-giving virtue as he beholds the dawn. But here we have an image of the sun at daybreak, when the sun itself appears in the sky and is not merely reflected in the moon. And, yet, the sun's "happiness," its overflowing joy as manifest in radiance, requires those on whom it shines—Zarathustra and his eagle and serpent. Even at dawn, Zarathustra suggests, the sun is not directly manifest. It comes into its own only through those who accept its overflow and offer a blessing in return. Zarathustra's blessing takes the form of not only gratitude but resolve. He will descend to man to share his wisdom: "Behold, I am weary of my wisdom, like a bee that has gathered too much honey; I need hands outstretched to receive it."[19] Zarathustra takes the sun's offering and accepts it as inspiration for his calling as a teacher. Through Zarathustra's exercise of that calling, the gift-giving resplendence of the sun animates the world anew.

Much later in *Thus Spoke Zarathustra*, after Zarathustra has offered his account of the gift-giving virtue, he presents another image of the daytime sun—now at sunset—as an emblem of gift-giving: "From the sun I learned this: when it goes down overrich, it pours gold into the sea out of inexhaustible riches, so that even the poorest fisherman rows with golden oars."[20] It is only in casting gold upon everything in its midst that the sun comes into its own as that which shines. But this means that even at daytime the sun transcends what is directly present. The golden ball that gradually disappears beneath the horizon is not the sun itself, but rather a manifestation of radiance no less shimmering and golden than everything that appears in its light. The sun itself, pure radiance, cannot be seen directly. Or wherever it comes to presence, it points beyond itself.

The paradox of a luminous presence that is always more than its appearance is the key to understating the self while "present on earth." And only in understanding this self can we understand the self "after death." We must therefore interpret the paradox of the sun closely. It is true that we can, in a sense, see the sun in luminous clarity during the day, if only for a few seconds, as we look up at the golden ball that radiates in overwhelming brightness against the sky. The paradox, however, is that the more brilliantly the sun radiates, the more it loses its definition, withdraws from direct manifestation, and becomes a blinding outpour. Its brilliance can appear only in what it makes visible, in the relation, for example, of land, sea, and sky. Whenever the sun appears as a golden ball, it is against a sky and above the earth, part of a connected variety of things, of a world, made possible by light. The sun, conceived as radiance, makes possible its own appearance as a thing among others and is thus more than anything that appears. Or, if we start with the appearances, we must admit that the beauty and definition of all things that shine point to a source that makes possible all definition and cannot itself take the form of a particular thing or arrangement. On the basis of what can be seen, we must infer a luminous realm in which they stand.

That luminous realm, radiance itself, cannot be pieced together from a successive inspection of particular appearances—the shimmering waves here, the rainbow on the horizon there. For all of these things, to even be seen together and compared, must stand in the light. Though each appearance can, in a sense, be regarded as a particular manifestation of the one radiance, such a relation cannot be captured in the familiar scheme of species and genus. It is not a conceptual relation, where the "one" that unifies a "many" is the same in each member. For example, in the relation of the concept of a "tree" to particular trees, the content of the unity, "having a trunk and branches," is identical in each case. Each tree conforms to "having a trunk and branches" and is thus a tree. By contrast, in the relation of radiance to what appears, the manifestation of radiance is *in each case its own*. The only thing, so to speak, that sea and sky share is that they shine. But in shining they belong together not as instances of some higher, more general concept "radiance," but as parts that need each other to be what they are, as parts of an articulated whole.

Just as the sun is the background light to everything that can be seen, and cannot be reduced to anything it allows to appear, so too is the self—the active, gift-giving self—in relation to its various perceptions and thoughts.

Everything that I perceive of myself and of the world is made possible by an active force—a simultaneous closure and openness of meaning expressed in my commitments—which, by its very nature as excess and becoming, I can never see directly or get entirely into my conceptual grasp. The face that I see in the mirror, for example, as I take stock of myself before a competition or big event, the thoughts of success and failure that pass through my mind, the feelings that lodge themselves in my throat or sit at the bottom of my stomach, are not really me or mine. Or, rather, they are mine only because I have turned myself into an object to be observed, analyzed, and compared to former states of myself, or to others against whom I might compete. More properly my own than any of the things I perceive is the possibility of perception itself, which depends upon the stance I take on the meaning of my life as a whole. Only because I already understand myself in what I do and because what I do is never simply "this here and now" but a reaching out into a web of relations and commitments, can I encounter "myself" as someone occupied with this particular thing and conceive of the thing as an object of success or failure and an occasion to take stock in my abilities.

My life in action—a reaching beyond itself that is at the same time a coming into itself—is the condition for everything I might perceive, including the things that can be seen to come and go "in time." To think of my life itself as something that comes and goes is to mistake the condition and source of perception for a phenomenon it makes possible.

The Circular Trajectory of Activity for the Sake of Itself

At the beginning of Nietzsche's *Zarathustra,* a brief but significant episode foreshadows and encapsulates his teaching on time. It is high noon, when the sun is at its peak. Zarathustra suddenly hears the sharp call of an eagle and looks into the air to behold a strange and miraculous sight: "An eagle soared through the sky in wide circles, and on him there hung a serpent, not like prey but like a friend: for she kept herself wound around his neck. 'These are my animals,' said Zarathustra . . . 'the proudest animal under the sun and the wisest animal under the sun . . . May my animals lead me.'"[21] From then on, the animals accompany him throughout his journey. In the broad circular flight of the eagle with his friend, the serpent, coiled around him, Nietzsche presents the trajectory of the self-possessed life: Throughout its far-ranging journeys, a life guided by the union of pride and wisdom circles back to its point of origin, each time from a higher vantage point, just as a soaring eagle circles upward, ascending toward the sun at high noon.

The image of circular ascension is meant to express the self-sufficiency of activity for the sake of itself: The eagle and serpent aim for no destination outside their flight; so they circle upward taking joy in each turn, expecting nothing but the circling itself.

The eagle and serpent represent the integrity for which Zarathustra aspires and later brings to expression in the midst of his lonely wanderings:

> Now as Zarathustra was climbing the mountain he thought
> how often since his youth he had wandered alone and how
> many mountains and ridges and peaks he had already
> climbed. I am a wanderer and a mountain climber, he said
> to his heart; I do not like the plains, and it seems I cannot
> sit still for long. And whatever may yet come to me as des-
> tiny and experience will include some wandering and
> mountain climbing: in the end, one experiences only one-
> self. The time is gone when mere accidents could still
> happen to me; and what could still come to me now that
> was not mine already? What returns, what finally comes
> home to me, is my own self and what of myself has long
> been in strange lands and scattered among all things and
> accidents.[22]

As we consider the phrase "only one's self," we must hold at bay the sense of isolation that the phrase appears to suggest. The self is the wanderer, the person defined by the journey who is never first an isolated individual but always a being who pervades "strange lands" and is "scattered among all things and accidents." So under-stood, the self comes into its own by understanding these lands and adventures as connected and as forming a single destiny. "Only one's self" means "nothing accidental." Throughout every new encounter—sudden, unexpected, terrible, an accident—Zarathustra returns to himself, just as the eagle and serpent return and circle back to their point of origin from a new and higher perspective.

Of course this is an ideal as much as a reality. There is something both natural and extraordinary in the effortless flight of the eagle and serpent. Nietzsche plays on our sense that these animals are typically opposed: Eagles swoop down from above to prey on serpents slithering below; serpents stealthily infiltrate eagle nests and devour their eggs. If ever we were to behold an eagle and serpent together in the sky, we would expect to find the serpent writhing desperately in the eagle's talons. When pride and wisdom part ways, Nietzsche suggests, they degenerate into thoughtless arrogance and life-sapping rationality: Our arrogance, with the sharp talons of an eagle, threatens to pierce and puncture our wisdom, as when we take ourselves to be all-powerful in virtue of some particular competence or skill and view the whole world from a little nook that we mistake for *the* perspective, or when we look upon the universe as but resource for our creative power, overlooking the significance of things already manifest in light of which our creative impulse would find direction.

Our rationality, with the constricting coils of a serpent, can also smother our pride, as when we self-consciously scrutinize our abilities and strengths in comparison to others, and define our worth in terms of relative accomplishment. What we ought to enjoy for its own sake, for the difference it makes in our life, becomes a means to an end.

Mired in the dissatisfaction into which goal-oriented striving always ultimately plunges us, we might be tempted to another form of rationality without pride: the attempted escape from comparison and competition that consists in examining ourselves scientifically, from afar, as if we were amoeba under a microscope, our movements but responses to the environment in which we find ourselves. Such rationality is comforting in that it seems to liberate us from the zero-sum striving that makes life so petty, providing us instead an objective perspective on things from which all pride is pointless. Thomas Hobbes's notion that the universe is nothing but matter in motion, a meaningless cycle of combination and dissolution, is one example of such a rationality at work. Hobbes promoted it with the explicit purpose of smothering our pride.

These are the ways in which pride and wisdom part ways, degenerate, and oppose each other. But they ultimately belong together. Their various modes of opposition are fallings out, not irreconcilable conflicts. Even the most domineering arrogance cannot entirely escape the sense that there is more to life than achievements, no matter how grand. The very desire to be recognized for one's dominance suggests, as we have seen, a longing for friendship. And even the coldest, most objectifying analysis of the world cannot quite extinguish the beauty and sublimity of nature that breaks into everyday life, arouses our wonder, and inspires us to self-possession.

Whether pride and wisdom remain bound in mutual strength, or part ways and degenerate, is decided by the way in which we respond to suffering: In the face of disappointment or misfortune do we give up on our vocations and commitments, conceiving the world as a pitiable battlefield of accidents to be accepted with resignation? Do we become arrogant birds of prey who resentfully look down on the world from on high and seek to dominate everything that scurries below? Or do we rise to the challenge of being ourselves anew, of circling back to ourselves from opposition and rising to further heights of self-possession?

The Passage of Time and the Deeper Meaning of Death

The ultimate source of suffering, teaches Nietzsche, is the passage of time—and not simply that such passage carries us and the ones we love to old age and death, conceived as the demise of the body or the extinction of consciousness. The passage of time that Nietzsche envisions is deeper, more pervasive. It has to do with facing a past—a dimension of ourselves that is still "here" but in the paradoxical and painful sense of what once was but now is not. The passage of time, according to Nietzsche, points to the sense in which our deeds, on the one hand, cannot be undone, and, on the other, cannot be relived. The passage of time has to do with the missteps that perpetually haunt us and the shimmering moments that fade away. Only by confronting this passage can we approach the deeper meaning of death.

Think back to a moment in your life at which you leapt for joy or faced a seemingly insurmountable hardship and overcame it. At the time, it was fresh and full of life, a focal point of the paths and commitments that defined who you were and aspired to be. Now it lies in your past. It hasn't flown away into oblivion; you can remember it and recount it to yourself and your friends. You can look back on it with a nostalgic smile. But you can't bring it back—at least not as it once was. That's what Nietzsche means by the passage of time: the sense in which events and moments "become past." It's not that they are extinguished or no longer the focal point of attention. Quite the opposite, they remain abidingly with us, but in the mode of what *was* and will never again be.

The passage of time characterizes the very structure of a journey: the way in which the next episode doesn't simply follow from the previous, but intervenes to recast its meaning. Imagine an artist in the midst of painting an infinite mural, striving for a beautiful, well-arranged image, but unable to efface any stroke of the brush. Every stroke carries consequences for the next, which, in turn, will recast what came before. Imagine this process with no beginning or end, no aim but to keep itself going and to be faithful to the image as a whole. Every mistake carries consequences that threaten to reach far and to discourage the artist from forging ahead. Every success, thrilling and inspirational in the moment, gradually loses its charm and recedes into the background as new strokes, new concerns, and new points of focus take center stage. Life itself presents something like this fundamental problem—that of eternal becoming and passing away.

How foolish our contemporary life-extension craze appears when we see the problem of death in this perspective. The problem is not, as the Stoics teach, that whatever extension of life we may achieve is puny by comparison to infinite time. The real issue is that the very meaning of time and death with which we must come to terms gets entirely passed over by the life-extension enthusiasts. What we fear in death is not simply the extinction of the body or of consciousness, which might somehow be postponed, but the sense in which the meaning and significance of things is slipping away and in need of being redeemed. But such loss is something we face at every moment, as the present is always becoming the past. Understood in terms of the passage of time, death is hardly something we could eradicate from our condition through medical intervention and biological technology. The more we busy ourselves with extending the measurable interval in which we persist in any which way, the more we distract ourselves from the fundamental task of coming to terms with the passage of time that we face in every moment.

This is what Zarathustra sets as his greatest project: "And this is all my creating and striving, that I create and carry together into One what is fragment and riddle and dreadful accident. And how could I bear to be a man if man were not also a creator and guesser of riddles and redeemer of accidents? . . . To redeem those who lived in the past and to recreate all 'it was' into 'thus I willed it'— that alone should I call redemption."[23]

We can't step out of the passage of time. We can't relive things as they once were. And, yet, as the eagle and serpent suggest in their circular ascent, we can redeem the past. We can return to it from a new and higher perspective. We can redeem the past because it is our own. It is our own action and creative power and orientation to the future that push moments behind us. Only because our lives do not move indifferently from one moment to the next but have a trajectory do we face the ultimate hardship of the passage of time. The strange paradox of life is that in facing challenges and coming into our own, we lose ourselves as well. Because we are responsible for that loss, we can redeem it.

Redeeming the Past

To remember, record, and recount is a first step toward redeeming the past, which too often we neglect in our abiding focus on what lies ahead. So much of the time, we find ourselves thinking ahead to the next step as compared to remembering people and events of old. It's worth asking yourself: In the thoughts that occupied my attention today, and in the conversations I had, how much of it was focused on how to deal with some upcoming event, and how much on how to make sense of what happened some time ago? When we do think of the past, it's often in the mode of fleeting and superficial nostalgia: We remember the past in terms of absence or loss, a grandmother or parent who is no longer with us, whose warm embrace we will never again feel. But rarely do we make an effort to recall the events and occasions we miss, to re-create them as they bear upon the character or essence of the life on which we reflect. The predominance we accord to the goal-oriented future suggests the need to find time for remembrance rather than striving. But as much as we might make a conscious effort to do so, we can at most prepare ourselves for the ultimate task: to seize upon the past as inspiration and insight for what may come.

I sometimes reflect how, with age, I've lost the carefree exuberance of earlier days. Today, I'm more cautious with my yesses and nos—both in the practice of philosophy and in the activity of training, in the way I select words as I write, and in the way I plan sets and execute reps as I work out. While such caution comes with maturity, it also threatens to shackle the spirit of adventure that says "make an attempt and worry about the fine points later." I think back wistfully to my early days of graduate school when I'd spray words like birdshot onto the page, unconcerned with what readers would think. I also remember my training attitude back in college, epitomized in a memorable single-rep power-clean, a lift that I still regard as one of my greatest triumphs, even though no one but my training partner was there to see it. It was at the end of a long day of summer work and my friend, who had preceded me to the gym, had just narrowly missed a power-clean attempt at 225 lbs. Seeing him frustrated by a weight that he'd lifted many times before, I brazenly approached the bar with a falsely confident "let me show you how it's done!" Without hesitation, I grabbed it with both hands, exploded upward, and hoisted it to my shoulders. I held it for a second to punctuate the completed lift, then dropped it to the ground with authority. The display, to which I gave scarcely a moment's thought in advance, and could have easily gone wrong, had its intended effect. My friend shook off his inexplicable hang-up and we carried each other through one of the most memorable workouts of the summer.

But that was then, not now. As much as I might like to relive that moment, it won't happen again. It's not that there's any natural or physical barrier to my attempting a reenactment of that lift. I could return to the same gym with my friend and power-clean the same weight with no warmup. But the experience wouldn't be the same. Even if I were to succeed in hoisting the 225 lbs. and replicate the event in some general and abstract way, the event would lack the meaning it once did. It would be devoid of the anticipation and thrill of the original moment.

Furthermore, my caution of today would intervene from the start and impose itself on the experience. And that caution is certainly not a mere loss. The reason I can't go back to the old days is that I can't unlearn what I know to be a more experienced, informed perspective—that a warmup is advisable, even crucial for a good workout.

At the same time, I recognize that my maturity has come at a price, at least at times, when the caution of adult life (whatever "adult" might mean) thwarts the youthful willingness to respond to the unbidden and to break the rules to which I've held myself. I'm thinking of obsessive adherence to a training plan that dictates a certain number of reps or miles per workout, even when a second

wind or sudden burst of inspiration suggests I could do more. Instead of stepping into a potential breakthrough moment, I save the
extra reps, or the extra mile, for the next time. Because that's what
my program tells me to do. Unlike the kid who got carried along
by things, sometimes to excess, I fall prey to the opposite extreme
of excessively looking ahead. I risk becoming the person who now
anxiously checks the weather forecast and carries an umbrella when
it's sunny, forgetting that as a kid, I ran outside to play in the rain.

Mired in excessive planning and analysis, as if I could control the
outcome of my training, or the meaning of my words, by ordering
everything neatly in advance, I long for the decaying spirit of "act
first, think second" and realize that it can be redeemed—not brought
back in the exact same way as before, but drawn up into the present, channeled through new insights and projects, to counteract a
moment of obsession, malaise, or timidity.

One day not so long ago, I had finished an exhausting pull-up
session. Proud of having followed the plan for the day and executed
every rep, I was ready to walk out when the voice suddenly came
to me: "Let me show you how it's done!" I remembered that power-
clean of '08 not as an object of nostalgia but as an unequivocal direction for my next move. This time, with muscles burning with
fatigue, feeling I had something left in the tank but not knowing
quite how much, I picked myself up for one more set, grabbed the
bar, and rocketed myself upward with the short, lightning burst of
energy that came to me back then.

In even small moments like these, we come to understand that
people, events, and experiences do not inevitably fly by us like the
scenery outside the window of a train barreling full speed ahead.
The past is in our hands to be redeemed, even though, at times, it
seems to slip away. When we face the past with tears or clenched
fists, we might ask ourselves: What have we lost that fuels our nostalgia? What lessons and insights does the past carry that today we
risk forgetting? How might we draw on the past to understand today

anew? What have we gained since back then such that we wouldn't want to simply repeat the past, even if we could? When we commit ourselves to redeeming the past, we come to realize that time does not move in a single direction, from past to future, but turns back on itself in each act of redemption, just as the eagle and serpent circle back in their ascending flight.

The Origin of the Passage of Time in the Openness and Closure of Every Moment

The conception of time as simply that which passes away, suggests Nietzsche, arises of our weakness in the face of suffering. Crushed by the burden of redeeming a distant moment of radiance now shrouded in clouds of hardship—the burden of recovering a passion that we let languish after it was thwarted by circumstances beyond our control, or of doing right by a loved one whom we failed and has since gone down a path of self-destruction—and unable to rise to the challenge, we regard the past as simply behind us and beyond our power. Thus arises a certain historical understanding according to which the gap between past and present is unbridgeable, the past lying forever behind us, closed and decided in its meaning, the future offering the prospect of forgetfulness as we move toward new and distant goals.

But we may also turn away from the past and delude ourselves into equating it with the present. In our frustration, we may conceive of the passage of time as a lie, a merely subjective view of the world that, in itself, knows nothing of past or future but simply undergoes endless change. We project onto nature the Stoic circle of life, which turns quite beyond our power, as elements combine and disperse within a sequence of undifferentiated moments, "now" followed by "now," rolling off into infinity: "whatever nature puts together, she undoes, and whatever she undoes, she puts back together," writes Seneca.[24] According to this conception of time, there is nothing new or old. Every event repeats itself, as a birth is nothing but the recombination of the same elements that eventually disperse and join once more. As time is infinite, all combinations have already been realized. Everything that *can* happen has happened— infinite times before.

In our despair, we come to regard this view of time as rational and objective, failing to recognize it as the repression of the past that hurts. And, yet, that repression subtly announces itself amid our supposedly rational conceptions. In Seneca, for example, "The day will come again which will return us to the light. Many would regret that day, were it not that it returns us without our memories."[25] The greatest source of pain, Seneca intimates, is not that our bodies are mortal but that we contend with memories that haunt us—that we face a past. We use the cyclical conception of time to comfort ourselves in the face of the passage of time, to talk ourselves into the idea that everything breaks and joins again, that we are all identical and composed of the same matter, swept up in the same eternal order of being. This is the ultimate form of knowledge without pride, the cold, observing eye of science without spirit, the conniving serpent without its proud friend the eagle.

Such knowledge, as Nietzsche puts it, is deadly. It offers comfort from the passage of time by depriving life of risk, adventure, and creative force. For such a life, there is nothing to fear but also nothing to await. Such a conception of time covers over but can never fully extinguish the original temporality of the soaring eagle and the serpent in unison—the collision of past and future characteristic of a journey in which each new episode redeems the past and each turn of the circular flight returns to a different, higher point. The active life for which Zarathustra aspires is not simply a contained, closed-circuit of striving that makes good on a narrative already given. It is an overflowing life force that always wants *more* of itself, that circles upward infinitely, back to itself and, at the same time, above itself.

Nietzsche makes this clear at the very end of *Zarathustra* in his final summation of the exuberant joy for life to which Zarathustra aspires: "What does joy not want? It is thirstier, more cordial, hungrier, more terrible, more secret than all woe; it wants *itself*, it bites into *itself*, the will of the ring strives in . . . it wants love, it wants hatred, it is over rich, gives, throws away, begs that one might take it, thanks the taker, it would like to be hated; so rich is joy that it thirsts for woe, for hell, for hatred, for disgrace, for the cripple, for *world*—this world, oh, you know it! . . . All eternal joy longs for failures. For all joy wants itself, hence it also wants agony . . . Joy wants the eternity of *all* things."[26]

Eternal joy, teaches Nietzsche, is not endless pleasure, experienced from one moment to the next, but activity that wants *itself*, that is intrinsically fulfilling and needs nothing external. But such activity, in wanting itself, also wants hardship and failure. For it is the possibility of redeeming the past in the confrontation with suffering that inspires life and makes it worth living.

6

What It Means to Be Free

Implicit in the idea of activity for the sake of itself is a certain understanding of what it means to be free—and one that challenges our familiar conceptions. In considering the problem of freedom, we are inclined to approach it in terms of the age-old debate between free will and determinism. Philosophers, theologians, and, these days, sociologists, psychologists, and biologists all have something to say, it seems, about the extent to which one has the power to choose one's own actions—thus to be free—when influences such as the norms of society, the contingency of upbringing, the will of God, or the blind forces of evolution may predetermine one's course. From this perspective, freedom gets interpreted as the capacity to break free of all external influences and make a choice for one's self, by one's own will. Freedom means the assertion of the self against or in spite of its circumstance. As Jack Nicholson's character, Frank Costello, asserts in the opening lines of *The Departed,* "I don't want to be a product of my environment. I want my environment to be a product of me."

There is something undeniably compelling in this aspiration, to the extent that we conceive of our environment as an impersonal context that threatens our independence. But from the perspective of the virtues we have examined, it is deeply misguided. The very distinction between free will and determinism makes sense only when one has assumed from the outset that the self is, in its essence, a subject vested with its own independent capacity for choice that is confronted by an external world of objects or by a society that exerts the pressure of oppressive conformity. Only then can the relative power of the will and of external influence become an endless topic for debate. But if we are defined by our relation to things from the start, at once solicited by the world and responsible for bringing it to expression, we have to reconceive the very meaning of freedom. The more thoroughly we find ourselves engaged with things—in the mode of caring for them, or responding to their promptings—the less we find ourselves in contrast to the world. The source of our deliberation and action turns out to be the world itself.

In the presence of a natural wonder that strikes us in its beauty or power and that presents a mysterious insight to be gleaned, or in the face of a friend who suddenly needs our help, our sense of self and agency cannot be separated from the thing that stands before us. The thing *itself*, in its own right, arrests us and elicits our care and interpretive power. Only from the abstract and superficial perspective of an onlooker with no stake in the situation can we be seen to have a choice to act this way or that. Of course, we remain "free" in a formal sense to turn away from what calls to us. But that is only because something else makes its claim and appears as a rival source of attention. Far more significant than the formal freedom to choose one thing over another is the freedom of responding to a world for which we are responsible. According to this view, we are paradoxically freest when we find ourselves subject to a necessity that flows from the very life we have participated in bringing to expression.

The Ideal of Free Will as a Symptom of World-Weary Cynicism

It is only when the things with which we are engaged and the people with whom we act in partnership no longer move us, because they have failed us in some way, or dwindled in significance as we lose sight of the stories that determine their meaning, that they may become features of a mere "environment" or "social context" and that we may get the idea of imposing ourselves on them, reconstituting them, or simply withdrawing from their sphere.

A willful stance thus becomes possible against the backdrop of a dejected and resigned mode of existence in which we close ourselves off to things, by depersonalizing or "objectifying" them, instead of making the effort to redeem them. As a way of coping with this dejection and resignation, we may interpret our situation as that of a subject—a sphere of consciousness and locus of choice—that faces an external "world" or "social setting" and can either be passively influenced by it or resist it. According to this view, all meaning of personal significance originates in the subjective consciousness. The world or society is but a realm of mere things and conventions to which people, over the years, have attached various subjective valuations. Nothing *in itself* makes a claim to special treatment or care. As individual subjects, we are free to accept or reject the influence of the external or socially constructed world according to our preference and in proportion to our strength of will.

By interpreting our identity and situation in terms of the distinction between subject and object, we suppress and forget the initial rapport with things that came to frustration. Having thus arisen as a sort of coping mechanism, the subject-object interpretation of the self may get recast in all sorts of ingenious ways that pose as properly critical and scientific. An example that has not ceased to work its influence since the seventeenth century is Cartesian doubt, according to which the very existence of the external world is held in suspension until one's own reason, guided by a sure method, can validate that it is not a mere dream world or figment of the imagination implanted by an evil demon.

Though dwelling on such radical doubt may seem, in one sense, bizarre and unsettling, it actually affords a certain existential comfort in the face of frustration with the world: It indulges a sort of theoretical escapism that can rest content with the thought that nothing really "is" until the subjective consciousness validates its objective existence. Such speculations also present the exhilarating challenge of overcoming the phoniness of what appears to be real and taking responsibility for one's self as a being who is independent from external forces. The excitement and sense of purpose that go with overcoming illusion account, I believe, for the widespread appeal of contemporary tales that trade on versions of Cartesian doubt, such as the hit films *The Matrix, Inception,* and *The Truman Show,* all of which present heroism as an escape from the apparent world, which turns out to be an illusion created by manipulative forces analogous to Descartes's evil demon.

But because the subject-object interpretation of the world is at bottom a flight from the reality of frustration and disappointment, which can arise only within an engaged and committed way of life that knows nothing of the difference between self and world, a close examination of what is presented as "subjective" and "objective," or "apparent" and "real," reveals far more of a kinship than first meets the eye. For example, the supposedly fabricated or dream worlds portrayed in films that play upon Cartesian doubt still, despite their strange inconsistencies, involve interactions and engagements that approximate life in the "real" world that is later uncovered. Ultimately, the films cannot help but present us with a certain continuity between the two worlds in which insights gained in one carry over to the other. Reflection upon this continuity leads us to the recognition that the very distinction between the fake and real, the subjective and objective, is undermined by a life oriented to self-understanding. For events within a dream cannot be dismissed as "unreal" if, in confronting them, one learns something of import for how to live in one's waking life. This is why, when we are gripped by a compelling fantasy or work of fiction, we don't think to wonder whether the events really took place. When the question of fact versus fiction does cross our mind, we either quickly recognize it as pointless speculation or indulge it to the extent that we have given up on finding a deeper meaning in what we consider and now view it in a disengaged, external fashion.

The same kinship of self and world, subject and object, can be discerned in the case of those who don't doubt the existence of their environment but stand aloof from it and seek to bend it to their design. Even in such cynical detachment, we find a mode of engaged and committed activity that cannot be understood simply in terms of willpower and imposition. Even Jack Nicholson's character in *The Departed*, the paradigmatic imposer (based loosely on the infamous South Boston gangster Whitey Bulger), relies for his "dominance" of that which "surrounds" him on certain loyalties and commitments that at least gesture toward friendship and solidarity. Even as he is overtaken by distrust of nearly everyone in his crew, he remains devoted to his dutiful right-hand man, a brutish fixer who sticks by him to the end. Most tellingly, his very obsession with smoking out the rats among his associates is born of an obsession with respect, which attests to the sense in which his environment is for him something more than the product of his will: a self-standing reality from which he seeks recognition. He cannot simply destroy this reality without depriving himself of the honor on which he stakes his life. He needs those who pay homage to his leadership and command. Thus, even in ways of life that claim to valorize willful dominion, we find intimations of a receptive and responsive mode of activity.

The Activity of Things Themselves

To fully appreciate the reciprocal relationship between ourselves and the things to which we respond, we could also consider activity from the perspective of the thing. Though we are in the habit of expressing activity in terms of a self that does some sort of work on the thing, as when we say "I play baseball," we may just as well say that the thing engages with us ("baseball plays *me*"). Though this way of speaking may sound strange from the perspective of the subject-object worldview, as it seems to spuriously invest the object with a life of its own, it finds familiar expression in the way that many languages express affinity. In Spanish, for example, the English phrase "I like" has no real equivalent, as the closet translation is "me gusta," literally, "it is pleasing *to me.*" The reversal of the subject and object of the sentence gives credit to the thing desired as more than a mere object but a living force in its own right. In contrast to the English formulation, which posits the subject, "I," as the locus of action, the Spanish expression speaks to the experience of being solicited by the world.

Even when the feature of the world at issue is an apparently inert object, such as a baseball bat, which may seem to exert its force only to the extent that we act *on it,* the thing can be seen to possess a force of its own. As any hitter knows, the bat itself demands respect: It must be swung in a certain very precise way if it is to connect squarely with a baseball and thus *be a baseball bat* rather than a long, oddly tapered cylindrical object that simply occupies space. The bat utterly defies the willful stance of a frustrated hitter who swings it angrily and without attention to its structure. In a larger sense, even when the bat just lies around, waiting to be used, it reverberates for the one who uses it with all of the occasions and stories of which it is a part. To the extent that the bat elicits for the player those occasions and stories, and instills in him, as he steps up to the plate, the calmness of someone who in light of his past can put the pressure of the moment in perspective, the bat itself, in partnership with the user, can be said to initiate the activity—to set the batter in motion.

Given the reciprocal relationship between self and world, which is really a single unfolding of activity, it would be a mistake to regard activity as a merely human possibility. Activity denotes the way in which *things offer themselves* to be interpreted, no matter how static they may appear. Activity is not something that we bring into the world but a force that defines the world insofar as it is a world at all.

That We Never Face an Abstract Either / Or

But what about those moments in which our freedom does seem to involve a choice, when we face forks in the road of life where the decision to go one way or the other seems to throw us into radically different possibilities of existence? What about conflicts of commitment that seem to offer us no recourse but our naked will, according to which we may leap one way or the other? Jean-Paul Sartre, one of the foremost proponents of the idea that freedom consists in self-making through choice, offers the following story in support of his view.

A student of his came to him during the war with a personal dilemma: whether to join the Free French Forces in England or remain in France to care for his ailing mother. Motivated by a devotion to the Resistance, and the chance to avenge his brother, who had been killed during the German offensive of 1940, the student was inclined to leave for England. At the same time, he felt duty-bound to remain by his mother's side, especially as she was grief-stricken in the wake of losing her eldest son, and embroiled in quarrels with her husband who, to her dismay, supported collaboration with Germany. The student believed that his absence and, were he to be killed in battle, his death, would plunge her into despair.

Sartre presents the student's dilemma as a conflict between two "very different kinds of action: one [was] concrete, immediate, but concerning only one individual; the other concerned an incomparably vaster group, a national collectivity." Sartre underscores the dilemma as also one between "two kinds of ethics": on the one hand, "an ethics of sympathy, of personal devotion," and on the other, "a broader ethics, but one whose efficacy was more dubious."[1]

Sartre concludes that the condition of being faced with such seemingly irreconcilable claims attests to the necessity of choosing for ourselves. What else do we have to fall back on, he asks, but our own individual will? Sartre considers recourse to several supposedly a priori standards of moral judgment that might guide us in the decision of such a conflict: the word of God, the dictates of human nature, the principles of Kantian morality—all of which he exposes as indecisive, as they might just as well point in one direction as the other. We are left, Sartre thinks, with but one option: to resolve to make a choice on the basis of which the course of our life will be decided. His advice to the student is that he must simply resolve to commit to one of the two paths and bear full responsibility for the choice.

There is surely something compelling in Sartre's account, at least in his critique of familiar "external" sources of decision and his call to decide for one's self. At the same time, there is something dissatisfying about the conception of freedom he proposes. According to his view, we are all alone in the decisions we make, without counsel or direction. Sartre does not hesitate to label such freedom "absurd," even "nauseating."

We could state the problem as follows: If all meaning originates in the self-governing will, it can be withdrawn by that very will and is therefore arbitrary. What appears to be an empowering conception of freedom when contrasted to forms of external pressure turns out to be, in itself, utterly aimless and, in a sense, impotent. What power is there in blind, baseless decision?

Dissatisfying though Sartre's account of freedom may be, we cannot reject it simply because it unsettles us. We must consider the sense in which it fails to adequately characterize the existential dilemmas we actually face. Though Sartre means to vindicate the will by presenting a messy, real-world dilemma that cannot be neatly resolved by supposedly clear standards of abstract morality, he falls victim to the very abstractions he wants to challenge. According to his presentation, there must be either some objective standard that lies outside the self (the word of God, Kantian morality, human nature) that the self may, as it were, reach out and grab hold of as a guide, or we are left with nothing but the purely subjective will. Sartre decides for the latter. In doing so, however, he leaves unquestioned the distinction between subject and object. Sartre overlooks the possibility that a life as it is lived, engaged with things and in concert with others, provides its own standard of action that is nether subjective nor objective.

If we examine the actual choice that the student faces, we can discern in each path a certain kinship to the other that Sartre overlooks and that undermines the existential significance of the choice. Even from what Sartre reports of the dilemma, the student's commitment to the Free French Forces cannot be neatly separated from his devotion to his mother. We know from Sartre's retelling that the student's mother is herself deeply devoted to the freedom of France and that a significant source of her domestic trouble is her husband's collaborationist sympathies. We also know that her grief is tied to the death of her eldest son, who was killed resisting the Germans. Given this background, it would not be implausible to interpret the student's decision to join the Free French Forces as an act of loyalty to country that is also an act of devotion to his mother. For in joining the Resistance, he would be fulfilling a mission with which she herself identifies and for which her elder son, his brother, gave his life. Though, in going to England, the student would not be in direct proximity to his mother, he would be supporting her in a different way: by redeeming the project of her son and engaging in a mission that connects all three of them.

Of course, the decision would come at a certain cost. In fighting for France, the student would risk getting killed and sending his mother into a deeper despair. He would also be leaving her to her own devices in the face of her troublesome husband. For these reasons, he may decide to stay. But the real question for assessing the sense in which he faces two very different options—such that his choice for one or the other can be conceived as an exercise of will—is not whether one comes at some cost but whether one can only be had to the exclusion of the other. Just as the student would not simply abandon his mother in fighting for France, he would not break all allegiance to France in remaining by her side.

We can readily imagine that the very way in which he would support his mother—reminding her of the importance of the cause for which her son died fighting, questioning her husband's political views—would involve a devotion to the freedom of France. It might be added that upon deciding to remain with his mother the student could still do everything in his power to support the Resistance movement from the home front.

Attentiveness to such connections among possibilities as actually lived reveals the sense in which Sartre has mischaracterized the student's choice as between "two very different modes of action" and "two kinds of morality."[2] The difference Sartre ascribes to the paths turns out to be an abstract characterization of the student's dilemma from a sort of bird's-eye view, as if different courses of action within a life were separate from each other and could be surveyed side-by-side and determined in advance to be irreconcilable. Sartre thus engages in a certain version of the a priori determination that he rejects: He believes it possible to attain a certain detached perspective on life from which one can know with certainty that two commitments cannot be reconciled. But from the engaged and committed perspective of life as a journey, the sense of each possibility depends to such an extent on its relation to the other that the two may, in a sense, be regarded as *the same*. This is not to say that they are identical and that the student faces no choice at all but that the student's freedom in the situation cannot be reduced to whatever choice he might make. For what gives rise to the occasion for the choice is the unity of the student's life as it has so far unfolded in which the love of his mother and the devotion to his country are inextricably bound. The student's true freedom consists in living out the open-ended narrative that has brought him to the moment in which two paths emerge.

Just how directed and prepared in advance his dilemma really is can be gleaned from a consideration of the infinity of paths that would be utterly out of keeping with the student's life as it has so far unfolded and that therefore do not present themselves at all—joining the Axis, for example, or abandoning both the Resistance and his mother for some frivolous allure, or simply embarking on neither course and burying his head in the sand. What makes the student's choice meaningful at all is the unity of self and world that precedes it. This means that in deciding to embark on one course, the student does not simply give up on the other but begins the challenge of fulfilling it in a different way.

Seen in this light, the significance of the choice is greatly diminished and so too the status of the will. It is not as though the student faces a fork in the road where he will become a different person, or create himself anew, depending on which path he takes. Both directions lead back, so to speak, to the same life.

Whatever choice the student can be said to make is but the next move in a course of action that has long been prepared by the web of relations in which he finds himself. Concretely, this means that in departing for England or in remaining by his mother's side the student has simply taken a step in the never-ending project of making good on two commitments that lend each other meaning.

In the final analysis, freedom is not a faculty of the will that can be exercised in certain moments but a way of being in which we are always engaged as we live out possibilities within the circle of a life already in the works. The opposite of freedom, so to speak, is not determination from the outside but forms of self-imposed enslavement, including the very view of the world in terms of the subject-object distinction. It is we who, in our despair, frustration, and loss of rapport with things, construct a world of subjects and objects and then fall into our own interpretation as if it were a self-evident description of the way things are. The opposite of freedom is thus itself a form of freedom: a boundless capacity to misinterpret and to lead astray—freedom turned against itself.

Too often in life we act as if so much were riding on the choices we make, as if going this way rather than that would lead to a different life. But this fork-in-the-road view of existence is the abstraction of a goal-oriented outlook, according to which everything is a discrete accomplishment or option rather than a possibility to be developed in partnership with others in the course of a journey. Attention to activity for the sake of itself reveals a corrective to this perspective. What matters is not what we choose but how we live out the choices we make.

Paradoxically, the choices that matter most *as choices* are ones for which we have already made up our mind, in that we know one course to be right but are still faced with the difficulty of choosing it against some tempting diversion. For example, I may confront the familiar difficulty of getting up for a run rather than hitting the snooze button. But the supposed freedom of this choice is actually quite limited, as I already take as given that the run, for me, is the right course. Though making the choice to roll out of bed may feel in some sense empowering as an exercise of will in the face of temptation, the choice itself, and the sense in which it is an exercise of freedom, rises to significance only in my actually *being on the run,* in the midst of a special form of exertion that has nothing to do with choice or will but consists in the union of self and world in which gravity and levity, sun, wind, and terrain are gathered in each stride. Whatever freedom we may be said to have in choosing depends on the deeper freedom of responding and interpreting.

This is the case in even those moments when we might feel all alone in the stand we take, liable to ascribe our resolve to naked willpower. The philosopher Maurice Merleau-Ponty gives an eloquent example:

> We torture a man to make him speak. If he refuses to give
> the names and addresses that we wish to extract from him,
> this is not through a solitary and ungrounded decision; he

still felt himself among his comrades and was still committed to their common struggle . . . or perhaps he had for
months, or even years, confronted this test in his thoughts
and staked his entire life upon it; or finally, he might
wish to prove what he had always thought and said
about freedom by overcoming this test. These motives do
not annul freedom, but they at least show that freedom is
not without supports within being. It is not ultimately the
bare consciousness that resists the pain, but the prisoner
along with his comrades or along with those he loves and
under whose gaze he lives.[3]

Thus we are always with others. Our freedom arises as much from
them as from ourselves.

Freedom and Openness to the Unknown

There is another dimension to freedom that, in conclusion, deserves
a final word. This is the relationship between freedom and openness to the unknown. In one sense, activity for the sake of itself—
in the forms of self-possession, friendship, and engagement with
nature—involves a certain "knowing in advance"—an understanding
of one's self and of the world as a whole that makes possible any
dilemma or occasion for choice. As soon as I find myself capable
of choice or decision, I already understand myself as a person
claimed by commitments that have come into tension only because
they already cohere in some provisional way, each dependent on
the other for its meaning and sense. The reciprocal relation among
commitments is itself dependent upon a larger whole of which I
am scarcely aware but understand with absolute certainty to the
extent that I am able to draw upon still other aspects of my life to
make sense of the difficulty I now face. It is this "knowing in advance"
that refutes the existential conception of the person as radically

self-creative, as if the self could, from nothing, piece together its identity through acts of choice.

Such an understanding can be more or less explicit. For example, I may know myself as a loyal son simply in the act of supporting my mother in a time of need without explicitly thinking of it as an act of loyalty and without even beginning to spell out the totality of relations to friends, coworkers, neighbors, fellow citizens, and so on in which the family, as a distinctive sphere of life, attains a special significance. But I may also conceive of myself in these terms, presenting to myself an image that is at once who I am and who I aspire to be. In either case, I can be said to understand myself in a way that encompasses any possible future and constitutes the security and closure of life. Whatever the future may bring, I will remain true to myself and to those with whom my destiny is bound. Such knowing in advance is of the essence of self-possession. It is that which makes one a self at all—a whole—and not a mere collection of disconnected and unintelligible bits of experience. Even in moments of radical doubt, we are never entirely without such an understanding, implicit and dim though it may be.

But in partnership with such a certainty of self, and constituting its very essence, is a radical openness to the unknown. For one comes to know one's self as a whole only in acts of comparison, analogy, and judgment, all of which are occasioned by some disruption, great or small. The whole that constitutes one's identity and that precedes any choice one might make is an active whole, a unity constantly being put to the test and discovered anew.

Another way to put it is this: In our deepest commitments we invite the radically unknown as much as declare an unshakable certainty. To say with conviction that "no matter what happens, I will stand by your side" or "remain faithful to this vocation" is to embrace the future in its unfathomable mystery. Without the possibility of radical disruption, our most certain commitments would lack meaning and weight.

Thus, in knowing one's self and securing the future, one at the same time embraces the exhilarating openness of life in which hardship and suffering are inseparable from redemption and joy. It is this openness that distinguishes activity for the sake of itself from goal-oriented striving. From the goal-oriented perspective, the only unknown is whether one will succeed or fail in actualizing the vision one beholds already. The more we get caught up in goal-oriented striving, the more we try to eliminate the uncertainty of the path to the end, by finding more efficient techniques of production and accomplishment. The goal-oriented outlook and a technological disposition thus go hand in hand. They conspire to render life predictable, within our control, and without adventure or risk. In the broadest sense, the technological outlook and the goal-oriented outlook are one and the same.

What the Greeks called *techne,* from which we derive the term "technology," is essentially goal-oriented: It denotes a knowledge of the means to make something, the form of which is already in view. For the Greeks, the paradigmatic *techne* is craft knowledge, that of the carpenter as he envisions the form of a table and sets to constructing it of wood. But *techne* applies just as much to the kind of self-making in which we engage when we understand our happiness to consist in a goal or life plan to be executed. The aim of *techne* is to produce reliable results and thus to eliminate the unexpected. Although technological knowledge has been and always will be a part of life, it has in our time risen to such prominence that it encroaches upon the basic experience of wonder and inspiration that lies at the origin of every form we take for granted. The reorientation to life that I suggest in terms of "activity for the sake of itself" comes with the recognition that what appears to be unimpeachably "there" in front of our gaze to be analyzed or constructed is given to us by an interpretation of life that is always in the works and that we never grasp or comprehend in its totality.

In contrast to the technological freedom of producing results, we may consider the freedom of stepping into the unknown, which takes us back to the reciprocal play of forces between self and world. Freedom, so understood, has not to do with the power to will, choose, construct, or foresee, but to *initiate*.

Consider the way in which even small gestures and deeds can play out in ways that far exceed whatever conscious motive lay behind them. We take a shot at a new project, accept an invitation, go out of our way to help a stranger, summon the courage to ask someone on a date. The next thing we know, we find ourselves immersed in a new vocation or relationship, on a path that at the time we could not possibly have envisioned. On the one hand, it was the power of our own action that set things into motion and sustained the unfolding of events. Were we not to have made an initial gesture, and followed up on its consequences, things would not have turned out as they did. But that power, we see in retrospect, far exceeds whatever conscious intention we had at the time, which, if we were to formulate it, is often something quite unremarkable or cliché.

Our action always exceeds our intention as it works its influence on a world, the response of which we cannot foresee. Only in the reciprocal play of forces that constitutes the unity of self and world does our action become what it is. Our action, in other words, can be an initiating force only in being received and thrown back as a new invitation to take up. We thus find ourselves thrown by our own actions into a perpetual game of catch, the meaning of which we arrive at only provisionally and in hindsight.

This is to say that what most bears our mark, and speaks to who we are, does so not in virtue of its being consciously chosen against other possibilities, or in its instituting a reality that once lay only in our imagination, but in its setting into motion a destiny that has since come to meet us, quite beyond our expectation or will. In retrospect, we can come to understand that the life we are living was prepared by a commitment or course of action in such a way that could not possibly have been foreseen at the time. We thereby catch a glimpse of the sense in which activity here and now, whether deliberate and conscious or not, is reaching beyond itself, opening a future, which as such is indeterminate. This power to initiate, and not our conscious efforts and constructions, is what constitutes genuine freedom.

So much of the time, we find ourselves in the thrall of goal-oriented striving—reaching for a milestone, trying to have an impact at work or in the world at large, completing a daily task, making an impression, attending to the future with an eye to health, safety, and stability. Often enough, these things keep us occupied and disciplined. We cling to them as antidotes to the myriad distractions and frivolities that threaten to plunge us into a mindless, helter-skelter mode of existence. But at times, at least, we sense that our focus and ambition are distractions from life in a larger sense. Perhaps in the face of failure, or in moments of anxious doubt, we wonder whether there is more to life than achieving goals, no matter how lofty or noble. Though we may jump back into our goal-oriented striving with renewed confidence, or turn to something new instead, we can never quite silence the thought that what we fight so hard to attain amounts to little in the greater scheme of things.

That thought may strike us all the more in moments of success, when we realize that what gave us purpose is now an accomplished fact and no longer a source of motivation. Reflection on the fleeting satisfaction of success may lead us to consider our striving in a larger scope, in terms of the infinite expanse of time and the fate of all human achievement. To the extent that we are focused on making, instituting, and constructing, we cannot escape the thought that even the greatest achievements grow old and the most celebrated names fade away.

In search of a perspective that will liberate us from the seemingly inescapable passage of time, we may turn to philosophies that locate eternity and ultimate satisfaction outside the realm of human affairs, in the cycles of nature, for example, according to which everything breaks and joins anew, or in a life after this one in which things never grow old. Stoicism, as we have seen, is one prominent version of such a philosophy. It teaches the impermanence of all human things and counsels us to seek refuge in the contemplation of an eternal nature. The perspective of activity for the sake of itself offers an alternative to the Stoic worldview and to all philosophies that regard the world in which we strive as but a way station to somewhere else. The greater meaning that we seek lies not in the eternal laws of an impersonal universe, or in some life after this one, but in the journey here and now through which the self—one's *own* self—comes to expression. To understand the journey is to recognize that every undertaking, no matter how circumscribed or goal-oriented it may seem, has meaning and significance as a vocation in relation to others, within a whole of connected activities that expresses an understanding of what it means to be, that speaks to a person, a self, and is not a mere collection of roles and enterprises that could be documented on a CV and replicated by someone else. Because the self is defined by the journey, which includes friends and foes, guideposts and diversions, rifts and bridges, the unfolding of the self is, at the same time, the unfolding of a world. Because the journey is, at every moment, a coming into one's own that is already in the works, it awaits no future for its completion or validation. In this sense it is eternal: not that it will last forever but that it evades measure by the familiar standards of duration or persistence in time. Life so conceived is itself the measure of time that passes—that which makes possible the experience of a sequence of moments and thus of time that can be displayed on a watch, quantified and calculated.

From within the journey, which is ultimately the only standpoint we have, the very notion of a future yet to be realized has no meaning or sense. For whatever the future may bring, it can do no more than reaffirm the life to which one is committed. This is to say that one's own moment, with its closure and possibility, is the one and only and that in living now, one understands what it means to live at all times.

The eternal now is a way of making sense of the openness and closure of every moment without which life would be impossible. It is a way of expressing how past and future are not points along a timeline, but essential dimensions of time that come together in any possible present. Without this simultaneous openness and closure, we would not be able to make sense of or experience the passage of time. Were our lives not radically open to the unknown, longing to be challenged, tested and affirmed, but fully determined in their meaning, we would never face a moment that lies behind us and will never simply return. Everything that we might identify as having happened to us would be but an event fully intelligible in light of the people we now know our selves to be. In this sense, what had passed away would be fully present, not past at all. We would not wish to put it behind us or long for its return precisely because it would be with us, integrated with an unshakable and static sense of self. From the perspective of total closure, the same could be said of a moment yet to come. Were our lives decided already in their essence, we would not look ahead to anything not yet here with anxiety or excitement. Tomorrow would be but a repetition of today.

At the same time, however, were our lives not closed and determined in their meaning but radically open, we would not encounter the passage of time either. Each moment, so to speak, would be a radical shift into a new existence, affording no basis for retrospection or anticipation. It is only because our lives are simultaneously decided and exposed to the unknown, permeated by past and future at every moment, that we can look back with wistful nostalgia or frustration and look ahead with eager anticipation or fear. When we look back on the past with longing to redeem a given moment or to restore to life one who is no longer with us, we do so precisely because the closure or direction of our lives has oriented us to the unknown in such a way that we need inspiration, guidance, or comfort. And as soon as we come to this awareness, we come to understand that the passage of time is not some external fact that we suffer but something that we enact. The passage of time is inseparable from the engaged and committed existence that constitutes the life we are living.

From the goal-oriented perspective, by contrast, we close ourselves off to the unity of past and future, closure and openness, that constitutes time in the most basic and essential sense. Everything is either completed, on its way to completion, or finished. Nothing strictly speaking is already in the works. What consists in anxious anticipation, and would therefore appear to concern itself with the future, has, in reality, closed itself off to the radical openness that constitutes the genuine future. Life, from the goal-oriented perspective, is merely one thing after the next, an endless repetition of the same. The flattening of time characteristic of goal-oriented striving is what ultimately unites it with the Stoic outlook, which seems, on the surface, to provide an alternative. Both ultimately understand time in terms of mere succession. Neither reckons with the authentic past and future that define the engaged and committed perspective of a journey and that make possible any succession we might encounter.

In a sense, the eternal "now" always has us in its possession, no matter how distracted by the goal-oriented future we might be. We experience such captivation in those moments when any thought of the not-yet-now gets held in check by an urgent claim of friendship, self-possession, or engagement with nature. Without even the slightest sense of self-sacrifice, we come to the aid of a friend, or make good on the claim that moves us, without regard for our most cherished goals or even the continuation of life. In doing so, we live up to the awareness that whatever we may accomplish or maintain tomorrow is of secondary importance to the immediacy of a claim that implicates the whole of who we are and will ever be.

But most of the time, we find ourselves in a middle position with regard to the eternal now of an ultimate claim and the fleeting moment yet-to-come of an alluring accomplishment or state of being. We recognize the intrinsic significance of attending a friend's wedding but feel too bogged down in work to make the trip. Or we realize that we really should stand up for ourselves but feel that doing so may jeopardize our social position. It is in these moments that reflection on our lives rises to special importance. Because life in its immediacy fails to move us alone, we need recourse to an interpretation of life that reminds us of what matters. With the help of philosophy, we may amplify the call of what we know to be true but often shirk or take lightly in the face of goal-oriented conceptions of happiness. In this way, philosophy and everyday life go hand in hand. Far from being a merely academic discipline that theorizes from on high and substitutes the abstract for the real, philosophy is an indispensable guide in returning us to what is most concrete.

Notes

Introduction

1. C. P. Cavafy, *The Collected Poems,* trans. Evangelos Sachperoglou (Oxford: Oxford University Press, 2007) 39.
2. Plato, *Phaedrus,* ed. Jeffrey Henderson (Cambridge, MA: Harvard University Press, 1914), 229b–230a.
3. Steven Pinker, "Enough with the Quackery, Pinker Says," interview in the *Harvard Gazette,* October 13, 2021, https://news.harvard.edu /gazette/story/2021/10/from-steven-pinker-a-paean-to-the-rational -mind/.
4. Marcus Aurelius, *Meditations,* trans. Gregory Hays (New York: Modern Library, 2003), 38.
5. Massimo Pigliucci, *How to Be a Stoic* (New York: Basic Books, 2017), 194.

1. Self-Possession I

1. Friedrich Nietzsche, "Aphorism 296," *Beyond Good and Evil,* in *Basic Writings of Nietzsche,* trans. Walter Kaufmann (New York: Modern Library, 2000), 426–427.
2. Plato, *Phaedo,* ed. Jeffrey Henderson (Cambridge, MA: Harvard University Press, 1914), 115c.
3. Daniel Kahneman, *Thinking, Fast and Slow* (New York: Farrar, Straus and Giroux, 2011), 377–390.
4. Thomas Hobbes, *Leviathan,* ed. Richard Tuck (Cambridge: Cambridge University Press, 1996), 70.

5. Ibid., 43.

6. Thomas Hobbes, _On the Citizen,_ ed. Richard Tuck (Cambridge: Cambridge University Press, 1998), 27.

7. Friedrich Nietzsche, _Thus Spoke Zarathustra,_ in _The Portable Nietzsche,_ trans. Walter Kaufmann (London: Chatto and Windus, 1971), 129–130.

8. Aristotle, _Nicomachian Ethics,_ ed. Jeffrey Henderson (Cambridge, MA: Harvard University Press, 1926), 1123b1–2.

9. Ibid., 1124a19.

10. Ibid., 1124a10–12.

11. Ibid., 1124b23–25.

12. Ibid., 1124a6–9.

13. Ibid., 1125a2–4.

14. Ibid., 1124b26–28.

15. Ibid., 1124b29.

16. Ibid., 1125a1217.

17. Ibid., 1124b19–21, 1124b30–31.

18. Ibid., 1124b19–20.

19. Plato, _Apology,_ ed. Jeffrey Henderson (Cambridge, MA: Harvard University Press, 1914), 22d.

20. Plato, _Symposium,_ trans. Seth Benardete (Chicago: University of Chicago Press, 1993), 176c–d.

21. Ibid., 186a.

22. Ibid., 176d.

23. _Curb Your Enthusiasm,_ "The Therapists," season 6, episode 9.

24. Aristotle, _Ethics,_ 1140a26–28.

25. Ibid., 1124a13–16.

26. Peter Abraham, "Red Sox Enjoy the All Star Game as the AL Outslugs the NL," _Boston Globe,_ July 18, 2018.

27. Aristotle, _Ethics,_ 1094a1–15.

28. Ibid., 1094a19–25.

29. Friedrich Nietzsche, _Schopenhauer as Educator,_ in _Unfashionable Observations,_ trans. Richard T. Gray (Stanford, CA: Stanford University Press, 1995), 174.

30. Aristotle, _Ethics,_ 1123b31–33.

31. Ibid., 1124a1–4.

32. _Curb Your Enthusiasm,_ "The Ida Funkhouser Roadside Memorial," season 6, episode 3.

2. Self-Possession II

1. Plato, *Gorgias,* ed. Jeffrey Henderson (Cambridge, MA: Harvard University Press, 1925), 458a.
2. Plato, *Republic,* trans. Allan Bloom (New York: Basic Books, 1991), 336d–e.
3. Ibid., 337d.
4. Ibid., 338b–339e.
5. See, e.g., ibid., 505d–e.
6. Plato, *Gorgias,* 485b–d.
7. Ibid.
8. Ibid., 486a–c.
9. Ibid., 486e–488a.
10. Ibid., 497e.
11. Plato, *Republic,* 349a–350d.
12. Aristotle, *Ethics,* 1125a8–10.
13. Plato, *Apology,* ed. Jeffrey Henderson (Cambridge, MA: Harvard University Press, 1914), 21b.
14. Plato, *Meno,* 90e10–92c7.
15. Plato, *Apology,* 38a.
16. Aristotle, *Ethics,* 1124b8–10.
17. Plato, *Phaedo,* ed. Jeffrey Henderson (Cambridge, MA: Harvard University Press, 1914), 58e.
18. Ibid., 88e–89a.
19. Ibid., 115b.
20. Ibid., 115c.
21. Ibid., 118a.
22. Ibid., 109a–110b.
23. Ibid., 110c–d.
24. Aristotle, *Ethics,* 1125a11–13.
25. Blaise Pascale, *Pensées,* ed. and trans. Roger Ariew (Indianapolis: Hackett, 2005), 58.

3. Friendship

1. Aristotle, *Nicomachian Ethics,* ed. Jeffrey Henderson (Cambridge, MA: Harvard University Press, 1926), 1156a10–25.
2. Ibid., 1155a27–28.

3. Ibid., 1155a.

4. Ibid., 1172a12–13.

5. Ibid., 1125a1.

6. Ibid., 1166a34–35.

7. Ibid., 1168b10.

8. Ibid., 1166a1–19.

9. Ibid., 1169b30–1170b12.

10. Nietzsche, *Thus Spoke Zarathustra,* in *The Portable Nietzsche,* trans. Walter Kaufmann (London: Chatto and Windus, 1971), 167–168.

11. Aristotle, *Ethics,* 1166a20–24.

12. Ibid., 1106b35–1107a2.

13. Ibid., 1156b26–30.

14. Ibid., 1168a5–8.

15. Massimo Pigliucci, *How to Be a Stoic* (New York: Basic Books, 2017), 194–195.

16. Adam Smith, *The Theory of Moral Sentiments,* ed. Ryan Patrick Hanley (New York: Penguin, [1759] 2009), 265.

17. Ibid., 277.

18. Montesquieu, *Mes Pensées, in Oeuvres completes,* ed. Roger Chaillois (Paris: Gallimard, 1949), no. 604, 1129–1130.

19. Smith, *Theory of Moral Sentiments,* 277.

20. Hans-Georg Gadamer, *Truth and Method,* trans. Joel Weinsheimer and Donald G. Marshall, rev. ed. (New York: Continuum, [1960] 1989), 480–484.

21. Nietzsche, *Thus Spoke Zarathustra,* in *The Portable Nietzsche,* 129.

22. Ibid., 121.

23. Muhammad Ali with Richard Durham, *The Greatest: My Own Story,* ed. Toni Morrison (Los Angeles: Graymalkin Media, [1975] 2015), 130–131.

24. Nietzsche, *Thus Spoke Zarathustra,* in *The Portable Nietzsche,* 214.

25. Plato, *Lysis,* ed. Jeffrey Henderson (Cambridge, MA: Harvard University Press, 1925), 214a–d.

26. Aristotle, *Ethics,* 1155b4–7.

4. Engagement with Nature

1. John Locke, *Second Treatise of Government,* ed. C. B. McPherson (Indianapolis: Hackett, [1690] 1980), sect. 40–43.

2. Homer, *The Odyssey,* trans. Allen Mandelbaum (New York: Random House, 2005), 41.

3. Ibid., 102.

4. Plato, *Republic,* trans. Allan Bloom (New York: Basic Books, 1991), 508a–509d.

5. See Martin Heidegger, "Modern Science, Metaphysics, and Mathematics," in *Martin Heidegger: Basic Writings,* ed. David Farrell Krell (New York: Harper and Row, 1977), 257–271.

6. Ibid., 262–263.

7. Nietzsche, *Thus Spoke Zarathustra,* in *The Portable Nietzsche,* trans. Walter Kaufmann (London: Chatto and Windus, 1971), 268.

8. Ibid., 269.

9. Seneca, Moral Epistle 36.7–12, in *How to Die,* trans. James S. Romm (Princeton, NJ: Princeton University Press, 2018), 6.

10. Seneca, To Marcia 26.1, in *How to Die,* 96–97.

11. Marcus Aurelius, *Meditations,* trans. Gregory Hays (New York: Modern Library, 2003), 56.

12. Ibid., 43.

13. Ibid., 8.

14. Ibid., 38.

15. Seneca, To Marcia 26.1–3, in *How to Die,* 35.

16. Ibid.

17. Nietzsche, *Thus Spoke Zarathustra,* in *The Portable Nietzsche,* 276–277.

18. Friedrich Nietzsche, *Schopenhauer as Educator,* in *Unfashionable Observations,* trans. Richard T. Gray (Stanford, CA: Stanford University Press, 1995), 213–214.

19. Nietzsche, *Thus Spoke Zarathustra,* in *The Portable Nietzsche,* 264.

20. Ibid., 189.

21. Ibid., 186.

5. Contending with Time

1. Todd May, *Death* (New York: Routledge, 2014), 5–6.

2. Friedrich Nietzsche, *The Birth of Tragedy,* in *Basic Writings of Nietzsche,* trans. Walter Kaufmann (New York: Modern Library, 2000), 52.

3. Plato, *Gorgias,* ed. Jeffrey Henderson (Cambridge, MA: Harvard University Press, 1925), 512e.

4. Friedrich Nietzsche, *Thus Spoke Zarathustra,* in *The Portable Nietzsche,* trans. Walter Kaufmann (London: Chatto and Windus, 1971), 183.

5. Ibid., 184.

6. Ibid., 127.

7. Ibid., 186.

8. Ibid., 185–186.

9. Plato, *Crito,* ed. Jeffrey Henderson (Cambridge, MA: Harvard University Press, 1914), 44a–b.

10. Friedrich Nietzsche, *Beyond Good and Evil,* in *Basic Writings of Nietzsche,* trans. Walter Kaufmann (New York: Modern Library, 2000), 296.

11. Plato, *Phaedo,* ed. Jeffrey Henderson (Cambridge, MA: Harvard University Press, 1914), 96e–97b.

12. Ibid., 275c–276a.

13. Nietzsche, *Thus Spoke Zarathustra,* in *The Portable Nietzsche,* 186.

14. Ibid., 244.

15. Ibid., 187.

16. Ibid., 190.

17. Ibid.

18. Ibid., 121–122.

19. Ibid., 122.

20. Ibid., 310.

21. Ibid., 136–137.

22. Ibid., 264.

23. Ibid., 251.

24. Seneca, Moral Epistle 30, in James S. Romm, *How to Die* (Princeton, NJ: Princeton University Press, 2018), 22.

25. Seneca, Moral Epistle 36.7–12, in ibid., 5.

26. Nietzsche, *Thus Spoke Zarathustra,* in *The Portable Nietzsche,* 435–436.

6. What It Means to Be Free

1. Jean-Paul Sartre, *Essays in Existentialism,* ed. Wade Baskin (New York: Citadel Press, 1993), 42–43.

2. Ibid.

3. Maurice Merleau-Ponty, *Phenomenology of Perception,* trans. Donald A. Landes (New York: Routledge, 2012), 481.

Acknowledgments

It is a joy to look back on the path I've taken in writing this book and to recount the many conversations and moments of support and friendship that have helped bring it into being.

Some of my first thoughts on the book took shape with the advice of my longtime friend and training partner Will Hauser, who encouraged me to connect my two seemingly disparate passions of fitness and philosophy. Since our early days of lifting weights together in college, Will and I have enjoyed many conversations on the subtle life lessons that can be gleaned from the activity of training. One of those lessons, which figures prominently in this book, is that friendship and competition can be mutually reinforcing. I'm all the more convinced of this as I reflect upon the friends I've made in the process of athletic competition, some of whom are major sources of inspiration for this book. An early archrival in a local "gym games" competition, Jay Fiset, has become a close friend and exemplar of the virtues of which I write. Scott Robertson, who knew me when I was just becoming interested in philosophy, has also been a source of inspiration for the spirit of friendly competitiveness that I take to be a vital dimension of friendship in general.

I've found stalwart support from Ron Cooper, a prolific Guinness World Record setter, who inspired me to pursue records myself, and who has become a good friend and training partner. I am grateful to

Ron not only for our memorable workout exploits, but for taking the time to read drafts and offer commentary in the final sprint to submitting the manuscript.

Matt Crawford, in his superb book *Shop Class as Soulcraft*, bolstered my faith in the project of combining philosophy, everyday life, and personal narrative. Since meeting Matt in 2014, when he invited me to give a talk on my first book at the University of Virginia, I've benefited greatly from our discussions on practical wisdom, the limits of technology, and the meaning of human agency.

As I was contemplating the unlikely union of fitness and philosophy, I was also gathering many notes and reflections on the meaning of time, a theme that has captivated me ever since my studies with Krzysztof Michalski, whose thinking on the relation of time to eternity has left a lasting impression on me.

There are several mentors to whom I owe special thanks for reading drafts at various stages and for providing generous commentary. I am grateful to Moshe Halbertal for helping me think through the meaning of activity for the sake of itself and for encouraging me to weave together the interpretation of ancient texts with an account of how to live in our own time. I am also very grateful to Sean Kelly, who helped me sharpen my critique of Stoic philosophy, clarify the concept of nature, and distinguish different meanings of activity. His support and enthusiasm for the project during the early days of the pandemic rejuvenated my own belief in it.

Since the beginning of my foray into political philosophy as an undergraduate student, Russ Muirhead has been a stalwart source of advice, support, and friendship. His playfulness with ideas and openness to questioning conventional wisdom have been inspirational. I am also grateful to Bryan Garsten, whose astute analysis of ancient philosophy and rhetoric has been a model for my own work.

I would like to give a big thanks to my friends Sergio Imparato, Julius Krein, Lowry Pressly, Peter Ganong, Julian Sempill, and Sungho Kimlee, all of whom took the time to read drafts of the book, and who enriched it with their commentary. The conversations I've had with Sungho are among the many occasions through which I will remember him. To Sergio, who has been at the nexus of my pursuits of philosophy and fitness for many years now, I owe a special thanks. He is at once cornerman for my record attempts, mental toughness exemplar, and philosophical kindred spirit.

For a good stretch of writing this book, I was also pursuing my JD at Harvard Law School. I owe thanks to Ruth Calderon, Dick Fallon, Mary Ann Glendon, Randy Kennedy, Tony Kronman, and Martha Minow, who all lent invaluable support to my dual project of writing a book and getting a law degree. I'm also grateful to Jack Corrigan for his practical wisdom and longtime mentorship, and to Abdallah Salam for our friendship and invigorating conversations on philosophy throughout the years.

I would like to thank Ian Malcolm of Harvard University Press for provided unwavering belief in this unconventional project, for his close reading of my manuscript, and for his encouragement to maintain the combination of philosophy and personal narrative. As I was refining my framing of the book, Sharmila Sen offered her insights and support and encouraged me to hone my critique of goal-oriented striving. Thanks also to Brian Ostrander of Westchester Publishing Services for his expert management of the book's production.

Finally, my deepest gratitude is to my parents, Michael Sandel and Kiku Adatto, my brother Aaron Sandel, and my fiancé Helena Ferreira—my greatest supporters and primary exemplars of self-possession, friendship, and engagement with nature. They also happen to be my most trusted advisers in all things related to writing. Their love, encouragement, and advice inspired and improved the book and transformed what can be the very solitary activity of writing into a family affair. The many conversations we've had on the themes of this book and on our respective writing projects, including "writers' house" sessions, in which we exchange critical commentary on drafts, have been a great source of the happiness in action that I attempt to express.

Thanks also to my uncle, Matthew Sandel, for his support and editorial acumen, and to my cousins Sam Adatto, Roberta Giubilini, Berto Ishida, and Lili Ishida, who helped me deliberate over many iterations of the book and offered much appreciated advice on how to connect philosophy and personal experience.

To Helena, whose love, support, and wisdom saw this book, and its author, through many ups and downs, I owe a special thanks. Her enthusiasm made the whole project worthwhile. When I was in doubt, she would often remind me that it was good just as it was, and then proceed to help me improve it infinitely with her incisive questions and literary and philosophical eye. I dedicate this book to her with love.

Index

fortune, happiness and, 47, 194–196
framing bias, 59
freedom, 31–32, 47, 253, 259–269
free will, 253–254, 254–257, 260
friendship: alliance versus, 7–8, 25,
117–118, 143; Aristotle's viewpoint
of, 24–25, 118, 120–121, 122, 125,
126–127, 128, 130, 138, 139–140, 157;
benefits of, 123–124; characteristics of, 117–118, 136–137, 157; claims
of, 139–142; commitment within,
128–129; competition and, 150–156;
creative dimension within, 128;
defined, 117, 125, 142–143; degradation of, 142–145; development
process of, 138–139; displacement
of, 3; goodness and, 127–128;
justice and, 129–135; modern bias
against, 135–139; nature as, 11;
Nietzsche's viewpoint of, 152–153;
opposites within, 156–157; over-
view of, 24–26; personal journey
within, 126; as philosophy form,
120; as preferred indifferent, 135;
progressivism and, 25; redemption
through, 145–150; for the sake of
itself, 124–129; self-criticism and,
122–123; self-friendship, 121–123;
self-possession and, 119–124,
139–140; Smith's viewpoint of, 137,
138–139; Stoics' viewpoint of, 17,
124; support within, 125; virtues
of, 126, 127
future: defined, 197; goal-oriented,
199–201, 247, 267, 272–273; as open
horizon, 30, 197–198, 205, 266,
270–271; in relation to past, 30,
198, 250–251, 271

generosity, 82–83, 233–241
gift-giving virtue, 232–241, 236
Glaucon, 92, 98–99
goal(s), 4–5, 220–222
goal-oriented outlook: challenges of,
38; characteristics of, 2, 13; criticism of, 54; as endless, 11–12;
examples of, 6; friendship within,
12; gift-giving virtue versus, 235;
judgment and, 58; limitations
within, 269, 272; living in the
moment approach versus, 3;
preoccupation within, 269; process of, 12; significance of, 220–221;
Stoicism within, 182; technology
and, 267; time concept within,
30, 199–201; unknown within,
267; writ large, 142
gold, 190–191, 235
golden ball, 221, 222, 223, 233–234, 239
good life, 6–7, 9–11, 12, 93, 96–97
goodness, 127–128
GPS navigation, 66–73
gravity, 176–178
greatness, 79–83
greatness of soul, 23, 51–54, 56–57,
74, 79–83, 120
Greeks, 46–47, 72–73, 143, 144–145, 267
guilt, 113–114

hallucination, 225
happiness, 10, 41–49, 50, 194–196
hardship, 114, 120–121, 124–125, 245, 250
health, 59–60, 62
Hegel, Georg Wilhelm Friedrich,
153–154, 164
Hobbes, Thomas, 47–49, 58, 220, 243
home, journey to, 5, 198, 202